WORKING IN GROUP CARE

Social work and social care in residential and day care settings

Adrian Ward

Consultant editor: Jo Campling

Revised Second Edition

First published in 1996 by Venture Press, 16 Kent Street, Birmingham, B5 6RD

This revised second edition published in Great Britain in 2007 by

The Policy Press
University of Bristol
Fourth Floor
Beacon House
Queen's Road
Bristol BS8 1QU
UK

Tel +44 (0)117 331 4054
Fax +44 (0)117 331 4093
e-mail tpp-info@bristol.ac.uk
www.policypress.org.uk

© Adrian Ward 2007

British Library Cataloguing in Publication Data
A catalogue record for this book is available from the British Library.

Library of Congress Cataloging-in-Publication Data
A catalog record for this book has been requested.

ISBN-10 1 86134 706 5 paperback
ISBN-13 978 1 86134 706 0 paperback
ISBN-10 1 86134 707 3 hardcover
ISBN-13 978 1 86134 707 7 hardcover

Cover design by Qube Design Associates, Bristol.
Front cover: photograph supplied by kind permission of Getty Images.
Printed and bound in Great Britain by Hobbs the Printers Ltd, Southampton.

To Mary, Lucy and Matt

Contents

Preface to second edition

This second edition of *Working in Group Care* has been revised, updated and refocused, first in order to bring the content and discussion in line with the many developments in practice, policy and research since the first edition, and second to incorporate further conceptual work that I have done on this topic in the intervening years. The book seems to have been valued by practitioners, students and academics in particular as it remains one of the few texts that explores the realities of practice right across the range of group care settings, and it is my aim in this second edition to build on the success of the first edition by keeping the original structure and adding new material (for example on 'Opportunity-led Work') within that existing framework.

The changes in policy and practice since the first edition have been enormous, with, for example, the increasing marketisation of welfare and the spread of private care facilities sometimes backed by large corporations with little expertise in 'care', the decline in the use of some types of residential facility and the continuing move towards smaller and more locally based units, and the equivalent shift from 'day care' to 'day services' and towards more inclusive and less stigmatising forms of care. There has also been the growth of the inspection and audit culture in which all forms of service are subjected to much closer (and sometimes intrusive) scrutiny at all levels, driven by understandable concern about the risk of abuse and neglect. Most importantly there has also been the growth of the service-user movement in which those using care and other services have developed a much fuller and stronger voice in the design and delivery of those services at both the broad policy and the immediate local levels. Government policy in the UK and elsewhere has been increasingly influenced by both research and direct pressure from service users and others to reform services. In some respects these shifts in policy have either affected direct practice or reflected existing trends and shifts of emphasis. For example in the UK, changes in patterns of adult care are reflected in the government publication *Independence, Well-being and Choice* (DH, 2005). Nevertheless, some fundamentals remain the same: in particular the people who use residential and day services continue to bring a similar range of personal needs and challenges, and 'ground-level' practitioners face exactly the same types of dilemmas and difficulties as ever. These realities of practice do not change and this remains a complex, challenging, but potentially deeply rewarding, field of practice. The focus of this book is largely on these unchanging realities of everyday care and support rather than on the ever-shifting context of government and agency policy.

However, another reality that does not change much is that public care remains a relatively under-resourced area not only in terms of direct practice but also in terms of training and staff development and programmes of research and policy development. While the UK has a comparatively good record of funding research in social care generally, there remain large questions that have never been fully addressed, especially around the difficult challenge of establishing connections between particular methods and processes of care and their likely outcomes. In producing a second edition I have not only wanted to reflect what is new in this field but also to continue to value that which is well established. For example, as well as using the latest research, I have continued to draw deeply upon some classic reviews of research and practice, especially the Wagner (1988) review of residential care and Jan Carter's (1981) comprehensive review of day care. Although in some respects the field has indeed moved on, in other ways these substantial reviews remain authoritative in their comprehensive coverage of their respective fields. Several other 'classic' texts are used, perhaps more than would be ordinarily expected, and this also reflects a reality that the whole field remains somewhat under-researched and certainly under-theorised. For example, I do not know of any modern English language texts that supersede or substantially update books for practitioners such as the volumes by Brearley et al entitled *Admission to Residential Care* and *Leaving Residential Care*, which both date from the early 1980s. Likewise the pioneering work of Ainsworth and Fulcher in 1981 remains current with the reissue of some of the original papers (Fulcher and Ainsworth, 2006).

The theme of this second edition is therefore one of continuity within change, and the need for sustained attention to the fundamental task of providing purposeful, respectful and positive care for those in need. It is my hope that the book will remain useful to practitioners at all levels, including both those learning about this field as new recruits or students and those responsible for managing and organising residential and day services. I have met many hundreds of dedicated group care workers over the years and I wish them all well in their continuing efforts to provide the best support to those in their care.

Introduction

The purpose of this book is to offer a framework for analysing what happens in social work in residential and day care settings, and to show how this framework can be usefully applied in practice, both by practitioners themselves and by students and those involved in teaching about this work. The method of the book is to bring together a number of different perspectives on group care work, and to show how they relate to each other. Some of the ideas are drawn directly from the existing literature and research, while some are drawn from my own experience both in group care practice and in the training of group care workers.

The book is aimed at all of those working in group care, whether as care staff, managers or trainers, although it is also intended for those undertaking placements in group care settings as part of social work and other programmes of learning and development. The field is extremely broad: in no sense can this book provide a full introduction to the issues arising in every group care setting – ranging from, for example, day care work with older people to respite residential care for children with learning difficulties – and for such depth and detail the reader will have to turn to some of the many books and articles referred to throughout the book, which do deal in particulars. What is attempted here is a bringing together of the themes arising for those working in *any* group care setting, with examples drawn from a wide variety of places, and with the aim of helping group care workers to be clear as to what the various settings have in common and where they differ. The message of the book is that, whatever group care setting you are working in, there are certain fundamental issues that you will have to address, and certain responsibilities that you will have to undertake – and that these issues and responsibilities are broadly similar across the board.

This is not, therefore, a book specifically about, for example, how to feed or bathe an individual in a home for older people with dementia or to plan the programme of a day centre for people with multiple disabilities: that level of detail would be better learned on the spot, with supervision and instruction as necessary, and backed up by the appropriate specific reading. What this book deals with is the context, purpose and philosophy of such work: for example, how and why do people reach particular care units, where will they eventually go on to, how can today's care be planned and delivered so as to help them on that journey? What are the worker's professional responsibilities, and how does her work fit in with the tasks of the rest of the team and with the life of the unit as a whole? Finally, how does the unit's 'internal' work connect with the client's family and community and with the work of the other agencies involved? These are the questions that are addressed in this book.

To write a book such as this feels like a considerable responsibility: although I have attempted to be comprehensive, it is inevitable that various aspects of my own bias will show through – and, in particular, that a greater proportion of the illustrative material will be drawn from residential child care than from other settings, since that is my own specialism and where my direct practice experience has been.

Since the book is aimed at practitioners and students rather than at a broad public readership, I will assume a degree of familiarity with some of the social work and social care practice and terminology – although I shall try to avoid jargon wherever possible, and will offer some thoughts on key terms and concepts during this Introduction and Chapter One. Moreover, because the scope of the book is so broad, readers looking for sustained critical evaluation of all the issues identified may be disappointed: while comments are offered on the various issues raised, the book is not intended primarily as a post-modern critique but as an aid for practitioners, student-practitioners and managers, to help them think more clearly about their work, and, ultimately, to help them deliver a better service.

Assumptions

Three assumptions have underpinned the writing of this book: first that group care is valuable and skilled work, although the value of the work and the skills required have often been under-recognised at all levels; second that a great deal of useful writing in this field has already been done, although it has never been satisfactorily brought together into a unified whole; and third that theories of professional practice are only of any value if they are accessible and can be used by practitioners and students to help them understand and improve their practice.

The first assumption derives from my own positive experience both as a practitioner and as a trainer, but also from the recorded views of many consumers of group care services and from the need to challenge the negative views that are propagated in some quarters, including some of the professional and academic literature (but see Jack, 1998, for a useful challenge to the more negative literature). Many readers will be aware of the continuing undervaluing of residential work in particular, and of the damaging effect that this undervaluing can have both on the providers and on the consumers of the service, for example in terms of low salaries, poor working conditions, inadequate budgets for building maintenance and the consequent low morale of all involved.

What is it that is valuable about this work? The potential value is that, when they are properly managed, residential and day services can provide a wide range of personal support, help and care to those in need, and that the group context allows for social interaction for the isolated and mutual support for those in distress, and the benefits of the shared expertise, concern and engagement of a closely cooperating team of workers.

It would be foolish to pretend that this potential value is always fully achieved: in fact, there is usually a ready supply of current scandals, which provide examples of the negation of these positives into the brutal abuse or wilful neglect of dependent people. However, there are many places in which the potential value *is* achieved, by thoughtful and dedicated staff in a very wide range of settings, and it is my belief that this success is more likely to be achieved when workers feel that the value of their task is fully recognised in the public domain, as well as by their colleagues and employers.

In what sense can this work be called highly skilled? There are those who argue that mere 'tending' does not require a high level of skill, since what is offered is often just substitute care for those who could in other circumstances have been adequately cared for by relatives using no special skills. This view, which may represent the less-than-conscious assumption of some policy makers and finance controllers, takes no proper account of the personal and professional skills required by those employed in enabling people to live 'private lives in public places' (Willcocks, 1987, p 1). It also represents an undervaluing of the skills and importance of all care work, whether provided by professional staff or by informal carers for their own relatives or friends. The details of the skills required for the group care task belong elsewhere in this book: what I wish to emphasise here is not only that group care workers provide much more than 'mere' substitute care, but also that even the provision of good-quality and purposeful substitute care is a complex and demanding task requiring high levels of skill, sensitivity and thoughtfulness. The bias of this book, therefore, will be towards making group care more purposeful and effective, and at the same time towards making it a humane and sensitive service to people in need rather than an insensitive and institutional response to 'problematic cases'.

The second assumption, that much useful writing in this field has already been done, will be seen to have a particular relevance in the main text of the book, where many of the practice-based examples for discussion have been drawn from the existing literature rather than all being brought from my own experience. The literature has been used in this way in order to emphasise both the value that I place on this material for teaching and learning purposes, and the validity of the claim that what has been lacking in this field is not so much a body of practice-wisdom or of theoretical statements, but a proper integration of this material into a coherent framework. A third source for the examples offered in the book is the work of students on placement in group care settings – many of the examples given are adapted from actual cases and incidents reported by students. In all cases, names and other identifying details have been changed to protect anonymity.

Most of the literature on residential and day care work has focused on discrete areas of practice, for example admission, or on particular user groups, for example children and older people, or on specific theoretical approaches, for example therapeutic communities. A few texts have covered residential work in general (for example, Burton, 1993; Stanley and Reed, 1999; Clough, 2000), while some others have covered aspects of day care (for example, Horobin, 1987; Clark, 2001). Although there is much useful work here, none of this material is really comprehensive or sufficiently integrative of the whole field. Even the Wagner Report (1988), a very full and influential survey on residential care, was criticised as being insufficiently broad or incisive in its range (see Chapter Two), although it remains an authoritative source in many ways and will be drawn upon in the present volume. Similarly, while Fulcher and Ainsworth's work on the concept of group care as encompassing both residential and day care (Ainsworth and Fulcher, 1981; Fulcher and Ainsworth, 1985, 2006) has been valuable and influential in the field of child care, little material relating to settings other than child care has yet been produced within this approach.

The literature has also included several useful surveys of the field, including the literature reviews in Part 2 of the Wagner Report (1988), and client-group-specific reviews such as those on residential child care by Berridge (2002) and Clough et al (2006). The day care field has been less fully researched, although helpful surveys of some of the literature may be found in Tester (1989) and in Clark (2001). However, while these various literature surveys and overviews offer well-categorised and descriptive listings, they do not attempt to provide an overall theoretical framework for students and practitioners.

The problem, then, is not that there is a lack of relevant theoretical material to draw upon. It is more complicated than that:

- First, as we have already seen, the material is widely dispersed and has never been satisfactorily synthesised into a coherent framework.
- Second, much of the literature tends to focus on the functions and dysfunctions of group care settings as a whole rather than on the responsibilities of the individual group care worker, which means that the material is not always as accessible for students and practitioners as it ought to be.
- Third, much of the existing material, while retaining considerable intrinsic value, has begun to appear rather 'dated' in its approach, and thus risks becoming of less value to students and practitioners. There is a real need for an up-to-date review of practice issues, incorporating findings from more recent research and legislation as well as integrating material on issues of anti-oppressive practice, and on the related themes of empowerment, inclusion, and so on. While one small volume cannot possibly provide answers to all these problems, it can at least bring together some possible approaches – even though it may still have to rely in part on some of these rather 'mature' sources!
- A fourth problem, specific to training, is that we have lacked a simple 'process' model for group care work. While the basic concept of the 'Social Work Process', as described by Payne (2005) and Parker and Bradley (2003) among others, not only provides a useful framework for teaching about fieldwork practice but also underpins the UK regulations for social work qualifying training, this concept has not translated easily into group care practice in such a way that students can readily use it as a set of guidelines for their own work.

This point brings us to the third assumption, that theory for professional practice is only worthwhile if it is accessible and of direct value to students and practitioners in improving their practice. The lack of a well-articulated body of theory-for-practice presents a major problem not only in group care practice, but also in the training of group care workers, for without conceptual clarity neither practice nor training can be effective. What is needed is a theoretical framework that group care workers and managers can use as a guide to practice, which students can use as they explore their way through practice on placement, and which practice teachers and tutors can use for teaching, supervision and the assessment of students' performance.

This book attempts to address these problems by presenting one formulation of the required framework and by articulating a version of the 'Social Work Process' for group care practitioners that is derived directly from a consideration of the issues arising in group care practice rather than from a mere reworking of the fieldwork model.

Terminology

Group care

The term 'group care' has been used throughout this book to cover both residential and day care work, following the approach taken by Fulcher and Ainsworth (2006), among others. The assumption behind the use of this umbrella term is that, from the practitioner's point of view as well as from the service user's, there are great similarities between what happens in residential care and in day care, and that the discussion of each of these fields will be enhanced and illuminated by their being brought together. Ainsworth and Fulcher (1981, p 2) use 'group care' to refer to all those settings 'which use the group and the shared life-space of the group as the primary focus', whether these are large or small institutions, and whether care is provided on an intensive 24-hours-a-day basis or on a much more intermittent and 'hands-off' basis. On the other hand, Fulcher and Ainsworth also appear to argue for the term to include settings as diverse as prisons and general hospitals, which are beyond the scope of the present volume. Meanwhile there is also an active movement towards reconfiguring 'day care' into 'day services', which aim to promote social inclusion by moving away from the use of 'day centres' (McIntosh and Whittaker, 2000; Clark, 2001). A fuller discussion as to what is and what is not 'group care' will be found in Chapter One.

For the purpose of distinguishing group care as a method of social work from other methods such as office-based fieldwork practice as well as from groupwork and community engagement, we can say that in group care there will always be some degree of emphasis on 'shared living and learning arrangements in a specified centre of activity' (Ainsworth and Fulcher, 1981, p 8). While workers in these settings will engage in some tasks equivalent to those in other settings (such as counselling and informal support), it is the sharing of living and learning arrangements (including facilities and resources) that provides the context for these tasks and which is now recognised as constituting a domain of practice in its own right. Referring to group care workers in child care settings, Ainsworth (1981, p 234) argues that they:

> ... take as the theatre for their work the actual living situations as shared with and experienced by the child. This is because of the view that it is through events that occur and experiences that are acquired in this life space that developmental opportunities are either reduced or enlarged for the child.

What is promoted by the use of the concept of group care, then, is the recognition that this creative exploiting of the opportunities for change and growth that arise in daily living is a valid method of social work, which happens in both residential and day care work but not normally (or not so fully) in other methods of social work.

It is the identification of this distinct nature of group care work that necessitates a body of theory-for-practice, in order to clarify the ways in which individuals and teams can identify, carry out and evaluate the tasks appropriate to this work. Such a body of theory needs to allow for the distinctive ways in which group care settings can make use of arrangements of 'time, space, objects, events, activities' (Ainsworth, 1981, p 234) – in other words, for the context of the work. It also has to allow for the context of teamwork, which is so central to this field of practice, and for the demands upon the worker's professional use of self in interaction with others, which is the main working method at the disposal of the worker. Some of these issues have been usefully addressed in Ainsworth and Fulcher's collections, others remain to be tackled.

Although the term 'group care' has not been universally adopted in the professional literature, my own view is that the term offers a useful, brief and appropriate way of referring to residential and day care practice in many different settings and contexts, and as such it has been used throughout this book. However, the use of the term should not be allowed to blur the real differences that do exist between residential and day care work – and, where necessary, these differences will be highlighted in the text. Consequently, the term 'group care setting' has been used as a cover-all term to refer to the workplace of the group care worker. The range of terms in actual daily usage is wide (for example, 'home', 'unit', 'centre'), and it seems preferable to stick to one admittedly clumsy term rather than to constantly offer the range of alternatives. The term 'setting' has been chosen as hopefully more neutral than most.

Social work and social care

Residential and day services sit uneasily across a number of other professional groupings including social work, nursing, education and that broad field known as 'social care'. These groupings continue to shift in significant ways, however, and not just in terms of their respective tasks but also in terms of their working assumptions as, for example, social work becomes more identified with a managerialist and procedural ethos (Postle, 2001, 2002) and nursing becomes more 'reflexive' (Redmond, 2004). Meanwhile new professional groupings (such as Connexions workers or Youth Justice workers) emerge as governments and others try to reconfigure services. In fact it is only really in the UK that group care has been so strongly located within the social work camp – elsewhere it has quite other identifications, such as with 'social pedagogy' in child care for example. In this book I have nevertheless retained a focus on the social work literature since this has continued to provide the nearest convenient reference group and to generate much of the relevant research and theory, as well as a well-articulated value base. 'Social care', meanwhile, is a much broader and perhaps over-inclusive term, although for the sake of argument I would locate group care alongside and overlapping with social work within this broader field of social care – which also includes many other forms of practice and subspecies of professional!

Clients/users

Wherever possible, I have referred to the people on the receiving end of group care as 'the individual' or 'the person', which I find greatly preferable to any professional jargon. However, it is often essential to distinguish the consumers from the providers of care, and, in these situations, I have generally used the term 'client'. This term is unpopular with some, as it is seen as implying subservience, and thus perpetuating the powerless position of consumers in the welfare services. However, while I will be seen to argue consistently for the empowerment of the group care 'consumer', I am also concerned about clarity and common sense in the use of language, and I have found the term 'client' preferable to the alternatives.

In particular, I have chosen not to adopt the term 'service user', which I find too ambiguous, despite its popularity in some quarters. For example, who is really the 'user' of group care services – is it the person who attends the day centre or lives in the residential home, is it the relative, friend or neighbour who needs relief from caring for the person in their own home, or is it perhaps the doctor or police officer who requests that this person be 'taken care of', or the field social worker who arranges a place in a given home or hostel for a person with whom they are working? All of these people are in some senses 'users' of group care services and facilities. Moreover, while the term 'user' does seem appropriate in relation to, for example, an adult choosing to attend a day centre, I find it less appropriate for some other groups, such as a child in residential care, and others whose situation does not necessarily include the degree of choice implied by 'user'. It can also be argued that to label people as 'service users' may serve to constrict and constrain their identity as people in their own right who do more than just 'use services'. In this book I will be proposing a model of practice based on principles of empowerment and choice, and on the recognition of the rights of those in group care. I retain the term 'client' as a necessary generalisation, but prefer where possible to use more personal and human terms such as 'person' and 'individual'.

Words and meanings

I have chosen generally to use the pronoun 'she' to refer both to workers and to clients, in recognition of the fact that in many group care settings the majority of both groups are female. This much-neglected fact about group care, and its implications for all of those working in group care, will be discussed at various points in the book, although there is still much more to be said on this issue. I have also used the term 'black' in both a general and a political sense to refer to people in the UK from 'black and minority ethnic' communities, in recognition of the view that despite the enormous diversity of cultures covered by the blanket term 'black' the political and social reality is that most of these groups face similar experiences of racism.

Choosing the right words when writing about groups of people requires care, awareness and sensitivity, and this reflects the need in group care practice to think carefully about the implications of one's use of language, and as far as possible to consult the people in question for their own views. In the more distinct context of writing a book, I have generally attempted to use terms that are currently accepted, for example, 'people with learning difficulties' rather than 'the mentally handicapped', but in full recognition of the fact that views change and practice develops, and that what is the preferred option today may be viewed with horror tomorrow. The debates around terminology are peculiarly susceptible to what in other contexts is known as 'churn' or the rapid reviewing and revision of language and concepts in an attempt to fit evolving and conflicting trends. In this context it is possible that some of my language may sit uncomfortably with some readers, which may be because of my own ignorance, prejudice or stubbornness or may at times be because these are very difficult areas to write about with sufficient sensitivity. If I give offence I apologise: we can only do our best.

Outline

Having defined our terms in this way, it is time to introduce the four perspectives that are covered in this book. The first point to be made is that what are presented here are perspectives, rather than theories. In other words, the book is concerned with examining group care from a number of viewpoints, with the aim of clarifying what the tasks and responsibilities of the workers consist of under each heading. Within each perspective, any number of different theories may be helpful – such as Goffman's (1968) social-psychological theory on stigma, Miller and Gwynne's (1972) version of 'Open Systems Theory' on the notion of the Primary Task, and so on. The fact of adopting one or other of the perspectives outlined here does not restrict us to adopting any one particular theory – although, not surprisingly, it will be found in the text that I am drawn more to some theoretical standpoints than to others.

The book consists of six chapters. There is first a general chapter on group care: what is distinctive about it compared to working in other settings, and what key issues and principles underpin the work? This is followed by a chapter on the contexts of working in group care, with particular emphasis on 'consumer power', and on the specific contexts of teamwork, shiftwork and 'centre-based' work. Towards the end of this chapter the first of the four perspectives on group care practice is introduced, that is, Opportunity-led Work, which addresses the use of opportunities for helpful communication during everyday life in group care. The following chapters deal in turn with each of the remaining perspectives: namely, The Client's Stay, The Worker's Shift, and The Team and its Task (see Figure 1). Taken together, these four perspectives complement each other to take account of each of the three main parties involved: respectively the client, the individual worker and the team.

The second perspective, The Client's Stay, draws largely on existing literature on group care practice, much of which does focus on the experience of the client – her 'career' in care from beginning to end, the extent to which this is planned and the extent to which it is integrated with other services. There will be a particular emphasis here on considering the client as a member of a network both within and outside the unit – her family, community, or living group. The third perspective, The Worker's Shift, on the other hand, represents a distinctive approach to thinking about group care practice in that it offers an account of the responsibilities of the individual group care worker throughout a day's work, from arriving at the start of a shift until leaving at the end of the day. The fourth perspective, The Team and its Task, focuses on the work of the team as a whole and on a 'systemic' view of what happens in group care.

These four perspectives are not intended to be an exhaustive listing – clearly there are other formulations that some would find preferable to those included, and certainly there are others that I would have liked to have space to discuss in more detail. These four have been chosen because, taken together, they represent four main strands of practice-theory, which experience shows to be essential for an understanding of group care. Indeed, it is worth stressing that, although some comments will be made about the relative strengths and weaknesses of each perspective, the view taken here is that it is only by taking account of all four perspectives that a reasonably accurate picture of the complex nature of this work can be gained. Moreover, although the four perspectives are presented in Figure 1 within a standardised format, suggesting parallel sequential stages, the four views are different in nature as well as in focus. While conceding the risk that this standardisation might be seen as inappropriate and potentially misleading, it is my belief that the potential gain from bringing the four perspectives into one framework is greater than any possible loss or confusion risked by shoehorning them into the occasional tight fit. In Figure 1 each perspective is delineated in terms of its focus, and each is then summarised into three main stages or elements.

In Chapter Six the four perspectives are drawn together to show where they overlap and complement each other, and to indicate some areas that are still obscured from view; finally there is a discussion on the implications both for practice and for training of taking this multidimensional approach to group care work. This was always intended to be a short book, and, while it covers a fair amount of ground, there are many implications of the approach taken here, which it will only be possible to outline in brief.

Figure 1: Four perspectives on group care practice

1. Opportunity-led Work	2. The Client's Stay	3. The Worker's Shift	4. The Team and its Task
Focus: quality of everyday communication	Focus: the needs of the client	Focus: the responsibilities of the worker	Focus: the task of the professional team
Observation and Assessment Detail: what is being said/done etc? Context: atmosphere, relationships, power	Preliminary: Referral, negotiation and agreement *Admission* *Joining*	Preliminary: Preparation and anticipation *Arrival* *Handover*	*Working in the Team* Team membership; the role of individual work; communication systems
Decision-making Priorities: urgency, feasibility, ethics Aims: task, time-scale, tactics Action: Opening the communication i) Short-term/behavioural/'first aid' interventions; choosing tactics ii) Longer-term/therapeutic interventions spotting opportunities and using them Sustaining the intervention	*Assessment* *Care/Treatment:* Individual 'Care Plan' based on Agreement, subject to review based on individual relationship incorporating links with family etc Group 'Care Plan' arrangements for daily living schedule of activities planned groupwork & meetings planned links with community etc. Balancing of individual & group needs	*Responsibilities:* Assessing Engaging Planning & anticipating Taking action Acting ethically Being reliable and diligent Monitoring Pacing oneself Using supervision & consultation Evaluating	*The Systems Approach* Principles of Systems thinking *Applications:* The group care unit as a system Wider systems and group care: Family systems The 'Unitary Approach': 'target, client, change-agent and action-systems 'The Primary Task and 'open systems'
Closure Closing the communication Further action and recording the incident Reviewing and evaluating	*Departure* Tasks of Leaving: Evaluation, disengagement, stabilisation	*Departure* Preparation for leaving Saying goodbye After departure – avoiding burnout	*Managing the system* Transition to management Levels of management Responsibilities of management: Systems for management

ONE

Group care: practice and principles

Introduction

We shall begin by considering the nature of group care work: what is group care, what is distinctive about it, and how does it differ from other forms of social work and professional practice? We shall consider what the distinctions and overlaps are between residential and day care work, and, in particular, what group care workers actually do. We shall then look at three key issues arising in all group care practice – issues of power, prejudice and dependency – and then at some basic principles of group care practice, which underpin all of the later discussions in Chapters Two to Five about the responsibilities and working methods of the group care worker. Finally in this chapter, we shall look at the problem of the prevalence of bad practice and the struggle to work towards positive high-quality group care.

Definitions

What is group care?

Group care is social work in a residential or day care setting. We may well then ask: what is a residential or day care setting? Such questions of definition have exercised others in the past and the boundaries of residential care are constantly shifting as policy evolves (for example, DH, 2005), while some have discarded the term 'day care' in preference for the idea of 'day services' (for example, McIntosh and Whittaker, 2000; Clark, 2001). For the sake of this book, a group care setting is a place that people attend for some form of organised and purposeful social work help on either a daily or a residential basis, and where, in addition to individual help, there is also some form of group or communal activity, which may range from a group meeting or shared mealtime at one end of the spectrum to full residential life at the other end.

In some respects group care is a *setting* for social work – in that some of the work is similar to the social work carried out in other settings such as fieldwork teams (for example, individual assessment of need, counselling) – in many other respects, however, it represents a distinctive *method* of social work, in that the distinctive context requires a very different combination of skills and knowledge. Indeed, there are some aspects of this distinctive method that are not usually found at all in fieldwork or clinical settings – particularly the ongoing and creative use of incidents and exchanges arising in everyday life, and the maximising of these informal opportunities to offer constructive help. Throughout this discussion we should also bear in mind that the nature and context of social work itself has changed enormously with the advent of care management (Postle, 2001, 2002) and the rise of managerialism and proceduralism (Adams et al, 2005). There is probably therefore no longer a single entity of 'social work' or 'fieldwork' with which to draw detailed comparisons: what we are doing here is to suggest general distinctions between different broad fields of practice, in order to become clearer about the nature and context of group care practice.

The term 'group care' suggests immediately two distinguishing features of this work: it involves working in groups – both groups of clients and groups of staff – and it involves caring for people, which is likely to entail becoming close to them both physically and emotionally. The implications of the 'group' element in group care vary enormously from one setting to the next: from the 'drop-in' day centre in which there may be very little notion of group identity among those attending, to the therapeutic community in which the entire group of 'members' (both clients and staff) meet together regularly to conduct the therapeutic work of the community. Most group care teams aim to be somewhere in the middle of this range, acknowledging and encouraging a sense of group identity and communality among both clients and staff, but at the same time not necessarily seeking to achieve overtly 'therapeutic' outcomes, and certainly wishing to avoid the 'totality' of the total institution.

The implications of the 'care' element in group care also vary from one setting to another. The levels and detail of care that may be necessary in a residential home for older people with dementia will of course be entirely different from what is appropriate in a probation day centre. As stated in the Introduction, I will not attempt to explore the detail of what is distinctive to either setting in particular, nor will I attempt here to define 'care' since the details of care and/or treatment are spelled out later in the book. What *is* offered in this book is an account of those elements of practice that may be held in common between the workers in any of these settings.

Who is the client?

For the purposes of this book, the client is the individual person who attends a group care setting – whether entirely by choice and without commitment or by some degree of compulsion or other people's choice, or with some longer-term commitment to continued attendance. We saw earlier that other people such as relatives and referrers may benefit both directly and indirectly from the person's attendance at the group care setting, and the 'systemic' approach described in Chapter Five argues for full acknowledgement of the involvement of these others. Nevertheless, it is of central importance that the needs, wishes and rights of the client remain the *primary focus of the work of the staff team* – see below for the full implications of this statement.

Who is the worker?

Most group care settings are organised so that there is a team of workers employed to offer services to a group of clients. The distinctions within and between these groups are not always totally clear-cut, however. For example, many units are staffed only partly by 'professional' workers, and rely also on volunteers, who may carry many of the same responsibilities as the professional staff, and on domiciliary staff, whose tasks may at times overlap considerably with the tasks of the professional workers, except in terms of planned formal contact with the clients. There are also further variations such as the role of waking night staff in residential care. For the purposes of this book, however, we shall define 'workers' as those staff who have regular direct contact with the clients in pursuance of the Primary Task of the setting – that is, those known as 'residential workers', 'care staff', or 'day care workers', but not usually those employed as ancillary or support workers such as clerical or domestic staff (see Chapter Two). Likewise I shall use the term 'manager' to refer to the head of the home or unit, while acknowledging that in practice a very wide range of terms is used.

What is the team?

For most purposes, the team referred to in this book is what we shall call the professional team of group care workers – including senior staff and the head of the unit, but again not usually including the domestic and ancillary staff. However, we shall also be looking (Chapter Two) at the concept of the full team – a broader network that includes all of those working within the group care setting plus some of those on the outside, both in the client's network and in the professional network.

Distinctive elements

Having defined our terms, we are now in a position to be clearer about what group care consists of, what its distinctive elements are, and particularly what distinguishes it from other forms of social work and social care practice such as 'field social work' and care management, which I will refer to broadly as 'office-based practice'. A number of these distinctive elements are outlined below – they will all be taken up again at later stages of the book, but for the moment it will be sufficient to outline their main elements, as shown in Box 1.1.

> **Box 1.1:** Distinctive elements of group care work
> * Coordinated use of time
> * Focus of work
> * The interdependent team
> * Multiple relationships
> * Public practice
> * Organisation of space

Coordinated use of time

In office-based practice the individual worker's time is usually her own responsibility to organise and plan, according to her own priorities and others' availability; in group care, time is usually organised into an overall cooperative routine, within which clients' and workers' activities are coordinated. Individuals are still responsible for managing their own time within the demands set by the agreed routine, but their work is also likely to be organised within a rota (Smith, M., 2005). The routine may have a mixture of formal and informal elements, and in many settings the workers will be with the clients during the informal as well as the formal times, and will aim to capitalise on the opportunities which these offer (see also Chapter Two). This element of 'prolonged exposure' to clients throughout a day's work can be experienced as quite stressful, especially for new or inexperienced workers, and in Chapter Three we shall consider how workers can plan and manage their day's work.

Focus of work

In office-based practice there is usually an emphasis on the formal interview or the planned group session as the main mode of direct practice with clients. In group care, on the other hand, whatever planned 'interview-based' work is carried out, there is usually a greater emphasis on the purposeful use of everyday interactions and events as opportunities for intervention, as in the concepts of the 'life-space interview' (Redl, 1966) and the 'Work of the Day' (Kennedy, 1987). This 'Opportunity-led Work' (Ward, 1995b) is done in addition to the other planned or formal work of the unit, and in some settings is given great emphasis. This aspect of practice has implications throughout the system, for example in terms of patterns of supervision and approaches to the recording of work. See Chapter Two for further discussion of Opportunity-led Work.

The interdependent team

In many office-based settings, a team consists of a collection of individuals who mainly carry separate caseloads from each other and who for the most part rely on each other more for occasional support and informal consultation rather than for active and sustained co-working. In most group care settings, however, the team can be said to be more *inter*dependent, in that workers rely directly on each other, and on the team as a whole, during everyday work with the clients. This greater interdependence of the group care team has widespread implications for the organisation and delivery of the service – for example in terms of the arrangements for supervision and staff meetings. We shall look further at the implications for teamwork in Chapter Five.

Multiple relationships: the team and the group of clients

In office-based practice, most of the clients are seen on an individual-case basis, either as individuals or as families, with the same worker always working on the same case. In group care, each client is likely to relate to more than one worker, and even where there is a system of 'keyworkers', each of these may work with many different clients within the same group during the day, as well as carrying other responsibilities such as managerial, administrative, or domestic/practical tasks. There is often an emphasis on working with groups and groupings of clients (see Brown and Clough, 1989), and sometimes with the whole group, rather than solely on working with them as individuals. Again there are important implications here for the workers in terms of the way they carry out their work with individuals and groups – and particularly in terms of learning to use systemic thinking (see Chapter Five).

Public practice

Not only is the team interdependent and tied in to a whole network of relationships with the group of clients, but much of the work undertaken between workers and clients is carried out in a public or semi-public forum. Workers observe each other's practice as they work alongside each other, and the clients and their relatives and friends will also be aware of how other clients are responded to: again this provides quite a different context from the largely individualised and in a sense 'private' practice of office-based practice, and one which may bring stresses as well as benefits. Few other professionals conduct so much of their work under the gaze of peers and other clients, and the combination of the intimacy of much group care work with the vulnerability of some of the clients (and, in another way, of the workers) means that the issue of what is public and what is private is a constant dilemma in group care. On the other hand, in some settings, much less work is done in the 'working alongside' mode than might be expected – where the demands of shiftwork or the geography of a large building means that individuals may find themselves working in isolation for considerable stretches of time, with all the risks of vulnerability for workers and clients that this may bring. Further, most group care work is only 'public' within the four walls of the unit itself, and one of the criticisms sometimes levelled at group care units in the past was that they became too isolated from public scrutiny: here again there is a tension, this time between the need for privacy and the risk of isolation.

Organisation of space

Most group care settings are 'centre based' – that is, workers and clients all use one building or 'centre' for most of the working day, rather than most of the work being done either in an office or in the client's home. Paralleling the use of time described above, most group care settings have both public and private spaces, and some spaces that are used for formal work as well as others that are mainly used informally by clients and workers together during 'in-between times'. Many office-based professional settings specifically exclude such informal or overlapping use of space – workers do not use clients' waiting rooms, and clients and workers do not share refreshment or toilet facilities. In group care, decisions about the use of space, and issues arising from its use, often assume major proportions both on a daily basis and in the longer term (see Chapter Two). For an interesting discussion of the use of physical space in therapeutic group care environments, see von Sommaruga Howard (2004), while at a broader level Warren-Adamson (2001) explores some of the dynamics and broader implications of centre-based practice for all parties.

None of the above factors taken alone would be sufficient to distinguish all group care settings from all office-based settings – indeed, the distinctions between different types of group care setting may sometimes appear just as great as these broader distinctions between group care and fieldwork. Nor is it necessarily productive to lump together all the other forms and settings of social work as 'office-based practice' and then to polarise the two. There remains a valid distinction, however: when taken together these factors indicate that there *are* important broad differences between these modes of practice, and that group care work is sufficiently different from other forms of social work to require its own body of practice-theory. The implications of these distinctions will be seen throughout this book, as they set the context for the planning and delivery of every aspect of practice, from assessment to evaluation, and from management and supervision to patterns of training and consultancy.

Distinctions between residential and day care

As we have seen, the term 'group care' is used to cover both residential and day care settings, and by now readers will be aware that it is a premise of this book that there is a great deal in common between these settings. However, there are some important differences between residential and day care that should be acknowledged, and which will be highlighted at various points during the following chapters when the distinction is seen as being important.

First, residential work is usually intended to provide a more comprehensive service than day care, in that much greater amounts of time are involved, and a wider range of space is required, including much more private or personal space for sleeping, bathing, and so on.

Residential care can therefore feel more complex and intensive than some day care settings and greater amounts of planning may be needed to coordinate the total operation.

Second, residential work often involves closer dependent relationships between clients and workers than those in day care, because of the greater quantities of personal care and living alongside involved. This generalisation does not always hold true, however, since the Primary Task of the unit (see Chapter Five) will also influence the nature of these relationships. For example, some day centres for older people promote much closer relationships between workers and clients than some residential projects offering 'semi-independent living' for adolescents or people recovering from a mental illness.

Third, from the workers' point of view, whereas in most day care settings the working day is broadly equivalent to 'office hours', residential work requires that much greater proportions of the waking day are 'covered', so that, for example, shift systems are required, bringing their own logistical problems and the consequent need for 'handover' and other meetings. Staff groups may also be considerably larger, in order to provide 'cover' throughout each 24-hour period. On the other hand, as day services are reconfigured and, for example, people move from long-term institutional care into the community, some of the evolving forms of day services require considerable flexibility and creativity by staff in terms of their use of time and other resources (McIntosh and Whittaker, 1998).

The field of day care and day services began to evolve significantly in the 1990s, and whereas previous research evidence on consumer views had suggested a largely positive evaluation of services, it became increasingly clear that reform was needed in keeping with the principles of social inclusion and normalisation. Studies began to highlight complaints about inappropriate activities, boredom and lack of direction in day services (Scottish Executive, 2000) and groups such as the King's Fund promoted major programmes and change and development in this field (for example, McIntosh and Whittaker, 1998). It may be that life in day care was previously assumed to be a less intense experience, usually involving less compulsion and thus fewer strong feelings on the key issues of power, prejudice and dependency. It may also be, however, that those using day care services were previously cautious about voicing their frustrations with the services: what is increasingly clear is that as, for example, adults with complex disabilities become more involved in evaluating services, the need for reform and change is much more evident.

These differences do mean that day care settings may at times feel different from residential settings in significant ways, both for the users and for the workers. Nevertheless, having acknowledged the potential differences, we shall now proceed on the basis that for most purposes there is more in common between these two types of setting than separates them, and generally much more in common between them than there is between either of them and other social work settings.

It is not just an academic exercise to insist on this common ground: it is part of the argument of this book that group care represents both a different setting and a different method of social work practice, and that there is a distinctive and rich blend of features operating in such settings, which requires that the work be described and conceptualised in its own terms rather than as an offshoot or lesser version of something else.

Key issues

Three key issues underpin many of the challenges facing group care practitioners, as shown in Box 1.2.

Box 1.2: Three key issues in group care work
- Power
- Prejudice
- Dependency

These issues are not being proposed as unique to group care, as they arise in all social work practice – but they have been shown by some notable research reviews, for example Clough (1987), to be especially significant in group care work.

Power

People in group care settings frequently feel that they have been placed at the receiving end of a complex set of power relationships. Issues of personal and political power operate not only within the group care setting itself, but also on the outside or the boundaries of the setting.

Power issues within the unit

At the level of the power to make decisions about one's own life, people in group care may feel excluded from decision-making processes. For example, even when they are present at their own 'reviews', young people in residential care often find that decisions have already been made elsewhere, while at the level of day-to-day decisions about rules and behaviour, they sometimes feel at the mercy of arbitrary rules and adhoc decision making by staff (Sinclair and Gibbs, 1998). At the level of personal power in relationships, clients may have been taken advantage of at home or elsewhere in terms of physical cruelty, exploitative sexual relationships, and other ways. A further irony is that it is often not only the client who feels powerless, but also the relative, the group care worker and even the field social worker – all tend to feel at times that events and people are beyond their control (Clough, 1987; Sinclair and Gibbs, 1998). Important questions therefore arise as to whether group care workers really have the 'power to care' in terms of proper access to information and resources (Baldwin, 1990). Nevertheless we must remember that it is generally the client who is in the most vulnerable position of all, and professional workers have a particular responsibility to be aware of issues of power and to ensure that they are addressed. Where these issues of personal power can be constructively addressed in daily practice, and when care can also be based upon a commitment to the human rights of service users (Frost et al, 1999), then group care can become a more positive and liberating process in people's lives (Stanley and Reed, 1999).

Power outside the unit

At the level of political and social power, people in group care – at least those in the public welfare system – are likely to come predominantly from those groups which hold the least power in society, and especially the least economic power. For some groups this situation is highlighted starkly upon admission and departure, when the poverty and hardship of people's lives is contrasted with their experience in the group care unit itself, while, for others, financial powerlessness sets the context within which the whole system of group care operates – for example, night shelters for homeless people, which are often woefully underfunded. This aspect of power connects with the elements of stigma often attached to group care services, both locally in terms of the prejudice that is attached to certain units and their users, as well as at a broader political level. Thus group care is often largely absent from consideration in terms of policy making, and remains a residual and neglected service even though it consumes huge amounts of public money. Despite the close connection between economic power, personal power, and the quality of life in group care, it is worth reflecting that there are some private group care facilities for those with both power and money, although consumers' views suggest that the quality of life in such units is not necessarily any better than in public facilities.

Prejudice

In particular, people in group care may have been at the receiving end of a combination of power with prejudice: the combination of the structural power held by the dominant groups in society with the prejudices held by those groups and which they have the power to enact or enforce. Many of our welfare services, it has been argued (for example, Patel, 1990), serve largely to perpetuate the disadvantage experienced by the less powerful groups. Moreover, people in group care may fall into more than one category of disadvantage (Norman, 1985), and simply by being in group care they may experience further prejudice in the form of stigma. The issue of prejudice, then, is inextricably linked with the issue of power, since those individuals and groups who hold the least power in society tend to be kept in that position by the prejudice-based actions of others at individual, institutional and societal levels. While the position of any of the disadvantaged groups might be used to illustrate this point, I shall draw examples here from the position of people from black groups, because their position has been relatively well documented.

The position of black people in British society vis-à-vis welfare provision has been dominated by the experience of racism at various levels – personal, organisational and institutional. Here we shall concentrate on institutional racism. An indication of the strength of institutional racism in the welfare system is that some local authorities continue to provide services based on a 'colour-blind' approach to the issues of 'race' and racism – an approach which assumes that everyone has equal power, equal opportunity and equal access to services, despite the great amount of evidence contradicting this assumption. Thus these local authorities tend to make no special effort to design and deliver their services in such a way that black people will feel able to make use of them, and black people then feel unable to use them for a number of reasons.

For example, one study in Birmingham revealed the following reasons given by black elders for not using day centre facilities:

- concern over speaking and understanding English;
- concern over the type of food offered and the catering arrangements;

- inability to participate fully in leisure pursuits because of health/physical reasons. (Patel, 1990, p 23)

To which a commentator added two further reasons:

- black elders were subjected to racist abuse and experienced hostility from the white elders at day centres;
- there was little to share and exchange with white elders (e.g. the leisure and educational facilities were inappropriate); and the 'feelings of being the only black person around' clearly made establishing relationships difficult. (Patel, 1990, p 23)

Eventually, if they are to have any welfare services at all, the black community often ends up providing its own services through the voluntary sector. Thus their needs are marginalised and are then less likely to be specifically considered by mainstream providers, and this situation soon becomes a self-perpetuating pattern. Meanwhile, in contrast to the under-provision of services for some groups, prejudice in welfare agencies may lead to *over*-referral for others, for example young people in residential care, and people within certain categories of psychiatric diagnosis (Rack, 1982).

This brief analysis of the effects of racism in welfare provision nevertheless gives an example of the twin roles which the issues of power and prejudice play in the provision of group care facilities, and it also demonstrates that these are not only questions of 'macro'-effects – there are also effects experienced directly and personally within the group care setting itself. These direct experiences of racism may happen at the hands of other clients or of members of the staff team; the racism may be overt in the form of abusive language, or it may be enacted more subtly and even unconsciously in a wide range of ways. The racism may also be experienced by black staff as well as by clients: for example one black social work student undertook 'agency' residential care work in a predominantly white rural English county but found that in one unit she was asked not to return to work after her first day, a decision that appeared to be based solely (although not openly) on her skin colour. If staff are receiving such treatment then clients are probably even more likely to experience it. It is for this reason that one of the principles set out later in this chapter is that of 'demonstrating an active commitment to anti-oppressive practice', since each worker has a responsibility to identify and prevent prejudiced actions at whatever level they occur within the system.

Although I have used the example of racism here, many other sorts of prejudice may operate in the group care setting. Variations on this theme will include the predicament of the gay or lesbian client in a setting where staff and clients are assumed to be heterosexual and where heterosexual images prevail and a subculture of discriminatory remarks may go unchallenged by the staff team; the girls in a mixed-sex adolescent residential unit where male 'macho' images and activities perpetuate stereotypes, which tend to attack or undermine the girls' self-image and self-respect (see Barter et al, 2004, for useful discussion of such issues); and the working-class parent and toddler who feel alienated and therefore misunderstood by the middle-class values and attitudes of some professional staff in family centres.

A further version of the prejudice which tends to disadvantage people in group care, as we have already seen, is the *stigma* associated with being seen to live in residential care or to attend a 'centre'. This stigma is often increased by the public labelling of buildings and vehicles, and may be reinforced by bureaucratic structures such as bulk-ordering of food and the 'order-book' purchase of clothes. While most agencies have attempted to move away from these more obvious forms of stigmatisation, it sometimes seems that, almost whatever measures are taken by staff to reduce it, the perceived stigma of the client is experienced as profoundly damaging, as Sinason and Hollins (2004) found when they consulted people with learning disabilities about their views of 'home' and 'community'. Furthermore, many social workers and other professionals may themselves contribute unwittingly to the stigma by continuing to view group care as a 'last resort' to be used (and thought about) only when all else has failed – an unhelpful attitude that needs to be challenged at all levels, since it so easily leads to a self-fulfilling prophecy.

For these reasons, group care workers have a responsibility to address issues of prejudice at whatever level they encounter them, and to develop an approach to their work that is truly anti-oppressive – that is, committed to recognising, challenging and redressing the kinds of imbalance of power and prejudice described above. A useful example of a residential service providing care for black children can be found in a chapter by Jones and Waul (2005), and, at a more general level, discussions of anti-oppressive and anti-racist practice may be found in Thompson (2002) and Dominelli (2002). The examples of group care practice presented throughout this book have been set within this anti-oppressive framework, although it would be foolhardy to claim that all of these examples represent effective anti-oppressive practice: it must be acknowledged that there is further work to be done in this area, in the theory as well as in the practice. The responsibility to address these issues must be taken on at a team as well as at an individual level, and the need to take these responsibilities seriously has big implications for the training, support and management of group care.

Dependency

It is in the nature of all 'care' work that the people on the receiving end are in a relatively dependent position – depending on others for a proportion of their physical, emotional and spiritual needs. The extent to which the clients enact this dependency will vary according to many factors, including their 'actual' needs and wishes, their own perceptions of their needs and of what the staff can offer, and according to the expectations of the staff (Stanley and Reed, 2001). The way in which dependency is handled is an issue of central importance in group care: how appropriate is it, in any given setting, for dependency to be allowed and even encouraged, and what are the risks and possible benefits for client and carer where the dependency is necessarily great?

For many of the people in group care, dependency may not only be a reality but it may also be a very fraught area. For children, their previous experience of dependency may have been traumatic. Perhaps they have not felt safe or happy with their parents or others upon whom they have had to depend, or they may not have stayed long enough in any one setting to achieve any lasting sense of dependency, while in some cases they may have had unrealistic levels of independence expected of them at far too early an age. For adults with learning difficulties, inappropriately high levels of dependency may have been expected or imposed in the past, sometimes leaving them with a legacy of institutionalised dependent habits. For others coming into group care, dependency may be equally difficult – adults with physical impairments may have understandably strong feelings about having to depend upon others for things which most adults can do for themselves, while older people who can no longer safely look after themselves may be most unhappy at returning to an apparently childlike state of dependence – although a move into residential care may actually bring increased personal *in*dependence for those who have been having to rely on relatives for personal and emotional support (Oldman et al, 1998). Thus, many people come into group care settings with great ambivalence about dependency, which may challenge the assumptions of those trying to help them. Colin Barnes (1990) provides a particularly sharp and challenging analysis of the handling of dependency in his study of day centres for young physically impaired adults.

The risk for the clients is that this element of dependency may be exaggerated and exploited by the staff for their own convenience, and that the clients may thus become institutionalised into a state of excessive and inescapable dependence. On the other hand, many workers feel considerable uncertainty and ambivalence about their clients' dependency needs, and especially about how 'involved' with one's clients it is appropriate to become (Clough, 2000, p 124). Indeed, some group care workers are so uncomfortable with the dependency element in their work that they wish to minimise it or even totally deny its existence, which in turn may risk creating situations in which clients feel unsafe because they cannot really depend on anyone. Dependency may have different connotations in a day care setting from those in a residential one; there may be a lack of clarity over, for example, who is really in charge of the children in a family centre (the parents or the staff?); or there may be difficulty for all concerned when a client forms an apparently strong attachment to a worker in a way that this client has not been able to achieve or sustain outside the centre. In this context, feelings (and especially anxieties) about dependency may obscure all other judgements and feelings about the client's situation.

The scenario is further complicated by the issues of power and prejudice outlined earlier, because the very people upon whom the client is more or less dependent also tend to be those people who are perceived as holding the greatest power, and who may additionally be enacting the prejudice, or who may themselves be affected by the prejudiced actions of others. In this context, it is worth remembering that much of group care involves women caring for women, and that these female group care workers are often juggling multiple caring responsibilities and multiple dependencies between home and work. It has been pointed out that some sectors of group care recruit:

> almost exclusively from a pool of local, otherwise unwaged, carers whose experiences as housewives, mothers and daughters substitute for formal training and whose availability for low paid shift work is directly related to their status as dependent women with domestic ties. (Bond, 1989, p 17)

The issue of dependency, then, is one that affects people at all levels in group care work, although it may be experienced as a gender-laden issue. Teams need to evolve a range of ways of handling dependency both in their clients and in themselves if they are not to become excessively stressed (see McDerment, 1988; Goodwin and Gore, 2000). The argument of this book will be that a proper awareness of dependency issues and a proper response to their expression are fundamental to good practice in group care. One useful way of formulating the aim for the group care team is to think in terms of offering clients the opportunity for 'dependency with dignity' (Wade, 1983). See Clough (2000, pp 123-7) for a further useful discussion of 'dependency and interdependency' in residential work.

These three key issues form the context within which all of those involved in group care must operate, and an understanding of the impact of these issues on the client must inform the daily practice both of the individual and of the staff team as a whole. In particular, addressing these issues leads us directly into participative approaches to practice such as advocacy and community meetings; see Chapter Two.

Principles

So far in this chapter we have been concerned with defining group care and highlighting some key issues that arise. In the light of this material, it is clear that working in group care poses many challenges. The distinctive elements of group care outlined above suggest a very different mode of working from other forms of professional practice, while the three key issues raise important questions in terms of the personal and professional value systems of the workers, and particularly in terms of their willingness and ability to translate values into action. We now need to be clearer, in relation to these and other issues, as to what guiding principles should underlie the practice of group care.

We should start by acknowledging that all those employed in social care are bound by certain guiding principles, which may be set down either by their employers, their professional bodies or by government. In the UK there are 'Codes of Practice' set down by the General Social Care Council (GSCC, 2002), the Scottish Social Services Council (SSSC, 2005) and other care councils, and all of these operate in the context of provisions such as the 1998 Human Rights Act. Requirements such as these provide the formal context within which we all have to work, but we need to think in a more focused way about our own individual and collective principles for practice.

The Wagner Report (1988) listed five principles as forming the basis of good practice, as follows:

Caring – this should be personal, and residents should feel valued, safe and secure;

Choice – each resident's right to exercise choice over their daily life should be respected;

Continuity – this includes both consistency of care from staff, and the maintenance of links with a resident's previous life;

Change – for residents, the opportunity for continued development; for staff, a commitment to respond to changing needs;

Common Values – ensuring that practice is based on a shared philosophy and values. (Wagner, 1988, p 60)

While nobody could object to principles such as these, I am not sure that they take us much further – nor are they all the same kind of principles. The first four relate mainly to the individual resident's rights in the group care setting, while the fifth is more about the underlying principles of the team's approach.

This is a complicated subject – every reader will have different views as to what the fundamental principles of this work should be, and some will object strongly to the inclusion or exclusion of certain elements. I must also admit to some scepticism here, for although I do think people may use books such as this one to pick up ideas about ways of working or new frameworks for understanding their work, I am not so sure that this is how people actually derive their own principles of professional practice. Most people probably refer to their relevant Code of Practice and rely on a combination of their own intuition, their personal value system, and whatever they pick up about the implicit working philosophy of their workplace – what has been described as the 'Working Myth' of the unit (Atherton, 1989). There is a risk, therefore, that anything spelled out here in terms of guiding principles will at best gain lip service from the average reader, and will at worst be ignored as well meaning but irrelevant. As with other themes in this book, the key to working out and working *to* one's principles will be to use the team as the focus for our thoughts.

For these reasons, I shall restrict my proposed guiding principles to four (see Box 1.3), which are outlined with some explanatory comments, and which will be illustrated throughout the book in the practice examples given – although the extent to which they do *not* underpin those examples will demonstrate that, like everyone else, I have some difficulty in putting principles into practice.

> **Box 1.3:** Principles of professional group care
> * Placing the *individual* at the heart of the system.
> * Demonstrating an active commitment to *anti-oppressive* practice.
> * Underpinning individual caring with a *team* approach.
> * Taking a *holistic* or 'systems'-based approach to the overall task.

Placing the individual at the heart of the system

This means always keeping in mind the individual client's needs, rights and wishes as the top priority. Unless this element is constantly placed at the top of the agenda, the risk is that teams and whole agencies 'drift' off course into other priorities, such as administrative convenience. This principle means that group care should be based on an agenda of participation, involvement and consultation with clients as far as possible (Frost et al, 1999). On the other hand, it also means balancing this participative and empowering work with the duties and responsibilities of care – including assessing people's needs and offering an appropriate response to those assessed needs, then monitoring and evaluating the help offered. Here the concept of a 'working alliance' between the helper and the 'helped' is useful (Brechin and Swain, 1990). This balancing of needs, rights and risks on a daily and longer-term basis is a large part of the challenge of group care. The subject has been covered by Clough (2000) and Burton (1993, 1998) in terms of residential care, and by Hunter and Watt (2001), for example, in terms of developing more open, responsive and imaginative day services for older people.

Demonstrating an active commitment to anti-oppressive practice

This means ensuring that one's practice always aims to identify, challenge and redress those issues of power and prejudice outlined earlier in this chapter. This will include a commitment to ensuring that one's practice is based upon a genuine and sustained concern to address the issues at all levels – from handling daily interactions between clients and between oneself and one's colleagues and the clients, to implementing appropriate management policies and procedures. While some of the implications of a commitment to anti-racist and anti-oppressive practice in group care have been described in the existing literature on group care, for example Fulcher (1998), Gunaratnam (2001), Okitikpi (2004) and Singh (2005), there is still much further work to be done on this theme.

Underpinning individual caring with a team approach

This means first that any individual's work must always be planned, carried out and evaluated with full regard to the work of the whole team and the life of the whole place (see Chapters Two and Four). Second, it also means ensuring that the work of the whole team is based upon an agreed system of personal and professional values, for example offering a commitment to providing dependency with dignity, and respect for privacy, individuality, confidentiality, and so on. This principle therefore requires that every group care unit works towards establishing a team approach, with a full programme of team-building and team meetings, staff supervision and training, and consultancy (see Chapter Five). This subject has been addressed by Atherton (1986) and Stanley and Reed (1999), while Clough (2000) has an excellent chapter on an 'ethical basis for practice' in residential work.

Taking a holistic or 'systems'-based approach

This is perhaps a different sort of principle from the others, but I regard it as equally fundamental to good practice. It means that, even when working in depth with an individual client, the worker must retain a full awareness of the *context* of her work – in terms of all the other aspects of the client's life, the rest of the group of clients and workers, the social and political context of the work, and so on. Working to this principle requires the worker to think laterally, to make connections, and to hold many different aspects of her work in mind, while not losing track of the immediate daily tasks of personal care. This principle is not only about 'systems thinking' however, it requires an attitude based on a 'holistic' approach, in which the people using the service are fully accepted as real and 'whole' people from real families and neighbourhoods: this approach represents a challenge to the 'little boxes' and 'pathologising' thinking that continues to characterise much of professional practice. It is an approach that also resonates with the 'strengths' perspective on social work practice (Saleebey, 2005), which values people as whole, real and human rather than as defective, problematic or even just as 'users of services'.

These four principles are only a beginning, a shorthand way of summarising the approach taken in this book, and thus they inevitably do less than justice to a complicated field. Yet in another sense, they could never be any more than that: a principle can never be a final pronouncement on an end-state, as things are always changing and developing, with new ideologies rising and fading. In this context, a principle is simply a proposal about a way of working that is 'always in a state of becoming' (Bettelheim, 1950).

Working for positive high-quality group care

Having considered these principles of professional group care, we must face the fact that they are neither universally recognised, nor always achieved in practice. While there is certainly plenty of good-quality 'principled' group care, there is also much that is mediocre, and some that is simply bad. If we are aiming for good practice, it is essential to recognise what can go wrong and why – and in particular to identify the major obstacles to good practice that people working in group care typically face.

In order to understand these obstacles, we must first recognise the societal context in which the work is set. Society's broad and clumsy definitions of social and personal problems clearly affect the ways in which welfare organisations make decisions about their services. These decisions will in turn affect not only the ways in which referrals are made to group care settings, but also the expectations that are thereby made on the settings, and ultimately the day-to-day tasks of the group care worker. For example, in relation to institutions for people with degenerative diseases, it has been argued that many of the people in these units have experienced powerful rejection (largely because of fears and stereotypes about people with disabilities) not only at an individual level but also at the broader social level, amounting to a sort of 'social death' (Miller and Gwynne, 1972), and that the task of such units may be strongly influenced both by this rejection and by the anxiety that it evokes in all involved. The challenge that such arguments pose to those designing and managing group care services is this: to what extent does society's general ambivalence about and even prejudice against the group of people you are attempting to help influence the assumptions underpinning the services that you provide? For the group care workers themselves, the challenge might be put somewhat differently: to what extent are you prepared to examine and modify your individual and collective helping efforts so as to genuinely address the situation of your clients and empower them to take remedial action where appropriate, rather than basing your efforts on your own or your organisation's attempts to cope with the anxiety associated with your task? These broad issues (to which we will return in Chapter Five when we examine the Primary Task of group care settings) set the overall context within which we can address the specifics of working towards good practice.

Obstacles to good practice

Wagner (1988) identified five common 'barriers to good practice in residential care': lack of planning and organisation, lack of leadership, fear of risk-taking, stigma and lack of resources (Wagner, 1988, p 65). Lack of planning and organisation includes such items as poor design features and poor location, some aspects of which are not in the immediate control of the group care staff, but also poor diet and failure to plan for individual needs, which certainly are in their control. Lack of leadership refers to evidence of 'an absence of caring and committed attitudes' on the part of some staff, and a suggestion that this may be due to such factors as 'poor management, staff shortages, lack of effective delegation and lack of training' (Wagner, 1988, p 66). The fear of risk-taking may derive from a mishandling of the dependency issues mentioned earlier in this chapter, while the stigma referred to has been described under the heading of prejudice. Several of these apparent 'barriers to good practice', therefore, turn out to be *symptoms* of poorly managed group care rather than either external or intrinsic constraining factors: they are thus largely within the responsibility of those working in or managing group care to identify and correct.

Lack of resources, on the other hand, may well be a real barrier to good practice in some settings, and may contribute to some of these symptoms of bad practice. Two examples will illustrate the point: buildings and people. Both Carter and Wagner report many examples of unsuitable buildings made even more unsuitable by a lack of proper investment in care and maintenance. Carter reports on day care thus:

> the biggest amenity sought most often by users and staff was more space. Overcrowding was seen by both users and staff as an inhibitor to developing new activities. One-room day centres came in for particular criticism. 'Space is our problem', said a nurse in a day hospital for the elderly. 'Everything is virtually done in one room. Moving furniture every time you want a different activity or lunch is no fun'. (Carter, 1981, p 311)

There is no doubt here that lack of appropriate resources is inhibiting the quality of the service offered – in terms of the range and variety of activities, and in terms of extra demands imposed on staff.

Similarly, lack of proper investment in staff can create real problems in group care. Again Carter comments:

> The most common opinion from staff was that the main improvement needed was to have more staff, particularly more direct service staff … more staff would allow more time to be spent with individual users. (Carter, 1981, p 317)

The lack of full professional staff training for group care workers has frequently been identified in official reports as a contributory factor to poor practice and as a serious inhibitor of positive improvements in practice (Residential Forum, 1998), and we shall return to this issue in the closing chapter. These problems of the under-resourcing of group care are serious and should be of concern to every group care worker, and they affect not just the numbers of staff but also the facilities for staff support, training and supervision. They stem from political decisions taken at every level about the relative economic importance of the group care task itself, and until more effective pressure is consistently put on the political decision makers, the situation will persist, with both clients and workers in group care continuing to be disadvantaged. It is especially important that those working in group care are aware of these issues and learn how to take appropriate steps towards improving the situation.

A second external barrier to good practice is the frequently poor fit between management and practice – particularly in terms of the pattern of 'distanced decision making' found in many welfare organisations, which places unnecessary constraints on group care workers' power to make relevant decisions (see Baldwin, 1990). Baldwin (1990, p 180) identifies a number of 'preconditions for constructive child centred care', including important proposals about the way that residential child care – and, by implication, all group care – should be managed. Group care is complicated and sensitive work, and it is essential that those managing it respect and support the difficult task facing the team, and that they operate within appropriately supportive management structures. Whereas earlier research perhaps tended to over-apply business models of management to the care sector, a growing literature has increasingly helped to clarify and theorise the management task in social care in its own terms, for example Seden and Reynolds (2003).

A third type of barrier to good practice, linked to the first two, is shown in the frequent failure of staff teams and managers to translate good ideas into practice. This problem was most clearly highlighted by a major survey of staff attitudes and caring practices in homes for older people, which found that, even when teams were aware of what might make for good practice, and even when they felt such ideas could be applied in their own settings, they often did not manage to actually put them into practice (Booth et al, 1990). This pattern, which the researchers called the 'cooling effect', was interpreted as being caused by a variety of possible reasons, similar to those identified by Wagner – that is, reasons related to design, to policy, to resources, to the residents themselves and to the staff, specifically 'from inertia through lack of vision, conviction or commitment to simple self-interest' (Booth et al, 1990, p 122). It is this inertia of group care staff and managers that represents the third of our barriers to good practice. The solutions proposed by the researchers include targeting staff training on two main objectives: first, 'on persuading the management tier within homes that good practices are not just the stuff of dreams but can be made to work', and, second, 'on demonstrating to care staff that good practices can be accommodated on a workaday basis within their daily caring routines' (Booth et al, 1990, pp 127-8). There are further implications of this phenomenon for the supervision and management of group care teams, and we shall return to these in the final chapter.

A fourth and sometimes very powerful factor in contributing to poor practice relates to the psychosocial processes that potentially complicate all care settings, such as the contagious and sometimes unconscious effects of anxiety. Thus, even 'good' staff may unwittingly distort and divert their best efforts and risk creating 'bad' or harmful care environments. Psychodynamic and systemic thinking have contributed greatly to the understanding of such processes as the 'projection' of difficult or unmanageable feelings by one group or individual onto another and the unhelpful 'splitting' mechanisms through which people tend to ascribe all 'bad' characteristics to one group or individual and all 'good' qualities to another. Helpful introductions to this approach can be found in Obholzer and Roberts (1994a), Hardwick and Woodhead (1999), Hinshelwood (2001) and Campling et al (2004).

Nevertheless, despite the reality of these barriers to good practice, we must also accept the validity of Wagner's caution:

> While scarcity of resources is undoubtedly an objective
> barrier to ideal practice, nevertheless this should not be
> made the excuse for lack of regard for the preservation of
> human dignity. (Wagner, 1988, p 65)

In other words, whatever external constraints they face in terms of
lack of resources or the effects of poor management structures, group
care workers must still endeavour to follow their professional principles
and carry out their responsibilities. It may be the case that structural
factors often make for extra difficulties for group care workers, but
such factors can never in themselves excuse or explain away bad or
even mediocre practice. The buck stops with the worker and her team.

Underlying all of these anxieties about poor practice, however, there
are deeper concerns about the real and serious damage that may be
done to people in abusive institutions (Stanley et al, 1999). There have
been enough examples of exploitative, harsh and actively abusive
regimes, especially in residential care settings, to have tainted this sector
irredeemably in some people's view, and a succession of governmental
inquiries in the UK and elsewhere have repeatedly highlighted serious
failings of systems of management and inspection that failed to detect
or prevent the worst practices (Corby et al, 2001). Some seek to explain
this 'corruption of care' (Wardhaugh and Wilding, 1998) through
examining not so much the motives of the staff but the 'conditions in
which the usual moral inhibitions against violence become weakened'
(Wardhaugh and Wilding, 1998, p 213), exploring factors such as
management failure and the inward-looking nature of some welfare
organisations. Others add to such explanations by analysing
unconscious factors operating in individuals and teams such as the
wish to deny or avoid others' (or our own) pain (Obholzer and Roberts,
1994a). In terms of trying to remedy the tendency towards bad and
abusive practice, some have emphasised the human rights of service
users (Manthorpe and Stanley, 1999; Willow, 2000) while others have
sought to build organisational systems on principles of empowerment
(Frost et al, 1999), 'ethical audit' (Stanley and Reed, 1999), improved
systems of inspection (Morgan, 2000), or structural and human
resources factors such as better staff training and development
(Residential Forum, 1998). In reality, probably all of the above apply:
care becomes corrupted and abusive when whole systems are distorted,
neglected and manipulated, and the prevention of such distortion, like
the prevention of terrorism, probably depends upon careful monitoring,
constant vigilance and a sense of individual responsibility to ensure
the best outcomes.

Finally, however, I want to conclude this chapter by emphasising a more positive and upbeat view of the potential of group care. There may be some who will find the tone adopted in this book over-optimistic and even idealistic: they will object that there is so much evidence of poor practice in group care that higher standards can never be reached or sustained. While not denying the difficulty of providing good-quality care, for the moment I want to put the case for optimism and idealism: there is evidence elsewhere in social work of the power of the self-fulfilling prophecy (Smale, 1977), and it is important that group care workers keep themselves away from negative prophecies and aim always for something more positive. If those working in group care succumb to the widespread cynicism that undermines the potential value of their work, things will never improve. Instead they must think of themselves as advocates for the potential benefits of the service that they can offer – other professionals will rarely plead on their behalf, so they will have to do it for themselves. I am not arguing for a naively uncritical defence of the group care 'corner', but for a reasoned yet enthusiastic advocacy of the value of this mode of working.

Conclusion

This chapter has aimed to define group care and to say what is special about it, to highlight some key issues that arise, and to show how these factors all fit together within some basic guiding principles for those working in this setting, and finally to show what group care workers are sometimes 'up against' in terms of the impingement on their task of various undermining factors. In the next chapter we move from the general to the specific, to look in detail at the context of daily practice in group care.

TWO

The contexts of working in group care

Introduction

We looked in Chapter One at certain features of group care that distinguish it as a mode of working from other settings. In this chapter we shall explore some of these features in greater detail, and consider their implications for those working in this setting. In respect of each of these factors, we shall be asking: what impact does this factor have on those involved in group care (both as workers and as clients), and how can the workers respond appropriately to the challenges set by these factors? However, we shall start by considering perhaps the most important aspect of context: the consumer's viewpoint.

The voice of the client

If we are to place the individual client at the heart of the system, as declared in Chapter One, it is essential that we listen to what people say about being in group care settings. We must listen to them *now* – that is, consider the available evidence here before moving to the next stage of this book – and we must listen to them *in practice*, by whatever means are the most effective, so that we can come to understand the experience of the person we are working with, and so that we can plan, carry out and evaluate our work accordingly. Listening to these voices now means taking a brief overview of the published material on the experience of people in group care. Some of this material is published in survey form or as part of the evidence in research reports or inquiries; some has been written by the people involved themselves or by their relatives or friends: all of it is powerful and worth listening to.

Published sources

Residential care

In general terms, it is clear that group care can be either a better or a worse experience for people for a very wide range of reasons, but we need answers to the specific question: what sorts of things do people value about being in group care, and what do they dislike? Although there has never been a great deal of first-hand published evidence to draw upon, the situation is gradually being remedied, and the Wagner Report (1988) did attempt a comprehensive answer to this question in relation to residential care. This report summarised the personal evidence submitted to it in terms of:

> Correspondents appear to be happy in situations where:
>
> Admission has been the resident's own choice.
>
> There is good food, warmth, physical and medical care and provisions for disability.
>
> Furnishings and facilities are satisfactory in both public and private areas.
>
> Services such as chiropody and hairdressing are available.
>
> Visitors are always welcome and there are facilities for their entertainment.
>
> There is provision for a variety of activities and outings.
>
> Birthdays and special occasions are celebrated.
>
> The resident is free to come and go or choose what to do at any time.
>
> Relationships are such as to allow the use of Christian names [sic] and reassuring physical contact.
>
> Conversation and companionship are encouraged both between residents and between residents and staff. (Wagner, 1988, p 138)

Conversely, the report's findings as to what made for negative experiences of care were the following:

> Correspondents appeared to be unhappy with homes where:
>
> Cruelty, ill treatment or neglect are overlooked by those in charge.
>
> Admission has not resulted from a resident's own considered decision.
>
> Regimes are designed for the convenience of an inadequate staff rather than to maintain the choice and comfort of residents.
>
> Activities and outings are few or non-existent.
>
> Visitors are not made welcome.
>
> Food, furnishings and facilities are poor.
>
> There is no respect for residents' dignity, individual personality or ability.
>
> Conversation, shared enjoyment and affection are not valued or encouraged. (Wagner, 1988, p 146)

Valuable though these findings are, we should remember that what they offer is by no means a fully representative sample. The Wagner committee acknowledged that the great majority of the personal evidence that they received came from elderly people, and they regretted the fact that they had heard very little from 'the mentally ill, the mentally handicapped [sic] and children', adding that 'this inability of three of the five major consumer groups to make their voices heard must itself be a cause for concern' (Wagner, 1988, p 129). Furthermore, Wagner was also criticised at the time for paying insufficient attention to the views and needs of black people (Nzira, 1989), women (Phillipson, 1989) and other groups:

> The blindness to gender differences in the report is accompanied by an absence of the words sexism, racism

and ageism, despite the fact that all are endemic in residential care. Like the massive presence of women, these dynamics go unexplained and all but unnoticed. (Phillipson, 1989)

Nevertheless, the voices of some of these other groups can be heard elsewhere: the views of children have been increasingly heard through the Who Cares? publications (for example Who Cares? Scotland, 1998), through the activities of groups such as 'A National Voice', and in the reminiscences of those who have grown up in care (Kahan, 1979). Two of the founding members of A National Voice were interviewed by Ann Wheal (Wheal, 2000) and offer powerful evidence about both the positive and the negative aspects of the care system. One in particular, 'Ronnie', felt that the system was cold, harsh and unresponsive and that the complaints system was 'a complicated joke' (Wheal, 2000, p 103). The views of people with psychiatric difficulties have been powerfully presented by groups such as Women in MIND (1986), and by David Brandon (1991) and others, while the views of people with learning difficulties may be found in Brechin and Walmsley (1989). There are many other groups whose voice is more rarely heard, such as children with autistic spectrum disorder, although research has begun to explore the challenges involved in consulting them (Preece, 2002). Much of this material suggests broadly similar findings to the Wagner evidence – although, if anything, feelings about the issues of power, prejudice and dependency emerge even more strongly from these groups than from others. The remaining uncomfortable fact, however, is that it is the groups of structurally disadvantaged people in group care who have gone largely unheard – especially women and black people. This situation reproduces and perpetuates the disadvantage that these groups experience in practice, and it is a situation which urgently needs to be remedied.

Day care

If the published evidence on the views of consumers of residential services has been sparse, the views of consumers of day care services are even harder to track down. The most important and comprehensive published source of such evidence remains the National Institute for Social Work survey, *Day Services for Adults* (Carter, 1981), although work by the King's Fund in the 1990s has aimed to build better day services by involving service users right from the start in giving their views on existing services. Views on day care sometimes appear to be more positive than those on residential care – perhaps for the reasons suggested in Chapter One. Thus, many of the findings reported by Carter are positive and appreciative:

> The point made most often was that coming to the unit helped them by giving users social contacts, friendship, or company with others. For just under half, the unit influenced their relationships with other users, and (for many) this was the foremost thing that coming to the unit had achieved for them.... In short, most users got most from the personal and interactive aspects of the day unit. (Carter, 1981, pp 278–9)

On the other hand, when people were asked about what *improvements* they would like to see in day care settings, a clearer picture emerged. Many of the issues raised about the various types of day care programme foreshadowed the later findings of the Wagner Report. For instance, there were complaints about the physical environment of the units, and some complaints about the attitudes of staff members:

> A minority of users pointed out that they felt a few staff members had adverse attitudes to users or showed little interest in them.... Other unhelpful staff attitudes were 'bossiness' and infantilisation of users. (Carter, 1981, pp 316–17)

In those day centres for adults where contract or industrial work was provided, many users complained about dull and tedious tasks; and in centres where a programme of social activities was provided, people raised two themes for reform: 'first, more feeling of involvement in social activities, and second, a livelier atmosphere' (Carter, 1981, p 293).

In the light of the themes of communication and participation highlighted elsewhere in this chapter, the users' comments on meetings and groups are especially interesting:

> The requests for improvement were for more meetings rather than for less, particularly from those users classed as mentally ill and those in family centres. 'We should', said a user in a day hospital, 'have, all of us, a discussion with all those concerned with what we do. If we patients could freely chat to these people, then they could find out how we feel. We could all meet here, knots would be unravelled

and discussed, we don't get any of that'. (Carter, 1981, p 302)

Evidence on this point is somewhat mixed, however, and Carter does point out that there were a 'few users who wanted *less* not more groups and meetings ... because they found them boring, frightening or too big (in that order)' (Carter, 1981, p 302). The work of the King's Fund project on 'Changing Days' (Wertheimer, 1996) demonstrates the power and clarity of the voice of people with learning difficulties when these are properly sought and acted on.

At the risk of excessive generalisation, then, a broad summary of the evidence suggests that being in group care is for most people a powerful and potentially traumatic experience. People in group care naturally tend to appreciate good physical provision, appropriate social opportunities, and the care, concern and engagement of humane staff who respect their dignity and their rights. Many people also feel vulnerable, powerless and uncomfortable in their dependency on others; and those who already felt in relatively powerless situations in their lives are likely to feel even more vulnerable in group care. Most of all, however, people in group care want to be *heard* – to be able to express their views and enter into dialogue with their carers and others about their situation, and thereby to be able to influence and improve their situation.

Everyday experience

Listening to what the client says, however, is far from an academic exercise, and reading the research reports is no substitute for engaging directly with the people you are caring for and consistently seeking their views on the services that you have offered or are planning to offer. There are numerous ways of achieving this communication, some of them formal, others less so; some of them more likely to lead to an honest and equal sharing of experiences – and thus to action and change – others less so. In particular, if important aspects of the way a unit is run convey an implicit message of ignoring or overriding people's needs, rights or views, then it is unlikely that a formal exercise in consultation will gain much trust or respect. The dangers of a half-hearted or insincere attempt at participation were illustrated graphically in the patients' meetings in *One Flew Over the Cuckoo's Nest* (Kesey, 2003).

The basic precondition for fully hearing people's views on their situation is the provision of a range of *opportunities for open communication*, including the following:

Communication within the unit

- *Individual relationships* between workers and clients will form the central arena of communication for most people. It is such relationships that can 'make or break' someone's stay in group care, according to whether or not they feel that those most closely involved in their care are sympathetic, engaged and responsive. In some cases, this relationship is formalised under the heading of a 'keyworker' or similar arrangement, but even in the informal everyday interactions between workers and clients, opportunities for real communication constantly arise, and it is the worker's responsibility to identify and use these opportunities. Indeed it can be argued that the relationship forms the core or heart of the discipline of group care practice, just as it has been argued is the case in other forms of social work (Trevithick, 2003; Ruch, 2005).
- *Small groups:* Much of the informal everyday communication takes place in small groupings – perhaps while engaged in some practical task or just relaxing after an activity. These occasions provide many opportunities for people to begin sharing their experiences and comparing views, often starting with views on the smallest details of the experience of care. In a team that is genuinely committed to listening to the consumer's view, the workers will regularly use these informal groupings to encourage open communication on themes of shared concern to the clients.
- *Community meetings:* If the team is really going to seek out and listen to the client's voice, there will have to be some occasions on which *everybody* comes together to talk about and listen to each other's experience. The use of such house meetings or community meetings is still underdeveloped in many branches of group care, which is unfortunate. A well-operating system of regular and open meetings between clients and workers can certainly be used to encourage people in group care to articulate their views and assert their rights, and to encourage workers and management to listen to and act upon these statements (see Ward, 1996; Firth, 2004), although it has to be acknowledged that research sometimes shows such meetings to be perceived as dominated by staff concerns rather than a genuine listening forum (Barter et al, 2004, pp 146-9). For such a system to work, people (including those with formal

power) need to be committed to make it work and to acting upon the views and feelings expressed, and, as Firth argues, it 'needs to be organised so that it does not have the feeling of a 'free for all' (Firth, 2004, p 185).

Communication with those outside the unit

Group care units vary widely in the 'inclusiveness' of the relationships that they promote and support between clients and their social worlds. Given that the issues of dependency and power are so great in group care, everyone using a group care unit has the right to some connection with independent people on the outside who will hear their voice and help them to achieve change and improvement where necessary – not only through informal friendships and family connections, but also through complaints procedures and advocacy schemes (see below) and through 'befriending' schemes. However, we should start with people's most immediate and personal connections, that is, with their family and friends.

- *Family and friends:* It is clear that the client's voice needs to be heard by her family and friends, and it is therefore essential both that individuals have unrestricted access to such contacts and that these are positively encouraged and facilitated (see Hill, 2000, for the full implications of this requirement). Indeed it has been argued (Ainsworth, 1997) that the 'traditional' models of group care (especially child care) have been built upon negative assumptions about family and parental connections, and an alternative model of 'family-centred group care' has been proposed and piloted to challenge these traditional assumptions. In the context of care for older people the role of family members has been shown to be of great importance for some residents (Wright, 2000). Of course, not all family contact is positive or even wanted, especially by those who may have been abused or assaulted at home, so this is a complicated debate (see Sinclair and Gibbs, 1998, p 158; Clough et al, 2006). For some people the group care experience offers a safe haven from oppressive or abusive family situations, and the dilemmas arising from such tensions may need to be taken into account in the plans for communication with family.
- *Formal and informal complaints procedures:* In many areas of group care, listening to the client in the sense of listening to formal complaints is no longer simply a matter of good practice – it is also a legal requirement. A complaints procedure will only work

'if people are confident that something positive will happen if they do complain' (Brearley, C.P., 1990, p 197), and implementing such a procedure will therefore involve detailed planning and consultation in order to ensure that it is perceived as fair, accessible and speedy. Moreover, it has also been pointed out that 'any complaints system is only as good as the system for putting things right where there are found to be faults' (Brearley, C.P., 1990, p 197). It is clear from research in the child care field that if a complaints system is going to be perceived as genuinely helpful and responsive, then service users need information, support and reassurance throughout the process (Frost and Wallis, 2000).

- *Inspection:* As with complaints procedures, there has been an increasing move towards tighter systems of inspection of group care settings. This is especially true of residential units, where the risks of abuse and of poor-quality care are thought to be greater – although experience has shown that inspection is no guarantee against the well-concealed operation of an abusive system. An effective system of inspection will naturally hinge on a well-informed, sensitive and highly skilled team of inspectors, operating to a clear and precise agenda in terms of what they are looking for and how they will assess what they find – none of which is easy (Morgan, 2000). Most inspections of social care services now include extensive consultation with service users and other stakeholders. For a fuller analysis of inspection issues in group care settings see Clough (1994, 2000).

- *Advocacy schemes:* Another way in which the listening may involve those outside the unit is through advocacy schemes, in which individuals and groups of clients, often with the support of outside bodies or pressure groups, assert their own view of their experience, and press the case for change where necessary. There is a wide range of advocacy practice, especially among adult groups such as those with learning difficulties and with physical disabilities. See, for example, Brandon and Brandon (2001), who have surveyed the range of such schemes including advocacy by professionals, self-advocacy and citizen advocacy, and argued for the value of the advocacy movement in that it 'defines and fights for devalued people's rights' (Brandon, 1991, p 44).

- *Network/neighbourhood meetings:* Since there is a sense in which the 'user' of group care services is the client's family, friends and even the local community, the team needs to have appropriate channels for hearing the views of these people. This may involve bringing an individual client's 'network' together for a meeting to help towards resolving the situation that has brought her into the group care setting, or in the more general context it might involve a series of regular meetings between team members, clients and people from the local community to discuss the relationships between the unit and the community. Another variation on this theme will be meetings between clients in similar situations throughout an area to share and compare experiences. In addition, the team must aim to ensure that the unit as a whole establishes clear and open communication with other professional teams.

Listening to people in group care is not always easy or straightforward, of course, and even David Brandon, an unremitting champion of consumer power in psychiatric services, conceded that 'it is true that some users are difficult' (Brandon, 1991, p 99). Nevertheless, those working in group care do have an overriding responsibility to find appropriate and effective ways of hearing the consumer's voice, and to ensure that they are supported in this task by appropriate systems of management and supervision – which is likely to mean that staff themselves will also have to articulate their own needs and rights and assert their views. Despite the increasing regulation in this area, not all social care agencies are genuinely open and responsive to hearing the voice of either the consumer or the staff, and getting heard can still involve a considerable struggle.

No specific working method or combination of methods will in itself create a system of open communication and power sharing: what is needed is the creation of, that intangible but all-important quality, the right culture or 'atmosphere' in which people will be listened to. Atmosphere is a shorthand term for what has also been called the 'social climate' of the place (Moos, 1974). It refers to the spirit in which life is lived, a blend of the predominant emotional mood of the place, the pace at which business is conducted, and the collective attitudes of the staff team. Everyone contributes to the atmosphere in their own way, including those with very little formal power in the organisation, such as newly admitted clients or domestic and ancillary staff. To complicate matters, there may develop an unofficial atmosphere among a sub-group who are at variance with the officially declared staff attitudes and working practices – for example, the 'delinquent subculture' that has been described in some residential units for adolescents (for example, Tomlinson, 2004). Brown et al (1998) focus helpfully on the theme of the staff and resident 'cultures' in the group care of young people and demonstrate the clear connection between positive cultures and positive outcomes. Atmosphere and culture may seem elusive and unmeasurable concepts, although considerable work has been invested in devising research tools for measuring and evaluating such factors (for example, Timko and Moos, 2004).

The atmosphere is usually most strongly influenced by the professional staff team in the way in which they relate to each other, with the clients and with outsiders, and is in turn influenced by the leadership style of the manager. The team as a whole therefore has a responsibility to cultivate and sustain an atmosphere in which open communication can take place, and in which users will be encouraged to express their views and exert their rights. This is most likely to be achieved through the workers paying meticulous attention to clients' views and needs during everyday interactions, and demonstrating a concern to respond constructively to requests and complaints. Without such an atmosphere, the other more formal working methods described above may not become established at all, or may wither away or become so routinised as to be meaningless.

Implications

The implications of the material covered in this section will be seen throughout this book, and should permeate individual and team practice in group care. The main implications for practice are these: that being in a group care setting is for many people a powerful and often uncomfortable experience. In particular, people's feelings about the key issues of power, dependency and prejudice are likely to be strong, and if these feelings are not heard and responded to, then the value of all the rest of our work may be undermined. Seeking, listening and responding to the views of the people in our care cannot be regarded as optional extras – they must be built in to the system of care from before the individual's arrival until after their departure.

If such a system is to work, the implications for staff at all levels are great. Individuals and the team as a whole will need to cultivate the following qualities, among others:

- the determination to *listen* to what people are saying or trying to say about their experience in group care; and in particular:
- the ability to tolerate and respond to other people's *powerful emotions*, whether these are of love or hate, pain or joy, rage or indifference;
- the ability to use *power* humanely and to release it and share it as far as possible;
- the ability to recognise the existence and effects of personal and institutional *prejudice*, and to challenge and counteract these;

- the ability to handle other people's *dependency* maturely and responsibly, and to resolve one's own ambivalence about caring for other people; and

- finally, and most importantly of all, the willingness to *take responsibility and take action* to improve the situation of individuals and groups using group care services.

The encouraging thing for the workers is that, however difficult it may sound to establish a system for what has been called 'adventurous listening' (Brandon, 1991), once such a system is set in motion within a group care setting, it may well take on a life of its own, and become central to the whole work and life of the place, as people at all levels discover the benefits of real communication. It is also likely to bring increased job satisfaction for the workers, since the great majority of group care workers are strongly motivated to provide services that genuinely and fully help the people using them.

The teamwork context

Introduction

We have already seen in Chapter One that there are certain distinctive features of teamwork in the group care setting – the interdependence of the team, the multiple relationships between team members and clients, and the public nature of much of the team's work. In this section we shall examine these features more fully, in terms of the effect that they have on the quality and nature of the service offered, and in support of the argument that successful teamwork is essential for successful group care.

The boundaries of the professional team

The question first arises as to who exactly 'the team' is: does it include only those whose predominant focus of work is direct work with the clients, and if so where do the other staff belong? To what extent, for instance, are the domestic and secretarial staff members of the team? The role of domestic staff varies widely between settings: in some places there is a deliberate policy not to employ domestic staff, as it is felt appropriate for clients and/or care staff to carry out all such tasks between them. In many residential homes for older people, on the other hand, there remain clear hierarchical demarcations between the work of domestic staff and care assistants, or between 'manual staff' and 'officer staff' with all its echoes of the class system and even military hierarchies. Some of these hierarchical distinctions are contentious, however, and their rigid enforcement can be most unhelpful and divisive, especially when they are accompanied by powerful assumptions about the relative values of different types of work – the assumption, for instance, that domestic work is less valuable than the personal care of clients, or that personal care is less important than unit management or case management. Some of these assumptions also contain a thinly disguised gender bias, where domestic and personal care are presumed to be female tasks, whereas management is assumed to be a male task. Thus, issues of power and prejudice affect even such a fundamental matter as the composition and hierarchy of the group care team. The extent to which domestic and ancillary staff are involved as full team members will be determined by the whole approach to the task of the unit by the manager and other senior staff, and there is no single 'correct' solution here. What cannot be denied, however, is that, in many group care settings, the domestic staff have at least as much daily personal contact with the clients as some of the 'care staff', and that they are therefore highly influential in determining the quality of the client's experience.

The important question of the boundaries between the larger team and the 'care' team is one that has scarcely been addressed in the literature on group care. A realistic approach to this issue in everyday practice might well be to regard *all* staff as belonging to the 'full team', in the sense that everybody has a responsibility to support each other, and everybody's contribution is valid and valued, whether they are chairing a meeting, taking the minutes, or cleaning up the room afterwards. On the other hand, for the purposes of this book, it is necessary to distinguish between the full team and the professional team – those engaged *directly* in achieving the professional social work task of the unit, in other words the 'care staff'. This distinction may not always be so clear in practice, but it is both necessary and realistic to attempt some distinction.

Another example of the decisions to be faced as to who belongs to the team is the special case of night staff in residential settings. Where waking night staff are employed, for instance, it can happen that insufficient opportunities for communication between night staff and day staff lead to major problems, with the two sub-teams establishing different approaches to their work, and thus potentially causing confusion and disorientation for the residents, who have to cope with the two different approaches. Here a way has to be found to coordinate the work of day and night staff into a more integrated approach, as it is essential that both groups consider themselves as full members of the professional team. The means for achieving this consistency will probably be through a combination of regular staff meetings, daily handover meetings, and individual and group supervision, as well as through a determination in the senior staff to validate and integrate the work of the night staff.

Many other variations on team composition arise – the position of the 'attached' field social worker in some units, for example, and the roles of students, volunteers and temporary or 'agency' staff. Many group care units have multi-professional teams in which there may be the risk of tensions and misunderstandings between the various professional groupings, which places extra demands on people's team membership skills. There is also likely to be a significant difference between teamwork in residential and in day care settings, with shiftwork in residential care sometimes bringing frequent changes in the composition of sub-teams, compared to the relative continuity in day care teams; additionally, changes in employment legislation have sometimes led to much larger teams as each person's working hours are restricted, thus creating the unintended risk of overcomplicating the team's work. It should be for the team and the team leaders to come to a working agreement about exactly how teamwork is to operate in any given setting, and it would not be sensible to offer prescriptive pronouncements here, beyond reiterating the general principle that group care work is essentially teamwork, and that anyone engaged in the professional work of the place must be somehow included as a member of the professional team.

Teamwork and gender in group care

The issues of power, prejudice and dependency arise not only in terms of direct work with clients, of course, but are of importance for all the work of the team. For example, there are important issues of gender here, which may have a profound effect on the ability of a team to work together properly. We saw earlier that sexist assumptions may underpin some of the questions of the relative power and status held by workers at different levels in the hierarchy – and that such assumptions may also be enacted in other ways, such as in the area of allocation of duties.

There are some important parallels between the experience of the worker and that of the client, and the most striking of these is that the majority of group care workers are women, just as the majority of the clients are female. The implications of this parallel bias are enormous, in terms both of the needs and expectations of all involved, and of the relationships within staff teams and between staff and clients. Again this is a topic that is largely invisible in the group care literature, with the occasional exception such as a useful chapter by Ann Davis (1989) and another in the mental health context by Sarah Davenport describing 'a gender-sensitive therapeutic environment for women' (Davenport, 2004). One example of a white male manager attempting to address these issues can be found in John Burton's (1989) powerful account of starting work as a manager of a large residential home for older people.

This brief acknowledgement of the issue of gender in group care indicates that the reality of teamwork may be much less cosy than some of the writing on teams suggests, with team members under demand from needy individuals and groups, feeling misunderstood or disadvantaged within the organisation, and sometimes without adequate opportunities to reflect together on the potential benefits and satisfactions of working together (Ward, 2003a). In a book that is aimed at improving the quality of group care work, it is sobering to remember the nature of the struggle for some group care workers.

Working with the team in mind

Despite these difficulties, teamwork must never be regarded as an optional extra in this sort of work: it is the heart of the matter. All work in a group care setting should emanate from and be referred back to the team. A worker who initiates and tries to sustain a large amount of individual work without reference to the team is actually undermining the strength of the team and thereby also devaluing her own work, since it cannot then be supported and sustained by the rest of the team. This situation is sometimes known as 'private practice', and is a familiar pitfall for those working in group care. This is not to deny, of course, that individual workers must carry responsibility for their own work, but to emphasise that all group care work is first and foremost teamwork.

The interdependent nature of the group care team means that team members may be in constant interaction and having to rely upon each other in various ways throughout the working day. The permutations of these various interactions between team members and clients are enormous: each worker will be working sometimes with individual clients and sometimes with groups; sometimes operating alone and sometimes with one or more colleagues alongside or observing. In addition, there are many different ways in which the whole staff team may be subdivided into smaller teams with their own team leaders. Each different form of organisation will provide a different context for the individual worker's efforts. In particular, the 'working alongside' context offers one of the great potential strengths of the group care setting, in that workers can support and complement each other's work, and junior or less-experienced workers can work alongside more experienced colleagues and learn the skills of the work by observation and modelling, an opportunity that does not easily arise in other types of social work (see Payne and Scott, 1985; Chapter Five, this volume).

In some ways the worker needs to see herself as 'working alongside' even when apparently working alone. At any given time, for example, she needs to know roughly where each other member of the team is and what else is happening in the building, so that she can stay in contact with colleagues to request or offer support, and so that she can remain aware of the climate of the place and the current state of the whole group. Those who are new to group care work may take some time to recognise the importance of this awareness and of the consequent need to adapt one's own work in order to stay in clear communication with colleagues. This need to always 'work with the team in mind' does not mean that each worker must be continually checking the detailed movements of every team member and client, otherwise nothing would ever get done. What the average worker needs is a general awareness of what is happening and where (see section on 'Monitoring' in Chapter Four). Where a more detailed checking out *is* necessary, as it is in some settings, this will probably be the responsibility of the senior person on duty or the shift coordinator. Even in those small-scale settings in which there may only be one person on duty at a time, the workers still need to operate as part of a team *through time*, and to work at optimum levels of communication in order to maintain the team ethos, for example by full and conscientious use of handover meetings.

Each of the different aspects of the teamwork context has a different set of possibilities and problems, and the worker needs to be able to appreciate these factors and switch from one context to another without undue difficulty. The implications of this context are therefore that, in order to function well, a group care team must cultivate and encourage the skills of team membership in its members, and must be managed and supported in such a way that people can capitalise on each other's strengths. For a further discussion of teamwork and team leadership issues in group care, see the useful collection by Seden and Reynolds (2003).

The physical context: place and time

Having considered the 'human context' of group care, in terms of the voice of the client and the experience of working in the team, we now move to the physical context: the organisation of 'place' (the physical environment) and of time.

Place

As we have seen, group care work is almost always 'centre based': in other words, it is located in a building or part of a building set aside for this purpose. It is clear that both the location of the building and its design and the environment which this creates will have an important bearing on the effectiveness of the workers' efforts.

The building

Much has been written about the physical condition of some group care units, and about the effect that a poorly designed or poorly maintained building can have on the effectiveness of the workers' efforts (see Wagner, 1988; and Carter, 1981, for users' views on the physical environment of group care). For example, in their comparative study of residential institutions for children with learning difficulties, Mazis and Canter (1979) examined the relationship between the environmental conditions in these institutions and the child management practices used. The findings of this study suggest that in the institutions studied there was 'an interlinked set of relationships between how child oriented an institution is, its size and general organization structure and details of its physical environmental arrangements' (Mazis and Canter, 1979, p 147), although no causal link could be established either way. In other words, while it is not proved that a poor physical environment necessarily leads to poor standards of care, the two are certainly likely to occur in the same place. Sinclair and Gibbs (1998) comment further on these complexities in their detailed study of children's homes. Carter (1981) provides many examples that would support these findings, and which would suggest a clearer causal link, as reported in Chapter One.

By contrast, it is clear that 'good' buildings may support and enable good care practice, by providing appropriate space for a range and diversity of activities, by enabling both movement and rest, and by adding aesthetic dimensions such as light, colour and form to other aspects of people's quality of life (whether as staff or as clients). It can additionally be argued that good buildings can carry symbolic importance for their users by providing physical shape to the 'good-enough' facilitating that is necessary for growth and change (von Sommaruga Howard, 2004). Some therapeutic communities and other mental health units have been designed with such factors in mind (see, for example, Bettelheim, 1974; Rose, 1990), and the principles of such design are becoming more widely recognised (Hosking and Haggard, 1999; RIBA Client Forum, 1999).

There are many implications of such research for the design and management of buildings to be used for other group care units. Slater and Lipman (1980, p 219), for instance, argue that the:

> fundamental principle should be that the physical settings in which people live furnish opportunities for residents to be and to remain independent and autonomous, to maintain social contact, and to find privacy, in a manner consistent with the maximisation of their quality of life.

In terms of the context for the worker which spatial arrangements provide, it is clear that the standards of work that individuals and teams can offer are powerfully affected by the physical environment of the building. The responsibility of the worker will be to develop an awareness of how these factors may affect the work in her own setting, to share and compare these findings with colleagues and clients, and to take whatever steps may be agreed as necessary towards achieving a workable and conducive environment.

Location

A second way in which spatial arrangements provide an important context for the group care worker's work is in the location of the building. Perhaps reflecting the residual model of the asylum still just about current in the late 1970s, Howard Jones (1979, p 91) wrote in *The Residential Community*:

> The Residential Institution is a kind of 'social island': a community separated to some extent from the rest of society, and thus developing customs and relationships which are also distinct.

While I shall be arguing *against* seeing group care units as 'social islands', it is true that every unit does have some boundaries which distinguish it as a unit from the other places in which people live and work in any neighbourhood. What distinguishes it may be the size or design of the building, its age, its location in its grounds, and its proximity or otherwise to other facilities and to the homes and neighbourhoods of its clients.

These physical boundaries may have a considerable effect on the social integration of the unit into its community, and consequently on the quality of the service that is offered. In her study of 44 residential units for children, Berry (1975) found that 31 of the units studied were 'isolated' or 'fairly isolated'. Half of her sample (22 units) were geographically isolated: some of these, which she called 'architecturally isolated', were 'large old converted houses, usually standing in their own grounds' (p 41) while other units were purpose built in the 19th century – these she calls 'historically isolated'. Physical factors such as these may contribute to the social isolation both of the clients and of the staff. By the start of the 21st century many – though by no means all – of these older and more isolated places had been closed, although it is sad to find that in Sinclair and Gibbs' (1998) study of 48 children's homes nearly a quarter of a century later they still found almost half to be 'clearly institutional' in external appearance, many of them built in the 1970s! Berry (1975) found that of the units in her survey that offered the lowest quality of care, 90% were also rated as either 'isolated' or 'fairly isolated'. The consequences of physical isolation may be that local people have very little contact with the unit, and that clients' families, friends and other important contacts will find it difficult to visit. Additionally, Fulcher (1981, p 181) indicates the considerable problems created for staff (both resident and non-resident) working in isolated residential units, while Sinclair and Gibbs (1998) point to the difficulties that may arise for clients in terms of visits to and from families.

The consequences of the inappropriate location of a day care unit may be that large amounts of time and energy have to be invested in transport arrangements for clients, with proportionately less time available for other aspects of the service. Carter (1981, p 314) reports transport difficulties of this sort as a serious problem in many day care units, and transport factors were again highlighted in the King's Fund study (McIntosh and Whittaker, 1998). Time used for transporting clients or for getting oneself to and from work is not necessarily wasted time, of course: we shall see in Chapter Four how some workers make constructive use of their journeys to and from work, while time used in transporting clients can often be used productively for informal discussion. What is counterproductive, however, is the wasted expense and logistic hassle of arranging transport to and from a day centre, which, with better planning, could have been much more conveniently located.

Every institution must maintain some of its boundaries – staff need to know where their own responsibilities end and where other people's responsibilities begin. My concern here is to highlight the need for each group care worker to be aware of the impact that the location of the unit may have on her work, and on the work of the team as a whole, and to consider ways of addressing any difficulties that do arise.

Time

In considering the ways in which people's time is arranged in group care settings, we shall be distinguishing between *rotas* – the scheduling or timetabling of staff's work and tasks – and *routines* – the patterns of daily living.

Rotas

Group care involves workers and clients in spending large amounts of time together. Residential care in particular has always involved prolonged contact between worker and client, and, in earlier days, people were expected to work throughout every day of the week, out of dedication to their task and often with minimal remuneration. Conditions of service for residential workers have changed enormously, in that most now work a shift system, and indeed there has been a general move towards shorter working hours and thus towards more complicated shift systems – a move that has been criticised as representing an 'industrial model' (Douglas and Payne, 1981). There is a real dilemma here: if group care workers are not to be exploited, their working hours must be restricted and must be scheduled in a fair and reasonable way, but on the other hand, beyond a certain point, personal care that is excessively scheduled and parcelled out into shifts becomes counterproductive for everyone: clients feel uncared for, and workers lose the job satisfaction involved in working closely with their clients over a significant stretch of time. The other consequence of the improved working hours of residential staff is that there is a risk of staff teams growing so large as to become completely unwieldy, which poses another real challenge.

In day care, the amounts of time involved may be considerably less, but there is still the need to ensure 'cover' for the building and for the group of clients as well as sufficient staffing for the range of specific tasks to be undertaken. Some day care settings operate an 'extended day', well beyond the office hours of most fieldwork settings, so that some form of shiftwork is necessary. In addition, most group care units employ a proportion of part-time workers, who all have to join, leave and rejoin the team on duty.

We have already seen that patterns of shiftwork create special working conditions for individuals and teams – such as regular changes in the composition of the team on duty at any one time, with the consequent risk of inconsistency from one shift to the next if inadequate information is handed forward, plus the risk of subtle but significant differences between the 'shifts' in terms of their assumptions about the professional task. The way in which the comings and goings required by shift systems are scheduled, and the way in which they are handled day by day, are essential elements in the design and management of a group care setting. Thus, if a shift system is not to lead to negative consequences for workers and clients alike, there is a strong need for careful scheduling of shifts, for regular whole-team meetings to work towards consistency of approach, and for full and productive handover meetings.

All of these matters and more go into the design of a staff rota. The rota is one of the least studied and most important aspects of the management of group care: the person who draws up the rota holds considerable power in terms of putting together particular combinations of workers at certain times of day, allocating people to the more- and less-popular parts of the day or week, and so on. A poorly designed rota, which takes insufficient account of staff needs, is the quickest way to undermine morale and therefore levels of investment in the professional task; on the other hand, a rota that operates chiefly for the convenience of staff will prevent the accomplishment of the professional task and have a bad effect on the clients, leading to their needs and requests not being met, and their rights not being respected. Mark Smith (2005, p 119) argues that 'good quality care demands predictability' and that the rota should model and facilitate this predictability.

The issue for the group care worker is that, whereas her fieldwork colleagues can more or less schedule their own time without great effect on the work of the team, she must operate to some extent within a planned schedule for the whole team. Working in a shift system to a planned rota does not come easily to those who prefer to organise their work more autonomously, just as the prolonged contact with clients in group care does not suit those who like their professional boundaries drawn more tightly. Most workers do need to feel that they can influence the design and detail of the rota to some extent to suit their own situation, but ultimately the rota is a grand exercise in mutual compromise towards achieving the task of the unit.

Routine

By contrast with the staff rota, the routine consists of the whole pattern of arrangements for 'daily living', including both formal and informal activity. In a unit that is properly geared to its professional task, these routines will be based on the daily cycle of the activities, wishes and needs of the clients, balanced against the needs and responsibilities of the workers, and will be operated in a flexible style in order to allow for individual difference and for people's need for variety (Clough, 2000, pp 10-14). Maier (1981) argued for qualities of 'rhythm and ritual' in the use of routine, and Mark Smith (2005) offers examples of such rhythms in supporting a residential programme for young people. The maintenance of a well-designed routine requires considerable thought and debate on the part of the staff team: indeed, for the organisation of daily life to take proper account of the needs of the client group, both the staff and the clients should be fully and actively involved in its design, monitoring and regular review.

On the other hand, there are plenty of examples in the literature of poorly designed or inappropriate routines, and their effect on the clients' quality of life. For example, Martin (1978, p 8) describes a home for older people in which she completed a social work placement:

> [T]he home appeared to be run largely for the convenience of the staff, and contact (other than physical) with the residents was seen as a potential threat to the smooth running of the regime.... Institutional life is astonishingly relentless and it is easy to see how maintaining its momentum can become an end in itself. In this context, the care assistant's job can all too easily become reduced to a series of physical achievements accomplished at frenetic speed within the institutional timetable.

Here the rigid routine appears to have encouraged the workers to become alienated from the real purpose of their work – the care of the residents.

Decisions about the overall structuring of time for the group and for individuals are crucial decisions, and even the way in which these decisions are arrived at will have important consequences. Do the patterns of daily living reflect the real needs and concerns of the clients, or are they chiefly dictated by the preferences of the workers? Does the use of routine reflect institutional convenience or the happy synchronisation of the shared needs and interests of a group of clients and workers? How is the structuring of time influenced by cultural assumptions about matters such as appropriate mealtimes and the balance between periods of activity and of rest? Thus, questions about the balance between staff and client needs, and between individual and group needs, which might otherwise seem abstract and conceptual, become real and concrete through decisions about the structuring of time. Carter (1988, p 133), writing about a day care setting for people with learning difficulties, observes:

> A timetable which allows for the expression of the unexpected, the dynamic and the unpredictable by [people with learning difficulties] will help them become the masters, not the victims of time and assist them in the quest for competency, creativity and community.

Elements of the routine

The design of the routine has consequences for the workers as well as for the clients, in that the workers need to be able to offer appropriate help and support at key times, and to have other times when they are under less immediate demand in order to concentrate on other tasks. One way of understanding the routine is to divide it up into distinct elements, which I shall call set pieces, in-between times and critical incidents – although Ruth Emond makes the useful observation that in the real context of everyday life in group care time does not always divide up so easily into 'distinct and separate segments' (Emond, 2005, p 130).

Set pieces

The daily routine of a group care unit is often focused on a number of central and regular important events, or 'set-piece' events. These are usually events in which all take part, especially mealtimes, or which are designed for a sub-group, but they will also include fixed events such as planned individual work. In addition, the workers will be involved in some set-piece activities that do not involve the clients (such as administrative tasks and staff meetings), and other 'indirect work' on behalf of clients, such as 'working with others on the [clients'] behalf' (Whitaker et al, 1998, p 50). It is the scheduling of these various set pieces that forms the framework of the unit's routine, and which thus requires careful coordination and regular review: this scheduling determines the flow and 'flavour' of daily living, and the rhythms need plenty of fine-tuning (see Maier, 1981).

In-between times

In addition to the set pieces, the routine will also include some periods of time which are much less tightly and formally scheduled – these are what Bettelheim (1950) calls the 'in-between times', during the interval between one set piece and the next. In fact these in-between times may be thought of in some units as comprising the main substance of daily life, while in other settings they may just be seen as the times when both clients and workers have more choice as to what to do and where to be: a unit that had no in-between times would be oppressive in the extreme. The emphasis will change according to the needs of the client group and the task of the unit, and especially in terms of the extent to which clients are encouraged and empowered to exercise choice.

While it will be appropriate in many settings for the in-between times to be left virtually unscheduled, there are other settings in which the perceived needs of the client group are such that these times have to be much more clearly organised, or at least arranged, so that the rules of social interaction are still clear and boundaries between people, and between one event and the next, are spelled out. On the other hand, some of the most graphic accounts of bad institutional practice describe great oceans of unplanned time, in which the whole of life appears to have drifted off into one long in-between time (the classic example is Maureen Oswin's [1973] powerful book *The Empty Hours*). What is most important is that the routine is consciously designed with the needs, rights and wishes of the clients fully taken into account.

Critical incidents

The third element in the routine that we shall consider here deals with the fact that not all events *can* be planned. It is in the nature of this work that things happen in the course of a day's work that were not scheduled, but which require an appropriate response from the worker or from the team. Examples might include a client unexpectedly walking out of a group activity, the unscheduled arrival of an important visitor for one of the clients, a sudden hostile verbal exchange between a client and a worker, and so on.

Such events are covered by the term 'critical incidents' – 'critical' in the sense that they face the worker with a decision as to how to respond, rather than in the sense of necessarily referring to a particularly dramatic incident. Many such events are relatively low-key, although they may still present the worker with significant decisions. These incidents may happen during set pieces or in-between times, and often comprise a large proportion of a typical day's work for many group care workers. The way in which they are handled will have a major influence on the overall climate or atmosphere of the unit – indeed some researchers have attempted to measure the 'culture' of units partly by assessing how such incidents are typically handled (Brown et al, 1998). An appropriate blend of flexibility and consistency is important here, and a team that is working well will establish certain agreed ways of handling the various types of incident that may arise, while still allowing for interactions to remain live and spontaneous rather than stereotyped.

When events such as this occur, the worker has to assess the situation, decide upon one of a number of possible courses of action, then carry through that action and evaluate the results. One useful format for analysing this aspect of group care work is 'Critical Incident Analysis' (for example, Taylor, 2000; Thomas, 2004), which is designed to enable students to focus on the 'choice point' at which they had to choose between a number of courses of action, and to describe the assessment and evaluation processes in some detail. This is a format that has been used successfully by group care students on placements, as it allows for the detailed discussion in supervision of the handling of such incidents; it can also be used as part of a student's contribution to her Placement Report. The concept of the critical incident applies not only to incidents arising in direct work with clients: it may be just as productive to analyse a decision as to how to respond when a colleague says something challenging and unexpected, or perhaps fails to appear for a handover meeting.

The implication of the critical incident model is that, even in these incidents, there is a recognisable 'process' of work involved – although such incidents often unfold so quickly that the inexperienced or untrained worker may not have time to give conscious thought to the processes of assessment and evaluation, and may have to rely largely on intuition. The context in which the worker has to respond to a critical incident is quite different from the contexts of the planned management of a set piece, or the general overseeing of an in-between time, because this mode requires distinctive skills of on-the-spot decision making, communication and adjustment to evolving situations. It is primarily with the aim of identifying and conceptualising these skills that I have developed the model of 'Opportunity-led Work' (Ward, 1995b, 1996, 2003b), which will now be explored. It is presented here as the first of the four perspectives on group care practice that we shall be examining in this book and which are summarised in Figure 1, p 12. These various perspectives, it will be recalled from the Introduction, are not intended as alternative or competing views, but as complementary approaches that need to be taken together in order to understand the full scope of group care practice. While the other perspectives deal with The Client's View, The Worker's Shift and The Team and its Task, it seems appropriate to start here with the close detail of daily practice covered by Opportunity-led Work.

Opportunity-led Work

The concept of Opportunity-led Work is a framework that has been designed to enable workers to think through the stages of handling and responding to the many unplanned moments and events in a day's work in order to make their responses more productive and helpful. There are two principles involved here: one is that even in the briefest of incidents there is a 'process' (see Chapter Four) of thinking, responding and evaluating involved, and the second is that it is in the handling of these unscheduled moments that many opportunities for useful communication (and some would say the 'real work' of group care) may arise. The skill lies in spotting these opportunities and making good use of them, and one of the key distinctions made here is between 'reacting', by which I mean a hasty and ill-thought-out way of dealing with situations, and 'responding', by which I mean dealing with situations on the basis of a well-thought-through judgement and a skilful use of verbal and other communication.

The kind of decisions that workers will have to make at such points will be, for instance, between giving 'emotional first-aid on the spot' to an individual in some distress, or on the other hand attempting what Fritz Redl calls the 'Clinical Exploitation of Life Events' (Redl, 1966, p 44): reframing the moment into an impromptu counselling session with the aim of helping the individual or group to gain longer-term insight into the nature of a recurring difficulty.

It is possible, even in brief incidents and exchanges, to identify a number of stages that typically arise. For a new practitioner, these stages may initially be hard to put into practice in the heat of the moment, although in time the skills can be learned and practice improved. The stages are as follows:

(1) Observation and assessment
(2) Decision making
(3) Action
(4) Closure and evaluation

Observation and assessment

This stage refers to the need when handling any incident to observe the detail of what is happening and to make a careful assessment as to why it may be happening and what it may mean for the individual(s) concerned. 'Assessing' in this context will mean weighing up not just the event itself but also its context. Thus the worker will begin by asking herself questions such as:

• What is happening?
• Who is involved?
• What is likely to happen next and how should I respond?

Some of the observation may be of events that appear so minor as to be almost imperceptible, and their detection as significant details may depend largely on the worker's sensitivity and intuition. Meanwhile, she will also need to expand her horizons to think about other factors that may need to influence her response:

• Is this an isolated incident or does it connect with other events?
• What are the current concerns and needs of the individual(s) involved, and how may these be influencing events?

She will be assessing not only the individual, however, but the group as a whole:

• Why this person or group?
• Does the incident really 'belong' with this individual or group, or are others involved in the background?
• Why now? Has this sort of thing happened before at this time of day/week/month/year?

And even at this stage she may also be starting to weigh up her possible response:

- What is my instinctive response and is there a good reason to override this?
- In what sense does this event represent a challenge, and in what sense an opportunity?

The assessment is not complete, however, without reflecting on the broader context of the situation:

- What is the current atmosphere in the unit – for staff as well as clients, and for sub-groups as well as the whole group? How may the atmosphere have changed just before or during this incident?
- What are the key concerns of the day and how may they affect this incident or influence its handling?

She will also think about the network of relationships and about the whole emotional 'theatre' of the situation:

- Who is involved and who is not?
- Who may be influencing this event by their presence or absence?
- How is the interplay of feelings and concerns between individuals, groups and the large group affecting this incident? Which external people or events may be involved?
- What is the quality of my own relationship with this individual or group, and how might this determine my response to the incident?
- If, as sometimes happens, unaccountably strong emotions are being expressed or enacted, where does the strength of these emotions come from? Do the emotions 'belong' with this incident at all, or did they originate with other people or events inside or outside the unit?

Finally, assessment also involves taking account of the context of power, prejudice and dependency:

- Who holds the power in this situation (officially and unofficially) and why? How may the power balance need to shift?
- In what ways may prejudiced actions, involving racism or sexism for example, be influencing the situation? (Including actions of staff and clients, but also of outsiders, including parents, friends and neighbours who may be influential even though not present at the time of the incident itself.)

- Is there an issue relating to dependency needs, for example feelings in relation to being cared for away from home, or to being emotionally attached to one of the members of the total group?

Weighing up all these dynamics and possibilities in a short space of time may seem daunting, although in practice some of the issues come much more clearly to the foreground than others, and experienced workers probably develop 'short cuts' to enable them to weigh up situations quickly and effectively.

Decision making

The outcome of this assessment will be a judgement about the situation: it is 'this sort of an issue' or 'that sort of a problem'. This judgement does not in itself tell the worker what to do, but it does contribute to the decision. The decision itself will also be influenced by other factors, and especially by the priorities and aims of the worker and the team.

Priorities

In order to be clear about the aims of any intervention, the worker must first be clear about her priorities:

- First, she must decide what is most *urgent*. Her overriding priority must clearly be the safety and well-being of all of those present: in this respect she may need to operate on the basis of a 'hierarchy of needs', putting safety and survival needs first, followed by other sorts of needs. Only then can she decide about other questions of urgency, such as whether it is more important at this moment to maintain the predictability of everyday life and 'keep the show on the road', or whether life can be relied upon to keep itself going while she attends to the potential for constructive work within this particular situation. This decision also involves judging as to what must/can be done now and what can wait or would be better done later, elsewhere or by someone else.
- Second, she must decide what is *feasible* – in terms of the available resources of time, space and personnel, but also in terms of her own abilities, confidence and energy level, and in terms of the quality of her relationship with the individual and with the others involved.
- Third, she must consider the *ethics* of the situation, including the legal requirements and constraints upon her. This will involve

being aware of the rights and needs both of the client (and their family) and of the staff, as well as considering issues such as privacy and confidentiality.

Aims

The worker needs first to think about what sort of results she wants her intervention to achieve (for example calming a troubled individual, achieving contact with a depressed and isolated group member, enabling a group activity to continue without disruption), and second to think about how she proposes to achieve that result (for example by making a direct verbal appeal to the individual, or by seeking to influence another group member to reach out to the person in question). When planning to achieve these outcomes she will therefore need to think in terms of task, timescales and tactics:

- *Task:* How will her proposed action connect with what she is employed to do as an individual and as a team member, and with the task of the unit as a whole? Is she clear that her own perception of the current task accords with others' understanding, and as to how the short-term tasks of the day connect with the longer-term task of the unit as a whole?
- *Timescales:* What does she want to have achieved in the next two minutes, what by the end of the day and what by the end of that person's stay in the unit? For each of these, her intervention should be based upon a hypothesis as to what is happening and why, and as to what difference her actions will make. This hypothesis may not always be fully formed in her mind, but may nevertheless influence her decision at a subliminal level.
- *Tactics:* A central assumption of this framework is that the group care worker always has a choice as to what to do or say, even though it may not always feel like this. Indeed, the mark of an experienced practitioner is that, rather than being driven to react unthinkingly to situations, she is able, upon reflection, to select an appropriate response from her repertoire to any given situation.

At this point the worker is in a position to decide on a course of action, perhaps implicitly based upon a working hypothesis as to what is happening and why.

Action

In terms of the types of action or response that may be used, the range of possibilities is almost infinite, but one important distinction that we have already noted is that between shorter-term and longer-term interventions. This may also be viewed as a distinction between on the one hand 'managing the situation' in order to keep life going both for the individual(s) and the group and on the other hand opening up the possibilities of fuller or deeper communication. I have suggested some of the possibilities for action below, divided broadly into the short-term and longer-term interventions, and the reader should bear in mind that what follows has been drafted with the child care context in mind, and it will therefore need adapting to other contexts.

Short-term/behavioural/'first-aid' interventions: 'managing the situation'

Most everyday incidents require an everyday response, that is, one that will keep life going by acknowledging the situation but also allowing people to continue with their plans. The goals of this kind of intervention are likely to include maintaining or restoring a sense of order and calm, achieving control, establishing and maintaining communication, and so on.

In other words, these short-term responses usually involve 'managing the situation', rather than seeking to open up communication (although communication will still be the means towards the end), and I have categorised the types of response according to whether the intention is to influence an individual or a group, and according to how one hopes to exert that influence.

Some of the options include:

Supporting individuals through one-to-one work, for example by:

- clear and direct one-to-one communication – acknowledgement of the situation, and of the feelings that it is generating;
- 'emotional first-aid on the spot' (Redl, 1966, p 90), for example helping the person to express and leave behind an upsurge of unprocessed anger, sadness or anxiety; where such first-aid is not enough, the focus would move rapidly to the deeper/longer-term interventions.

Supporting individuals through group handling, for example by:

- promoting group sensitivity to an individual's situation or distress, to help them make allowances for the individual's behaviour or feelings;
- supporting the task-focused activities of the group in order to override the disruptive effects of one member;
- promoting a light-hearted atmosphere to boost people's ability to withstand the pressure of a depressive or aggressive individual.

Managing the group through focusing on a key individual, for example by:

- identifying an influential member and focusing significant public interventions on her;
- identifying an 'underdog' and implicitly challenging the group norms by 'promoting' her;
- drawing explicit attention to the way in which an individual may have been discriminated against by other group members.

Managing the small group through group handling, for example by:

- 'Regulation of behavioural and social traffic' (Redl, 1966, p 89), for example reminding people of the ground rules of social behaviour – respect for each other's privacy and safety, and so on;
- 'Umpire services – in decision crises as well as in loaded transactions' (Redl, 1966, p 89), for example actually sorting out disagreements, or helping people to manage 'loaded transactions' such as lending or swapping possessions.

Managing the large group through group handling, for example by:

- calling an 'extra meeting', either formal or informal, in which situations requiring urgent consideration or decision by the whole group can be dealt with.

Managing the large group through focusing on an individual in the group, for example by:

- highlighting in public the extent to which an individual's powerful feelings may have come to dominate the mood of the whole group, creating a mood of fear, anxiety or uncertainty.

Other tactics for managing conflict:

Where the situation to be managed is one of conflict, there are other tactical questions to bear in mind, including:

- offering people alternatives where possible;
- preventing the build-up of intolerable frustration by defusing the tension in the situation;
- allowing people to climb down from conflict, for example making a brief tactical retreat or taking a pause for reflection.

Many of the above actions may be seen as 'systemic' interventions, that is, seeking to influence the whole situation by an action targeted on one part of it, rather than necessarily focusing solely on the obvious 'target'. See Chapter Five for more on this approach.

Longer-term / therapeutic interventions

When the initial or subsequent assessment suggests the need to move beyond the short-term focus, the emphasis is likely to be less on 'managing' the situation so as to close it down fairly quickly, and more on seeking ways to open up and promote communication. The notion of Opportunity-led Work suggests that many such moments can offer opportunities for useful and significant communication that might not arise otherwise, and the worker may, for example, aim to engage an individual by suggesting a connection between the present incident and some deeper or longer-term concern of theirs. At the same time we must be wary of implying that workers should always be ready to 'pounce' on a client with some deep interpretation or connection, which may be quite inappropriate at that moment – thus the need for careful assessment and decision making. As before, we are again faced with the decision as to whether to talk with the person individually or in a group. For both the individual and the group approach, certain key questions arise, examples of which are shown below.

Individual discussion

Why? Will it be better to talk with the person individually or in a group? An individual approach may be preferable where there is only one person apparently involved, or where it is primarily an individual concern for this person that is indicated. Even where several individuals are involved, it may still be preferable tactically to focus initially on one key individual, or to deal with each individual's concerns first, before progressing to group discussion or bringing in outsiders or external issues.

When? Should the discussion be held right now, or immediately afterwards; or perhaps at a later time, for example by suggesting: 'Let's talk about this later/tonight/sometime'? Even if none of these is appropriate right now, the worker might yet say to the person later in the day: 'Remember what happened earlier? Shall we talk about that a bit more?'.

Where? Should the discussion be held right here on the spot, close by, or somewhere well away from the group, perhaps outside the unit – in the grounds or even well away from the site? Other factors will enter such as 'Whose home-ground?'. The best guide to choosing the location, of course, may be to ask the person herself.

Who? The worker must ask herself: 'Am I the right person to be pursuing this discussion with the person, or should I pass her on to her keyworker, who may hold more information and have a better rapport with the person?'.

How? There is such a wide range of possible techniques for communicating with people that it would be inappropriate to try to list them all here; instead I will highlight a few key themes:

- *Reflecting back:* helping the person to piece together the sequence of events (for example identifying and recalling significant details), and thereby promoting the person's ability to explain and predict their own and others' behaviour and feelings, and the person's understanding of consequences. For example: 'Let's just go back over all that and see what really happened'.

- *Making links:* helping the person to explore the possible connections between this incident and other events, such as issues from the person's own family life/earlier problems/current concerns. For example: 'Have you felt like this before/recently?', or 'I wonder if [X] reminds you of anybody else you may have had strong feelings about?'.
- *Promoting self-awareness and insight:* strong feelings emerging from out of the blue can be disconcerting and even frightening for the individual as well as for others; the development of greater self-awareness through exploring the significance of a powerful situation may help the individual to develop greater ability to handle the situation more autonomously next time around. For example: 'Did you realise you were getting so angry?', or 'Do you know what it was about this morning which left you feeling so sad?'.

Group meeting

Why? Will it be better to talk with the whole group or a sub-group rather than 'picking off' key individuals from a group incident? Sometimes it may be preferable tactically to focus initially on the whole group, and only to deal with individuals' concerns once a group phenomenon has been resolved.

When and where? Should an informal group discussion among those involved be convened immediately, or should the matter be brought to the next planned meeting, for example a house/community meeting, or should an 'extra meeting' of the large group be called at once?

Who? It may be appropriate to involve other key players, such as other clients/staff member(s), other professionals, or perhaps family members or other friends.

How? Again the range of groupwork techniques is large and readers should turn to other sources for the full range. Here I will simply highlight some key functions of therapeutic groupwork in this context, including the following:

- offering a collective sense of 'containment' for troubled individuals and groups, that is, the bearing of anxiety, and the ability to think about and recognise mental pain;

- providing a place for the large group to struggle with achieving its potential for mutual help and healing, and with comprehending its own group identity;
- providing a forum in which issues of personal and social power within the group may be safely raised and learned from, rather than being re-enacted in destructive ways, for example racist comments, bullying.

Sustaining the intervention

The discussion so far might appear to imply that Opportunity-led Work involves a single decision or set of decisions, after which the situation either closes quickly or evolves along a predictable path of interactions. In reality, of course, nothing could be further from the truth: while some events do require only the simplest of responses, many require a much more complex and evolving sequence of interactions, with the worker needing to reassess and re-evaluate at regular intervals. In one sense, the daily life of a busy group care unit consists of a virtually seamless flow of such events, one merging into or overlapping with another, one situation influencing the handling of the next, and so on. To have separated out one hypothetical 'opportunity' from this melee might be seen as wholly artificial, were it not for the fact that for the person and the worker involved, each incident does have its own significance and does require the same attention to detail: this is one reason why the work is so challenging but also so potentially rewarding. The task of 'sustaining the intervention' therefore begins almost as soon as the 'action' phase has begun, and may continue for some considerable time.

We should also note that, if the intervention is to be sustained, then the worker, too, may need to be sustained: she will certainly need to stay in touch with other staff or managers as the situation unfolds, and she may need the availability of ongoing support in the form of 'live supervision'. If this is to be reliably available, the organisation as a whole needs to be tuned in to the fact that people will sometimes need such support at very short notice. The question of sustaining the intervention therefore raises important organisational considerations: in general terms, what will be important is that the organisation is seen to value and support the opportunity-led mode of work, through implementing systems of planned supervision, handover meetings and full staff meetings as well as systems for short-notice consultation as situations unfold. There may also need to be considerable flexibility within the team in terms of people's roles and functions (see Chapter Five).

Closure and evaluation

There are three main things to consider in the 'closure' phase of an intervention, whether it has been a brief exchange of words or a more substantial group meeting.

First, it is obviously important to bring the situation to an agreed and clear ending so that the participants can resume their other activities and responsibilities, but also so that there will be less risk of the situation being misunderstood or misrepresented at a later stage. This can be thought of in terms of closing down the communication – making sure that no 'loose ends' have been left, in the sense of people who are not sure what has been said to them or not clear about or satisfied with the response that they have had. It may be important for the worker to actually say something like: 'Well, that's finished with now', or 'Let's leave it there for the moment'. It will not always be clear as to when this can be said, and the worker may need to check with the person, for example: 'Are you ready to leave it there?' or 'How do you think we should finish this off?'.

Sometimes she will find that she has to extricate herself from a situation which she feels has gone on long enough, even though the other(s) involved may see it differently. Here she might need to say something like: 'I would like to be able to talk about this more, but I'm afraid I have to go and ...' (*note:* the genuine reason will almost always be the best one to give!).

Second, decisions may need to be made as to what else has to be done in connection with the facts and feelings of the situation. For example, information may need to be conveyed to other people inside or outside the unit, or strong feelings may need to be allowed for during the ensuing period and may need to be raised again later elsewhere – perhaps at a handover or community meeting or at a family meeting, or with the person's social worker. Sometimes the worker may need to close the incident by giving a firm undertaking as to how it will be followed up, either with this individual/group, or with other people, for example: 'Now that I know how you are feeling, I will speak to [X] first thing in the morning, and then let you know what she says', or 'I really think we should go together to talk with [X] now, and get this cleared up'. The worker will also need to think about how an individual or group's learning from an incident can be incorporated into the mainstream of the work of the unit.

The written recording of incidents is a legal requirement in most care settings, so questions will arise as to who records what and why. There will also be questions about how far the private concerns of an individual are to be made public, either through discussion or recording, or in what way it will be appropriate and productive to convey the learning from an incident to others who may be affected. This will partly depend on the extent to which the concerns of an individual are judged to have impinged, or to be likely to impinge, on the whole group.

Third, after the situation has been resolved, there is the need for team review and evaluation – for people to evaluate their ways of working and to improve their understanding, incorporating any changes into their policies and procedures. Individuals (workers and clients) may need supervision, catharsis, free time, relief, and so on. If the situation has been an especially difficult one to handle, other people may not realise how strong the worker's feelings were, and she may need to seek out an appropriate team member and ask for immediate support. She has a responsibility to do this – a responsibility both to herself and to others – because it is likely that there is a good reason for her to have these strong feelings, and she needs to learn from these feelings rather than letting them stay with her. Moreover, if she has strong feelings, it is likely that the client and others involved will also have equivalent feelings, and somebody (not necessarily this same worker) may need to offer them some further support. The period immediately following a sustained piece of opportunity-led communication may be an especially sensitive time for some of those involved – including those only apparently involved at the fringes of the communication.

Here we conclude this relatively brief introduction to the concept of Opportunity-led Work. There is much more that might be said about this mode of practice, but space does not permit in the present volume; indeed the fine detail of working 'in the moment' with the wide range of people with differing needs in group care services remains to be explored. In the current context this concept is offered as the first of the four perspectives on group care practice to be outlined in this book. It offers a 'process'-based way of thinking about everyday practice, and is intended to be used in conjunction with the other perspectives presented in the following chapters.

Conclusion

To summarise this chapter, the contexts of group care work vary according to the different possible combinations of people involved and according to the ways in which time and space are structured and planned. We have also considered the experience of the consumers of group care services and the implications of this experience for those organising and delivering group care services. Finally we have examined the concept of Opportunity-led Work, the first of the four perspectives on working in group care.

THREE

The Client's Stay

Introduction

We now move to the second of the four perspectives on working in group care that were briefly introduced earlier in the book. As was pointed out in the Introduction, these perspectives are not intended to represent mutually exclusive theories of group care work. Indeed, they are not in themselves 'theories' at all: they simply represent different ways of looking at group care work, each of which allows for a wide range of theories to be drawn upon, but all of which need to be taken equally into account if we are to build up an accurate picture of the complex nature of the work.

In this second perspective – The Client's Stay – the focus is on the life situation of the client, and on the stages in the client's 'career' of contact with the unit from admission through to departure and beyond. This focus derives from that substantial proportion of the literature on residential work which addresses issues of admission, care and/or treatment, and departure. It offers a logical framework of sequential stages for describing the individual's experience of group care and for analysing the corresponding tasks at each stage for the group care workers.

Although this approach has been principally derived from the literature on residential care, it may also be usefully applied to the stages of a client's contact with a day care setting. For example, in many family centres, people are referred to the unit, attend over a given period of time, and eventually finish their involvement with the centre and leave. Other types of day services, however, are envisaged in different terms entirely – an example would be the community-based family centres described by Warren-Adamson (2001), where people use the centre as and when they wish on a self-help basis. In such settings it may be less appropriate to describe the work in terms of 'the Client's Stay', since those using the place are specifically not viewed as clients, and they are not attending for care or treatment so much as for mutual support and collective action. Nevertheless, people do arrive at and depart from such centres, and some of the other features of this perspective on group care may also still apply, such as the planning of daily life to meet group needs and wishes. This perspective on practice, then, is not intended to be imposed on every type of group care setting – where it does not fit exactly, readers are encouraged to simply use those elements that do fit, and to adapt or ignore the rest.

The process

'The Client's Stay' perspective represents a 'process' approach to group care, in which the focus is on the process through time of the individual's experience of care. At its simplest, this perspective describes group care as a sequence of:

Admission → Care/Treatment → Departure

This approach is helpful in demonstrating the importance for the worker of keeping a focus both on the nominated individual or client and on her family or social network, and in allowing for a clear analysis of the tasks of the unit and thereby of each worker in relation to the types of service offered at each stage. Another merit of this approach is that it matches well with the parallel tasks of the field social worker/ care manager at each stage – especially at the admission and discharge stages. Indeed, the interaction between field and residential workers can be seen constructively in terms of a collaborative partnership, in which responsibility is shared between the various workers, family members and others for work with the client at each stage of the process (Milligan and Stevens, 2006). This is a useful approach, since the role of the fieldworker during the care/treatment stage varies considerably in practice, and has long been a potential source of friction and misunderstanding.

It is easy, however, for a discussion on the client's 'career' to become preoccupied with the concerns of the worker, rather than those of the client: in this chapter we will try to maintain appropriate focus on both, by discussing at each stage first the experience of the client and second the tasks typically required of the workers. Moreover, there is a risk when concentrating on the individual's stay of discounting the role of other important parties such as the other clients, the families and social networks of the clients, and so on, so these factors have been included at each stage. The underlying themes of this chapter are first the importance of *planning*: knowing what you are aiming to do and why; second the importance of drawing up these plans in proper *partnership* with everyone involved; and third the individual's right to involvement and *participation* in decision making about individual and group life in the group care setting.

Admission

Introduction

The admission stage is probably the most fully researched of all aspects of group care practice. For example, Brearley et al (1980) analysed admission to residential care in terms of a 'risk-analysis' framework, which was designed to help workers recognise and weigh up the various hazards and strengths that a social worker has to assess when considering a planned admission to care. Decisions about admission to group care are complex decisions, and much of what has been written in this field analyses the decision-making process in some detail – but usually from the fieldworker/care manager's point of view, with the role of the group care worker only being considered after the important decisions have been taken, and often also with insufficient emphasis on the full involvement of the individual client herself who is entering the unit. These tendencies in the literature undoubtedly reflect the reality of practice in some settings, where group care workers do not get to meet their clients until after the admission process is complete, and where the voice of the client is not properly heard.

If group care is to be based upon a holistic approach in which the clients are valued as real and 'whole' people from real families and neighbourhoods it is essential that group care workers become more fully involved in *all* stages of the process of care, from before admission until after departure (Hill, 2000). They therefore need to become familiar with the home surroundings and family circumstances of the people likely to come into the unit, and with the details of the dilemmas involved for the person as well as for the other professionals in making decisions about admission. The logistics of this broader role for group care workers do need careful consideration, but they are certainly achievable.

People enter group care for a wide range of reasons, not all of them linked clearly to an assessed and agreed need for the group care programme itself, and workers will need to appreciate the implications for the work of the unit of some of these other reasons such as the protection of the individual's family or neighbourhood. We also know that conditions of poverty and homelessness often contribute powerfully to the decision to refer an individual for group care, and that among some client groups black people and women are greatly over-represented in referrals, so those working in group care have to be careful that their units do not become used as a further step in the disadvantaging of already powerless groups (Barn et al, 1998).

Taking account of factors such as these, some have argued that admission is not simply a stage in a sequence but a central issue or 'focus of work' in its own right, a critical point of decision making at which the key participants can be helped to face the true nature and extent of the problem they are facing, and the possible consequences of their proposed solutions. From this angle, the work that goes into the pre-admission stage of the group care 'process' may have a crucial effect on the person's whole experience of group care (see Bruggen and O'Brian, 1987).

In order to address the role of the worker in the admission process more fully, we need to consider both the client's and the worker's experience of admission, before setting out a fuller version of the sequence of events and of the tasks required of the workers.

The client's experience

Residential care

From the client's point of view, admission to group care is widely recognised as being potentially a highly traumatic experience. In an early but still relevant social work text, Juliet Berry (1972, p 428) suggested that:

> The first entry into any institution is particularly traumatic because of the fear of the unknown, the uncertainty about how one is expected to behave, the sudden loss of one's customary roles and pattern of living – these amongst other factors may cause severe shock.

This state of trauma probably results partly from the feelings that anyone has upon entering a major new situation or stage in their life, but also from factors such as the way in which the decision to admit was taken, the specific reasons for the admission, the type of unit and the degrees of restriction and compulsion involved, and the way in which the actual entry to the unit is planned and managed by the team.

In the literature on group care, many of the more horrific examples of bad practice at admission are drawn from what has been called the 'literature of dysfunction' (Jones and Fowles, 1980), for example texts by Goffman (1968) and others describing the worst extremes of institutional depersonalisation. While such accounts do offer sombre warnings to group care workers, they are now very outdated and quite unhelpful in specifying what would make for *good* practice. A more balanced view of the experience is given in the personal evidence submitted to the Wagner Report (1988), and for a useful analysis of the 'literature of dysfunction' see the excellent collection of papers by Raymond Jack (1998).

On the one hand, some residents report admission as a time of having been deceived or abandoned, while, on the other hand, for some admission is recollected as having been positive and a genuine relief. The Wagner Report also indicates that, in general, residents appear to be happier in situations where admission has been their own choice than where it 'has not resulted from a resident's own considered decision' (Wagner, 1988, p 146). This unsurprising finding supports the view that what happens *before* the actual admission may have as much effect on the experience of entering care as any particular dynamics of the institution itself (Tobin and Liebermann, 1976). For example, Jan Holloway (1999) contrasts the terrible distress that she experienced before admission to an in-patient psychiatric unit with the feelings of relief and safety upon being looked after once she was admitted. These findings are borne out in the work of Oldman et al (1997) on older people's experience of moving into residential care. In other words, the way in which the workers handle the planning and decision-making stage of the process, and specifically, the extent to which they listen to and act upon people's own views and preferences, may be critical to its overall success.

Nevertheless, it is clear that many people entering residential care do risk experiencing what I shall call 'admission trauma'. The potentially traumatic nature of the experience of admission may be said to have the components shown in Box 3.1.

Box 3.1: Some factors contributing to the risk of 'admission trauma' in group care
- Loss and separation from familiar people and places.
- Anxiety at being in a new situation, where expectations of behaviour and so on may be unknown or unclear.
- Fear of an uncertain future, and especially of losing control of one's circumstances.
- Feelings of stigmatisation and other consequences of prejudice.
- Feelings of powerlessness to influence decisions.
- Fear of imposed dependency.

This knowledge of the powerful impact that admission may have upon the individual effectively sets the agenda for the work of the staff in the planning and management of each new admission. In particular, the workers must achieve good communication with the person, so that the factors contributing to admission trauma may be addressed and hopefully resolved. They must work in such a way as to minimise any additional trauma caused by their own working methods, while they must also allow the individual space and time to reflect upon the meaning and reality of such a major life event.

Day care

While it may be relatively easy to identify the above phenomena as components in admission to residential care, it is not so widely recognised that similar experiences may be felt by those entering day care. Admission to day care is rarely as 'total' as admission to residential care, in that the person usually remains living in their own home base and is thus able to return everyday to a known environment with familiar people. On the other hand, in some circumstances the experience may be just as traumatic as admission to residential care. This may happen, for example, where attendance has an element of compulsion or where there is a lack of choice between resources for the client; where the admission follows closely after another important transition in the individual's life, such as the loss of a spouse or of one's mobility; where there is perceived stigma for the client in being seen to attend a place that is used by some of society's 'deviants', or a sense of shame in finding oneself in the company of other stigmatised people; or, finally, where the 'newness' or strangeness of the day care setting is sufficient to create disorientation or distress for the individual.

There is another reason why it is important not to underestimate the significance for some people of coming into day care. The very decision to become a user of day services may signify to the individual an unwelcome step along a one-way path to increasing dependence. Carter (1981, pp 51-2) shows that:

> the decision to admit a person to a centre for mental handicap [sic] is a critical one, for once in the training centre most clients are unlikely to leave it. In nearly three-quarters of the units [studied] managers predict that 90 per cent or more of the clients will stay in the centre for the rest of their lives.

While the proportion remaining in day care among other client groups varies considerably, and while one would advocate a much more flexible use of day care resources, it does seem that, for some adults, entering day care may be experienced as almost as 'final' a decision as entering residential care.

In conclusion, then, the client's experience of admission to group care is often a powerful and traumatic one, which is likely to be experienced as all the more threatening by those who are already disadvantaged in terms of power, oppressed by various forms of prejudice, and vulnerable because of increased dependency. It is the nature of this potential trauma which sets the agenda for the responsibilities of the group care team in planning and handling the admission.

The workers' response

When someone enters group care, the experience may be difficult not only for the individual in question but also for the others involved, including the other clients and the group care workers themselves. There may be strong feelings in all concerned and the way in which these feelings are understood and handled by the workers may have a considerable effect on the success or otherwise of the placement. Juliet Berry describes a new arrival as a 'special event-cum-crisis' for the group of established clients, and suggests that 'the reactions in the group are likely to be ambivalent in that every arrival and departure forcibly reminds each inmate of his own personal uncertainties' (Berry, 1972, p 427). Such ambivalence may also find an echo in the response of the workers to a new arrival: Berry argues that admissions can also 'cause something of a crisis to the staff, even though they are relatively secure' (Berry, 1972, p 429). While this disturbance to the staff will certainly not amount to the same trauma as for the new client, it is nevertheless important to acknowledge that for everyone involved admission may be an intense and unsettling experience.

The stages of the process

If admissions are to be planned in such a way as to empower the client to take an active role in the process, the main requirements from the individual's point of view will be facilities for *information, consultation* and *negotiation*, so that she has the facts upon which to make decisions, the opportunity to consult with and influence the relevant powerful people, and the right to negotiate the type of entry into the group care setting that will feel acceptable to her.

Pointers for good practice

Certain basic elements of good practice will therefore underpin any discussion on admission to group care. First, each *unit* (and agency) must have clear and written referral procedures and admission policies. Second, each *client* should have a written agreement or contract covering the reasons for the admission, the expected length of stay, and so on. Third, the workers should never underestimate the possible impact of admission trauma for those entering group care, and its ripples throughout the unit, and should always plan for appropriate support to be offered to the individual and their family during and after an admission. Fourth, admission should be planned in terms of the whole team's work with the whole group of clients, rather than solely in terms of the transition of the named individual.

Referral

For the individual, the actual admission is not usually the beginning of her contact with welfare agencies. There will usually have been a period of referral and negotiation, perhaps as part of a continuing social work plan with her and her family or social network. (Where an admission has had to be carried out in an emergency, the same negotiations may have to be condensed into a very short period of time, or may even have to be held immediately after the admission itself. In general, however, emergency admissions are even more traumatic and disruptive for all involved and need extremely careful handling.)

Decisions about admissions raise fundamental questions about the management of a unit, in terms of policy and procedure. Before considering admission of any particular individual, the team will need to be clear about:

(1) Where do referrals come from and what form should they take? What is the unit's policy as to what sort of people in what circumstances are normally accepted; what criteria are used to decide whether or not any particular referral (including emergency referrals) is appropriate?

(2) Does everyone know about and agree with these policies, and where are they written down? What is the balance of power between the client, their family, the professionals and others?

These important questions about the running of the unit cannot realistically be re-examined each time a referral is to be considered. What is needed is an established set of policies and procedures within which the unit can operate in a relatively consistent and predictable way, sanctioned and supported by the larger organisation in which it is set.

Negotiation

Not every appropriate referral to a group care unit results in an admission. Ideally, there should first be a period of negotiation, leading to decisions and to an appropriate agreement. It is at this stage of negotiating the details of an individual admission that issues of power are most crucial, and it will be important that the following items are addressed, among others:

(3) Is it really appropriate for this particular person to be coming into group care and why? What do the carers, relatives and the rest of the person's network think of the idea? Have the cultural assumptions and other possible stereotyping underpinning the referral of this individual been fully examined?
(4) How much is really negotiable, and is this clear to all parties? Are the language and time-span of these negotiations comprehensible to all parties?

Agreement

Once these general points have been covered, we are left with the task of agreeing upon the detail of the admission. This agreement should be recorded in writing, to achieve maximum clarity about the purpose and plans for the placement, and to provide a clear record for all parties as to what has been agreed and why. The details of such agreements will obviously vary widely according to client groups and circumstances, but the elements covered in a typical agreement will include the following:

(5) The *reason* for the admission – why does this person need help of this sort, and why at this particular unit? And the *aims* of the

placement — what are the intended outcomes of the placement, how will 'progress' be assessed, how long is the person expected to stay and where will she move to afterwards?

(6) The *arrangements* for the placement — what sort of contact will the person have with her family and network, at what frequency; in day care, when will the person attend, what transport arrangements will be made, and so on? How is the placement financed, and what arrangements will be made in respect of the person's own money and other possessions including furniture and perhaps pets? What basic rules and regulations do the person and her family need to be aware of? What possessions will the person actually bring with her on the day?

(7) The *needs, rights and strengths of the individual* — how will these be acknowledged and addressed during her stay, including issues of culture, religion, food, and so on, and the person's need for continuity of contact with her own community, as well as enabling the person to retain her interests, abilities and strengths?

(8) Questions about the *status* of the agreement — how long does this agreement last for, how and when will it be reviewed and by whom? What will happen if the agreement is broken unilaterally? And questions about the respective *roles and responsibilities* of the professional workers — who does what, who works with whom? What is the legal status of the agreement?

(9) Linked closely to the above item is the question of *complaints procedures*. It is essential that the individual knows from the start how to complain about any aspect of their experience in the unit that they find unsatisfactory — who to complain to, who may support them.

Much more might be said on the significance of the use of written agreements in group care (see Corden and Preston-Shoot, 1987, pp 65-9), and we shall consider later in this chapter the link between this agreement upon admission and the planning of the programmes for individual and group needs.

The moment of admission

Most people coming into group care seem to retain vivid memories of the moment of admission, and what happens on the first day may set the tone for the person's whole stay. It is also likely to be at the moment of admission that the fears and anxieties described earlier under the term 'admission trauma' may be at their greatest. It is therefore essential that, however careful the overall planning for the person's stay in group care may have been, the actual admission itself should be properly planned, and especially with an aim of addressing and reducing the types of fears and anxieties we have identified.

Again the details of such plans will vary widely, but among the methods used in some settings are the following:

- prior visits to the individual on her own territory by a keyworker, followed by visits by the individual to the unit;
- preparation of the unit by the team, including opportunities for workers and clients to discuss feelings and arrangements about the new arrival;
- on the day of arrival itself, ensuring that a familiar person meets and greets the individual, ensuring ample opportunities for the person to join the place and meet people at her own pace and in her own chosen style;
- after admission, providing opportunities for the person to reflect further upon the experience; ensuring that team members remain in clear communication with the person, supporting her through the early stages of joining the place; and creating opportunities for the newcomer to share experiences with others more established in the unit.

In this context, Claire Wendelken (1983) describes the useful idea of providing a 'bridge person' who will aim to offer support to the individual throughout the transition into the unit, meeting her well before admission, being present at the moment of admission itself, and staying in close contact with the person over the next few days and beyond.

Admitting the 'whole person' to the 'whole unit'

A holistic approach to group care suggests that it is not sufficient for admission to be thought of simply in terms of the physical transfer of a needy individual, neatly arranged between a fieldworker and the head of the unit. The person has a right to be seen as a 'whole person', with strengths, skills and history as well as with needs and problems (Saleebey, 2005). Moreover, each time someone enters group care, the person's family and network, plus the whole group of staff and clients, are all affected to some degree, and the reactions and responses of these groups may in turn have a powerful effect upon the individual in transition. For this reason, the whole team must take responsibility to *plan together* for the handling of each admission or departure, and will need to include in this plan not only the details of the individual work outlined above, but also other matters. For example, the other clients have a right to be informed and consulted about the impending new arrival, and may need the opportunity to reflect together or individually on the likely impact of this arrival on the life of the place. Similarly, there may be a mixture of feelings in the staff team about the admission, and unless team members are enabled to reflect together on their feelings, they may not provide the best possible reception for the new person.

In order to facilitate such planning, the team may find it helpful to use a form such as the one shown in Figure 3.1, which offers a framework within which they can plan their individual and collective efforts with each party at each stage of the process. Such a form might be used in two ways – first to agree upon a 'normal procedure' for the sorts of things that will usually be done at each stage, and second to plan the detail of each individual new admission, focusing on the particular people to be involved, the scheduling of dates, and so on. It should be possible to do some of this planning jointly with the client group in many settings: after all, the existing group of clients know far more than any of the staff what it is like to enter a group care setting

Figure 3.1: Admission to group care: outline for planning the team's work at various stages

	Referral	Negotiation and agreement	Admission
Work with the individual			
Work with relatives and others			
Work with the existing client group			
Work within the staff group			

as a client, and may have valuable contributions to make, both to the general planning and in terms of reaching out to an individual newcomer. If the planning and anticipation remains solely within the staff group we risk losing the potential benefit of the greatest resource within most group care units: the group itself.

Care/treatment

The second stage of 'The Client's Stay', described here as the care/treatment stage, covers the whole of what happens for the individual between entering and leaving the place. To examine this stage, we start by considering the implications of the terms 'care' and 'treatment', and looking at the client's experience. Approaches to care or treatment will be then discussed in two sections: first, assessment and planning, and, second, programmes, the latter of which is subdivided into the Programme for Individual Needs and the Programme for Group Needs.

'Care' and 'treatment'

The concepts of 'care' and 'treatment' need further comment: not all group care teams work with an agreed aim of offering 'treatment' with its connotations of therapy, and some are even reluctant to use the word 'care'. I am using 'care' here to mean *the organised provision of personal and other services* to the clients of the group care setting. In some settings, anything that might be called treatment is seen as something different and extra, while in others, treatment or therapy are not seen as forming any part of the work. In many places, however, there is an implicit assumption that daily life in the unit provides a kind of treatment in itself, in that *the way care is provided* is viewed as offering a range of opportunities for people to reflect on their experience, learn and develop, change and grow.

There is a strong argument for most group care to be organised on this latter basis. Group care settings are costly facilities, and are probably best used when they are offered to those who want and need something beyond mere 'accommodation'. It makes sense, therefore, that group care should provide planned and purposeful help, rather than simply offering a supposedly neutral and undirected 'care'. This is not to argue that all group care should follow the so-called 'horticultural' model (Miller and Gwynne, 1972), since, as we have seen, some people do not want to be 'treated' or expected to 'grow'. What I am proposing is that group care should be operated on the basis that, since care cannot be 'neutral' and the way in which everyday life is handled will inevitably have a more positive or more negative effect on those using the place, we may as well aim for the more positive!

This raises the question as to whose view prevails as to what is 'more positive' – the clients, the referring agency, society, the group care workers – and where and how such views about the quality of care are heard. First and foremost this is for those using the service to judge, and it is the responsibility of the group care team to empower these individuals to assess and assert their own needs, rights and wishes – to decide, for example, how everyday life should be structured and managed. The finely balanced task of the group care team is to offer planned help in the spirit of empowerment, without being patronising or excessively controlling on the one hand, and without denying some people's needs for dependency and even protection on the other hand.

Maintaining this balance highlights the important issue of people's rights, including their right not to receive 'treatment' if they do not wish to. Later in this chapter we shall be discussing people's needs and how they may be assessed and met. However, whatever is said or done about people's needs must be set in a framework of their rights: people have the right to private space and time, freedom of expression, and equality of opportunity, and such rights must all be built in to a code of ethics for group care. People's rights in group care are the same as their rights in any other context, and these rights will remain constant throughout their stay and broadly similar whatever the setting.

From the point of view of the client, the distinction between care and treatment may begin to seem rather over-elaborate: the question from their point of view may well be: 'What feels right, and what helps?'. The next section therefore considers the client's experience – in this case, the experience specifically of *being in group care*, rather than of entering or leaving it.

The experience of the client

We have already seen that what people value about group care is not only individual, personalised and sensitive care, but also opportunities for conversation and companionship, for a range of activities, for contact with visitors and others outside the place, and so on. There will not be space here for a survey of the whole range of consumer views about the experience of being in group care – and in any case, what is more important than a literature review is that practitioners themselves should regularly make the time and space with their 'consumers' to review the quality of the service offered. For this reason, what follows focuses on people's comments not so much on specific aspects of daily life, as on their right to participate in decisions about *all* aspects of life in group care, with the aim of establishing a link between the quality of the experience of group care and the clients' right to participation.

For example, the Wagner Report (1988, p 143) highlighted the need for an appropriate programme of activities by quoting a resident who is clearly not only bored but also deprived of the opportunity to argue for a better system:

> The sheer boredom causes real hardship.... There is a constant feeling that 'there is a great big world out there and I should be part of it', but residents are cut off completely from everything.

The connection between this kind of situation and the right to participate in decision making is established by a resident in a home for people with physical disabilities thus:

> I have always objected to the restrictions placed on my lifestyle and environment, not always because of the nature of my disability, but usually by so-called 'professional people' who say they 'know what's best' for me.... I find it very important to be able to speak for myself, and have people listen to me and treat me with respect. (Wagner, 1988, p 147)

Some of the strongest voices articulating the need for participation come from those with physical disabilities – Wagner (1988, p 148) quotes another resident who develops the need for consultation and respect into an argument for a complete change of emphasis:

> The emphasis of the entire establishment should be of the staff depending on the residents for their jobs and not the residents depending on the staff for anything other than 'hired muscle'.

Such a voice sounded wildly radical at the time but in some areas exactly such an approach has been implemented in the years since the Wagner Report. To do so requires a complete re-examination of the relationship between everyday practice and the assumptions made about the dependency needs of people in group care. Indeed, a version of this re-examination is offered by Colin Barnes, who argues that:

> User participation and mechanisms for user participation
> in day centre policy making should be mandatory, and
> should be organized around a formal constitution which
> stipulates users' rights as well as their responsibilities. (Barnes,
> 1990, p 199)

These views on the experience of being in group care show strong
support for a participative approach to practice, and indicate the logical
conclusion of developing such participation into a coherent working
method. This is an approach that presents a major challenge to those
working in group care: how far can such methods be developed with
other groups, such as older people or adults with severe learning
difficulties, and how would they apply in settings such as a 'drop-in'
day centre or a 'secure unit' for adolescents beyond control? I hope
that these examples suggest, not that this approach is in any way
unworkable in such settings, but that there are particular issues that
will arise in its implementation in each different setting. There is also
the major question as to how far any group care team will be allowed
the opportunity to use such an approach within the powerful constraints
imposed by many welfare organisations – and by legislation. Indeed, a
later review of the emerging pattern of user-led services for disabled
people confirms that:

> User-led organisations face a continuous struggle to ensure
> the availability of sufficient and appropriate resources –
> funding, staff and premises – to undertake their desired
> service role. (Barnes and Mercer, 2006, p 7)

Assessment and planning

Any planned work with an individual or group must be based on a
sound assessment or understanding of their needs and wishes, and the
method of assessment should be appropriate to the context. Assessment
in the fieldwork context is often carried out on an individual basis by
a single worker, but this model does not match with what we have
identified as the distinctive nature of group care. Assessment in group
care should draw on the shared observations and judgements of the
whole team, as well as on the contribution of the individual client and
her network, otherwise the rich potential of the group care context is
being wasted. This is not to undervalue the role of the individual
worker in assessment – the worker can still take responsibility to arrange
and record assessment meetings, draw together appropriate material,

consult relevant outsiders, and so on – but, with such a wealth of possible information and judgement available, it would be foolish to retain a purely individual model of assessment. A range of possible working methods for shared assessment is available, including team discussion, consultation with external experts, and 'network meetings' in which the individual client's family, friends and fellow clients contribute to the discussion. There is also a wide variety of possible criteria for assessment, varying according to the client group and to the 'philosophy' of the centre; readers will have to turn to more specialist texts for the details of such criteria.

Two further general points need clarifying. First, although we are considering assessment at the start of the care/treatment stage, assessment is not a once-and-for-all phenomenon, and a group care setting should have a schedule for reviewing and reassessing each person's and group's needs throughout their stay. 'Situational assessment' is also a component in managing daily life in group care, in terms of assessing the mood of the group and monitoring the atmosphere of the unit as a whole, and teams will need to evolve an agreed approach to this type of assessment. Second, it will be clear that individual and group needs sometimes overlap and sometimes conflict, and that part of the function of assessment will be to enable the workers to plan the coordination of individual and group needs within the overall task of the centre, and sometimes to replan or reschedule existing plans in the light of evolving assessments.

It is also important to recognise, however, that, because assessment has a subjective element, it is the area of practice in which there is the strongest risk of clients being disadvantaged through the cultural assumptions, racist stereotyping, and so on of the staff team. The workers as a team need to ensure that they develop an approach to assessment which is determinedly anti-discriminatory – that is, which is based on a sound awareness both of their own cultural assumptions, and of the disadvantage which some of their clients will have encountered, and which is targeted upon redressing this disadvantage (Barn et al, 1997; Fulcher, 1998).

Programmes

The aim of assessment will be to arrive at an agreed programme of care and/or treatment for each person. The whole notion of 'programme' remains unfamiliar to some group care workers in the UK (Smith, M., 2005), although elsewhere in the world the term is used to signify a theoretically informed plan for both group and individual care: in other words a plan for what we will offer to people in group care services and why. The term is perhaps becoming more familiar through innovations such as the Care Programme Approach in mental health care and Individual Programme Planning in work with people with learning difficulties. I will outline the two main aspects of any such programme: first, a programme covering the individual needs of each client, and, second, a programme relating to the shared needs of the group of clients.

Joining the group

As a prelude to considering the programmes for individual and group needs, we should acknowledge that any individual entering group care faces the potentially daunting task of joining what is often a well-established group of clients and workers. It is unfortunate that, despite the large amount of literature on admission to care, there is relatively little that deals with those subsequent days and weeks during which the new individual is still having to assimilate and adjust to many aspects of her changed circumstances. Indeed, a certain amount of very unwise 'folk wisdom' is still rumoured to persist in some places, such as the supposed need of a new client in residential care for a 'settling-in period', during which she should have little or no contact with family or friends – a monstrous idea, somehow reminiscent of the idea of 'breaking in' a horse. Crisis theory (Roberts, 2000), meanwhile, suggests that it is precisely during such critical times in people's lives that they may be amenable to intensive support as they re-evaluate their lives and their coping strategies: with this in mind the 'crisis' of admission could be regarded as offering important opportunities for people to be offered significant help.

Programme for Individual Needs

If we are really to 'place the individual at the heart of the system', then the Programme for Individual Needs will be a central means of implementing such an approach. As an absolute minimum, the individual person in group care is entitled to expect individualised care, and for it to be effective this care cannot be left to chance or to the day-to-day whims of those on duty: it must be based on an agreed plan drawn up on the basis of proper assessment. The Programme for Individual Needs will therefore need to take account of the elements shown in Box 3.2.

> **Box 3.2:** Aspects of the Programme for Individual Needs
> (1) A programme based on the original agreement, but subject to participatory review.
> (2) A programme built around an individual relationship with one of the workers.
> (3) A programme which incorporates links with family and network.

A programme based on the original agreement, but subject to participatory review

We saw earlier that the agreement at admission should include a plan as to how the person's needs and rights will be addressed, with clear links drawn between this plan, the purpose of that individual's stay, and the overall task of the whole unit. Naturally, it will not always be possible at the start of the person's stay to predict *all* that will need to be done, so regular review and reassessment will be needed. The Individual Programme should therefore always be viewed as an adaptable plan or 'work in progress', which can be altered in response to changing circumstances and current special needs, and all parties will need to be clear about how such changes can be called for and implemented. The individual should be fully involved in the review process, and there are many ways in which this can be achieved, from regular discussions between the individual and her keyworker, to the use of group meetings for review and evaluation.

A programme built around an individual relationship with one of the workers

Each client needs to know that at least one individual worker in the place has a clear understanding of her personal needs, wishes and rights and a clear commitment to ensuring that these are consistently met – one worker, that is, in addition to the head of the unit. Whether this worker plays a more administrative role, or whether she also takes on functions such as counselling or links with the family, will depend on many factors, and the nature of this relationship will therefore vary immensely from one setting to another. Without this allocation of an individual worker, however, the individual client may remain powerless and excessively dependent, and thus may risk sinking in the ocean of group life (see the section in Chapter Five on keyworkers).

A programme which incorporates links with family and network

Not all of the facilities and services offered to the individual will be within the centre, and it is important that consideration is given to the possibilities offered *outside* the centre's programme, especially links with the individual's family and community (Ainsworth, 1997; Hill, 2000). This will be especially important for those in residential care, where there is sometimes a real risk that essential contacts with family and community may wither if not nurtured. The worker has a responsibility to enable the individual to explore and maximise these contacts, which may also turn out to be critically important for her after leaving the centre (Wright, 2000; Paulus et al, 2005).

As with the keyworking relationship, all the other details of any Individual Programme will vary according to factors such as the wishes and needs of the individual, the nature, task and working methods of the setting, and the resources available. An Individual Programme will consist of a blend of planned individual and group activities as well as participation in the informal daily life of the place, and while these informal interactions, by their very nature, cannot always be specified in a programme, the part that they play is often so significant that a way must be found of acknowledging their importance. Every unit will have its own way of formulating programmes: see, for example, Jenkins et al (1988) on 'Individual Programme Planning' for people with learning difficulties. The way the programme is formulated will embody the team's whole approach to its task, and will be based on the assumptions (spoken or unspoken) within the team about the clients, their needs and their rights (see Atherton, 1989). However, research suggests that simply having a well-written plan is of little value to the client unless the plan is put into action clearly and consistently (Adams et al, 2006). To summarise, it is not the fact of the Individual Programme – or indeed of having any form of care plan or programme – that is important but rather the ways in which it is implemented.

Programme for Group Needs

In addition to the Individual Programme, there must be an overall programme to address the shared needs of the whole group. The Programme for Group Needs, like the Individual Programme, should be based on regular assessment of the needs and wishes both of the large group and of smaller groupings, and will have to be regularly reviewed and altered as circumstances change. There is therefore the same need for flexibility and adaptability as in the design of the Individual Programme, and the same need for consultation with the clients.

This programme will include elements such as those shown in Box 3.3.

Box 3.3: Elements of the Programme for Group Needs
- Arrangements for daily living, with each individual located in a 'home-base' group.
- A schedule of activities and opportunities.
- Planned groupwork and meetings.
- Planned links with the local community.

Arrangements for daily living

We have already considered the general importance of the routine of daily living in group care (Chapter Two). Here we look at three specific ways in which the planning and managing of daily life affect the experience of the individual. The assumption throughout this section will be that individuals are located in what might be called a 'home-base' group, that is, a stable and consistent group of clients and staff, small enough in number to be manageable (say, no more than eight clients and often fewer, plus the appropriate number of staff for the context), rather than simply belonging to what can be an amorphous total group in a large unit. One of the more positive trends in group care towards the end of the 20th century was the reduction in size of many units and the arrangement of smaller living groups in the remaining large units. This trend has certainly helped to create more positive and less institutionalised group care (Fulcher and Ainsworth, 2006).

First, the *quality of daily-life activities themselves* is of great importance, and each activity should be designed taking into account both the group's general needs and each individual's specific needs and choices (Clough, 2000). For example, every aspect of food is of great significance in group care, including the quality of the food itself, the care with which it is prepared and presented, the atmosphere in which mealtimes are conducted, the amount of choice that people have about where, when and what they will eat, the extent to which the food provided matches the ethnic, religious and other requirements of the individuals (for example, Gunaratnam, 2001), and so on. Moreover, the overlap between care and treatment is illustrated by the fact that in some settings the details of the arrangements for food may also be planned with an overall 'treatment' aim of, for instance, improving nutrition, or furthering psychotherapeutic aims (for example, Carter, 2003).

Second, the *pattern* or *routine* into which daily living is structured will affect people's overall experience. We have seen that the routine of daily life needs to be designed with a feel for the rhythm and flow of life, making allowance for people's needs for activity and rest, companionship and privacy, and for predictability as well as variety. It also needs to allow for difference as well as for similar needs in the group day by day, to prevent the risk of people being pushed into 'batch living', and to enable them to choose the pattern as well as the content of their day's activities.

Third, and in some ways most important of all, will be the *spirit* in which daily life is conducted. Whatever is planned, and however laudable the intentions of those doing the planning, what matters is the way in which these plans are translated into action: there is no benefit to the clients if what is on paper a splendidly positive and empowering programme is delivered by a staff team who do not have the motivation, skills or morale to make the programme come to life as intended. This 'spirit' or climate does not arise either by chance or by diktat and needs to be actively supported and nurtured by unit managers.

A schedule of activities and opportunities

The second element in the Programme for Group Needs is the scheduling of regular activities, including leisure or educational activities, plus (where appropriate) specific therapeutic activities such as the rehabilitation programmes in some day care settings. In some settings it may be quite inappropriate to have a 'schedule of activities' at all – especially where the task of the unit is to promote maximum independence on the part of the clients. Yet even in such units there may be some benefit in holding planned events such as a regular discussion group on 'how it feels to be struggling towards independence'. In general, the role of activities in group care seems to be undervalued in the literature, compared to the importance which many of those living and working in group care would attach to them. One useful example of the use of activities in support of a therapeutic programme can be found in Graham McCaffrey's account of the use of leisure activities in psychosocial nursing (McCaffrey, 1998).

For the details of the range of specific activities for any given group the reader will have to turn to a specialist text; here we shall mainly consider the role of activities in general and their scheduling into the programme. Despite the wide range of possible activities, the reality is that potential is not always fulfilled, and some researchers have commented on 'patronising' or 'belittling' activities (Clough, 2000, p 16) and on the 'dull and routinised programmes in some units' (Tibbitt, 1987, p 20), while, on the other hand, too much diversity of activities can become chaotic and counterproductive. Activities should be offered for a clear purpose, and these purposes should relate not only to the staff team's ideas but also to the clients' own views as to how they would like to use their time (see Van der Ven, 1985; Clough, 2000). In this context it is interesting to note that research into activities in day care has shown that the same activities may be classified under completely different purposes in different settings (Tibbitt, 1987). This finding suggests that in some units the planning of activities is done without taking full account of the views of the clients, and a cynical view might be that the overarching concern of the staff team may sometimes be simply to 'occupy' the clients in order to keep them quiet and easy to control.

Just as in the Individual Programme, group care workers should not assume that all activities will be inside the unit. Participation in activities outside the unit is valuable not only for those taking part, but also for those who, for whatever reason, do not take part. It ensures that the boundaries of the unit do not become too 'set', and it allows for a continual flow of ideas, people and sometimes artefacts, across these boundaries.

Before concluding this section, we should also acknowledge that in some units the 'activities' planned include work. In particular, some day centres provide 'paid' work for the users – although this is a highly contentious area, and important questions have been raised about the nature of the work and the levels of pay provided. Carter records strong views from some clients on this theme, and raises the question as to 'whether work in day units should parallel the opportunities, choices and variety of work experiences and industrial practices outside' (Carter, 1981, p 291) – concluding that the whole subject has not been adequately addressed in the planning of day care services. On the other hand the King's Fund development project to improve day services includes encouraging examples of much more positive experiences of real employment for people with learning difficulties (McIntosh and Whittaker, 1998) and people with complex disabilities (McIntosh and Whittaker, 2000).

Planned groupwork and meetings

The third element in the Programme for Group Needs is the use of groups and meetings. There is some overlap between this element and the previous two, since groups and groupings occur naturally throughout the day, whether in the set pieces of daily living such as mealtimes, or in the 'in-between times'. It is in the more informal 'groupings' that much of the 'Opportunity-led Work' described in Chapter Five happens. Sometimes this simply involves helping people to resolve the tensions and conflicts that will arise in the life of any group, while at other times the workers will capitalise further on everyday interactions by offering particular help on individual issues or on the shared concerns of the group. The task of the worker in such situations is to spot the opportunity when it arises, and then to find appropriate ways of using this opportunity without causing unnecessary disruption to the life of the group. Whitaker et al (1998) describe how 'staff strive to maximise the occurrence of constructive group situations' (p 69) and where possible may try to adjust the composition of informal group situations, 'trying to avoid mixes which staff predict will create serious problems' (p 73).

In a sense, group care is entirely about being in groups of various sorts, and several useful texts address this subject (for example, Douglas, 1986; Brown and Clough, 1989; Stokoe, 2003), while research also indicates the positive potential of the resident group for its members (Emond, 2002). The team therefore needs to be aware of the interrelationships within and between the various groups in the place, and to try to take account of these issues in planning their work. Planned groupwork will therefore include contingency plans for handling group situations as they occur in everyday life (see above), as well as formal small groups for discussion, and the use of the large group for decision making and so on.

Small groups

However much informal and opportunity-led groupwork happens in a unit, planned groupwork should always be considered as an option. Some people – staff as well as clients – feel threatened by the idea of planned groupwork for a variety of reasons, but the benefits of such work for many clients has so frequently been demonstrated that such fears should always be explored rather than being allowed to inhibit creative practice. The fears may relate to anxiety about people being forced to disclose personal material, or, for some workers, apprehension about the challenge to the established order, which, for example, a group on the theme of empowerment might represent. Nevertheless, small groupwork may provide an ideal setting for some of the psychosocial support and confidence-building that many people will value, perhaps through working together on common interests, or through sharing aspects of themselves through work on reminiscence or life-story work for instance.

Many of the problems of organising groupwork in field social work settings, for example identifying an appropriate membership, agreeing on shared concerns, and finding suitable space, are handled much more easily in the group care context, since the people, the space and the shared concerns are often readily identifiable. Nevertheless, planned groupwork in the group care context still requires careful preparation and consultation: for example, it is not only those who are to be included in a group who will have to be consulted, but also those who will not be included, since everyone will be aware of their inclusion or otherwise, and may have strong feelings about this issue. Similarly, booking a room for a regular group meeting may be straightforward in some units, but establishing the boundaries so that other clients and staff do not intrude on the group's work may take much longer to achieve. There are a few papers on working with small groups in this context (for example, Brown, 1990), to which readers are referred for further ideas.

Large groups

Groupwork in group care also includes working with large groups. The central fact about group care is that it involves groups of people – staff and residents – living and working together. They all belong to one large group, whether or not they identify strongly with that group, and whether or not that group becomes formalised into an identified meeting. They all affect each other for better or worse, and while some of these effects are very obvious for all to see, others are much more difficult to detect, although potentially just as powerful. In some settings the opportunities of this situation are exploited through the use of the 'community meeting', although in many other places there is considerable anxiety and uncertainty about working with the large group (but see Brown and Clough, 1989, pp 194-5). My own experience in practice was that, although establishing a system in which people in group care can work together productively in large groups may be difficult and anxiety provoking, this way of working can eventually become the central reference point of daily living and indeed of all the work of the unit – 'the heart of the system' (Ward, 1993b). In particular, the large group is the ideal forum within which to address issues of power and dependency in group care, by encouraging people throughout the system to reflect on their personal power within the place and to begin to redress the balance where necessary.

While the community meeting is often seen as a method specific to the therapeutic community approach, there are many straightforward and productive ways in which large groupwork can operate in group care, and can usefully address many of the same issues as the community meeting. For example, Moya Sadler (1984) gives an account of setting up a residents' committee in a home for older people, while Duffy and McCarthy describe the 'conversion of a routine house meeting in a hostel for teenage girls to a therapeutic group with more emphasis on personal growth and relationships' (Duffy and McCarthy, 1998, p 145), and Tomlinson (2004) has a more substantial discussion on the therapeutic use of meetings.

Planned links with the local community

The fourth element in the Programme for Group Needs will be the way in which the internal life of the unit is connected with the life and activities of the local community. Here again, practice varies widely according to the setting and its task, but especially according to the attitude and assumptions of the staff team. If the team sees its task as predominantly providing an all-inclusive service for an inward-looking group of dependent people, then the links with the community may be minimal – and in some settings this might possibly be appropriate. There are some units whose task is so delicate or profound that too much coming and going across the boundaries can seriously disrupt the work. For example, the manager of a small hospice for dying and seriously ill children would not consider taking a social work student on placement because she felt that at that particular time the intrusion on the task of the unit would be too great – which felt an entirely appropriate decision. Yet at the same time many hospices and other palliative care settings are quite public about their work (Hearn and Myers, 2001) and see this openness as an important part of their 'mission'.

By contrast, then, some units aim for extensive contact with the local community, as in the case of the team of a residential centre for older people, who ensured that, as far as possible, all medical, dental and other appointments for the users should be arranged off-site in local clinics. Thus the users retained maximum contact with the widest network of local facilities, rather than sinking into the administrative convenience of using visiting professionals. All units have to achieve a sensible balance between what is provided within the unit and what remains on the outside, just as they also have to decide whether the unit can offer to the community certain resources or facilities beyond its immediate primary task, such as opening up day centres for use by local groups needing a venue for evening meetings. These should be shared decisions between staff and clients, based on genuine recognition of the pros and cons, rather than solely on the assumptions of the workers – or, worse still, the prejudice or financial 'eye' of the manager.

Balancing of individual and group needs

Since there may be considerable overlap between the Programme for Individual Needs and the Programme for Group Needs, there will always be a balance to be achieved between the two. It is a key responsibility of the workers to monitor this balance, and to help individuals recognise and act upon their own needs and rights if these are at risk of being overridden by the group. The tasks of the worker will be to remain aware of the issue, to monitor people's experience by listening and watching, and to take appropriate action to support individuals in redressing the balance if it is lost.

Departure

Introduction

In comparison to the extensive literature on admission, there has been much less written on departure, although increasing concerns both about young people leaving care and about adults leaving long-term institutional care have been reflected in more recent literature. This lack of attention mirrors the extent to which the importance of achieving an appropriate departure is often overlooked in practice, which itself is perhaps an indication of how hard most people find it to face endings and departures in general. Both admission and departure are important transitions, and the transition out of group care may be just as difficult as the transition into it: it tends to arouse similarly strong ambivalence and anxiety all round, and it therefore merits equal emphasis with the earlier stages in the process. The focus here will be on the client's experience of the ending of their stay, and on the tasks and challenges that consequently face the workers at each stage.

The client's experience

How do people experience departure from group care settings? The range of experience is wide: some might echo the psychiatric patient quoted as saying, 'Discharge is hell' (Brandon, 1981, p 17), and we should not underestimate the sense of abandonment and even betrayal that some may feel upon leaving (Stein, 2002). Thus one young person told a researcher:

> I don't think they realise how big a step you are taking when [you move] into your own place, but ... they never seem to take what you say seriously. I don't think I should have been pressurised the way I was into my flat. (Sinclair and Gibbs, 1998, p 68)

On the other hand, not all departures from care are traumatic: indeed, some people experience departure as the positive culmination and fulfilment of all their experiences during their stay, and when departure is appropriately planned and supported the experience holds far less fear for those anticipating leaving. A young person who has been adequately prepared for independent living, a family that has been helped at a Family Centre to overcome conflicts and tensions that were placing the children of the family 'at risk', an adult with learning difficulties who finally manages to make the transition from the 'total shelter' of a large institution to live in a shared house with perhaps two others, will all anticipate departure with a mixture of excitement and apprehension, but at least with the possibility that the future will be more positive and rewarding than the past.

In some group care settings, there may be little prospect of departure other than through death, and, in these circumstances, it may be feelings about death itself, rather than just about departure, that predominate. Yvonne Shemmings (1996, 1998) writes sensitively and constructively about the way death is handled in the residential care of older people. It has been argued that some institutions for those with physical disabilities or degenerative diseases provide 'lifetime care' to people who may be perceived as having no role in society or positive social status, and that the task of these institutions thus becomes in some senses 'to cater for the socially dead during the interval between social death and physical death' (Miller and Gwynne, 1972, p 80). See Chapter Five for a fuller discussion of this provocative interpretation and its implications for the task of residential care.

Among the factors that will determine the wide range of experiences of people leaving group care will be the following: (i) the sort of place the person is departing from, (ii) the nature and quality of that person's experience while in the unit; and (iii) the sort of place she is going to, and the reasons for the departure.

Where is the person leaving from?

There are significant differences between leaving residential care and leaving day care. Leaving residential care might be expected to be a more profound experience than leaving day care, since it involves a change of place of living as well as of daytime activity, support and companionship, and many accounts of the experience do describe feelings of rejection and abandonment, heightened by the fact that people have often felt inadequately prepared for the departure itself or for living outside the institution. Moreover, for some people, *any* change may be experienced as stressful and even life-threatening, and this factor may make leaving group care stressful for these people however much preparation is carried out. Leaving residential care is not always a permanent or unanticipated transition, however. For example, where the person has been in respite care, the period in residence may have been as short as a few days, and the departure may become a relatively regular and familiar event. On the other hand, the comings and goings of respite care may be unpredictable, poorly planned and profoundly disturbing for the person involved, and if a pattern of respite care becomes either haphazard or over-routinised, there is a risk that the impact of the experience on the individual constantly in transit will be overlooked. See Stalker (1996) for a collection of papers on the experience of short-term and respite care, Moriarty and Levin (1998) for a very useful discussion of respite services for adults, and Laverty and Reet (2001) for a practical account of planning for respite care provision for children with disabilities.

Leaving a day care setting, meanwhile, will not necessarily be any less complicated than leaving residential care. An indication of the difficulties faced by some people in leaving day care is found in Carter's comment that three quarters of the heads of the day hospitals covered in her survey:

> had trouble persuading people to leave, most often because of the fears of the old person: 'Some patients become very attached to the unit and are therefore very upset about discharge. Some have been known to, for instance, aggravate

ulcers so that treatment can continue'…. (Carter, 1981, p 196)

This observation certainly confirms the view that people who feel vulnerable may experience *any* change as stressful, and especially when the change involves leaving a situation in which dependency needs have been met and in which the future looks uncertain.

It should also be recognised that the views of the parties involved may differ: while the professionals may assess a need on the part of an individual to return to independent living, the views of that individual may indicate quite different priorities, such as wanting to retain the social network offered by a day care setting. The questions then arise as to who has the power to influence the decision, and as to how the original offer of help may have been construed by the individual and/ or their family. As the head occupational therapist in a day hospital commented: 'It is so difficult to give an old person a physical, psychological and social crutch and then take it away' (Carter, 1981, p 197).

One important finding is that there are wide differences between day care settings in terms of the proportion of people who leave: Carter (1981) found that in those day centres for older people based in residential homes, some had virtually no 'turnover' in the client group during a given year, while others had several complete turnovers (Carter, 1981, p 30). The researchers found it impossible to explain these differences, and Carter later comments that 'more work needs to be done on what constitutes a successful discharge from a day unit' (Carter, 1981, p 80). One other significant feature of day care is that, since people arrive and depart on a daily basis, some of the feelings associated with such transitions permeate the work of the place. This feature can be turned to useful effect if opportunities for reflective discussion are created, since it offers people frequent examples and rehearsals of the feelings associated with departures and other transitions.

What has the person's experience of group care been like?

Departure is the stage of 'The Client's Stay' in which everything comes to fruition or comes home to roost; that which was not resolved at earlier stages will return; people are likely to feel a mixture of excitement and apprehension, validation and rejection. All of these feelings will naturally vary according to individual circumstances, including the way in which the key issues of power, prejudice and dependency have been handled during the stay. If the person has been enabled to feel increasingly in control of her life, then however much apprehension is felt, the experience of departure may be more positive. On the other hand, if the person has been made to feel powerless, lacking in confidence and inappropriately dependent, for example, then the experience of departure may serve to confirm these feelings. Some young people will have experienced 'a high degree of movement and disruption during the time they were 'looked after'" (Frost et al, 1999, p 117). Moreover, for some people, departure comes about not so much from a considered decision about the individual's needs but more as a consequence of policy or other pragmatic decisions taken at local or national level. Thus, people discharged from long-stay psychiatric hospitals under 'Care in the Community' plans have sometimes experienced this move as just as impersonal and alienating as the institutionalising experience that they endured in hospital. Similarly, Johnson and Traustadottir (2005) collect many moving accounts of the experience of people with learning difficulties moving out of long-stay institutions, sometimes into what Gardner and Glanville (2005, p 222) call 'new forms of institutionalization in the community'.

The sort of place she is going to

The experience of leaving group care will also vary according to where the person is going *to*. Some people leave one group care setting to go to another: to move, for example, to a less-protected or (for some) a more-protected environment. Many others are leaving group care altogether to return home – and some of these are returning to a situation that may have changed dramatically during their absence (see Millham et al, 1986). This situation naturally brings special anxieties that will require skilled support (Fariss, 2000; Stevens, 2000). Other people are returning to a situation that feels just as unsafe as it may have been when they originally left – for example, children returning to a family in which they may previously have been neglected or even abused, or other individuals who may have been 'placed' in group care as part of a scapegoating process in their family or community, and who may find themselves returning to an unchanged situation, in which stigmatising and scapegoating may restart immediately upon their return. Departure may also mark other major transitions, as in the case of young people leaving residential care to live independently, who have to face all the hazards of entering adult responsibility in addition to the trauma of leaving the security of dependent care, and similarly in the case of people with learning difficulties making the transitions from large-scale institutions to much smaller households, who may be having to face the responsibilities of independent adult life for the first time (Astor and Jeffereys, 2000).

As will have been noticed in the above examples, two particular groups figure largely in the literature on departure from group care: first, young people leaving residential care, and, second, the large number of patients discharged from long-stay hospitals. The fact that in both cases those leaving frequently experience isolation, homelessness and poverty reminds us that many people come into group care not simply because they have certain social, psychological or other problems, but also because they lack the financial resources to sort out these problems without help, or because they are stigmatised through their poverty. When these people move on, to risk further poverty or homelessness, those working in the units themselves may not always have much further involvement, but they may be powerfully affected by the knowledge that these are the circumstances facing those who leave. Some places, however, do evolve successful ways of offering continuing support and involvement of those leaving their care – see below under 'Aftercare'.

Other responses to departure

It is not only the client herself who will have strong feelings about departure, but also her relatives and her community, plus the workers both individually and as a team.

Impact on other clients

The departure of any individual may have a general impact on the life of the group, as well as special resonance for some individuals. Since everyone in the place will eventually leave, the actual departure of an individual may reawaken in others some version of their own fears or hopes, or remind them of previous departures, or may perhaps put them in mind of other wished-for departures, leading to questions such as, 'will I be next – and have I got anywhere to go to?', 'why is it her rather than me?', 'why can't I stay here forever?' or 'why am I still here?'. Within the group as a whole there may be a collective – although sometimes unspoken – response to an individual's departure, according to the role that she played in the group: sometimes a feeling of mourning when a much-loved person is leaving, of denial if the group does not wish to face the loss of that person, or of relief if an unpopular person is leaving. One of the key responsibilities of the team at this time will be to help both individuals and groups to say what they need to say about such feelings – both to each other and (where appropriate) to the person who is leaving. The use of group discussions and community meetings can be especially helpful for handling feelings such as these, and such discussions may require sensitive and skilled responses from staff. Since some reference has been made here to unpopular or 'difficult' clients, it should be noted that the process of scapegoating, both among staff and client groups, are powerful and potentially destructive (Douglas, 1986). Peer group hierarchies arise in most group care settings (Barter et al, 2004) but where they lead to 'acting-out' behaviour they may be best addressed through support from external consultancy (for example, Obholzer and Roberts, 1994b).

Impact on family and social network

Just as the individual may be ambivalent about departure, so too may her family – if dependency is reverting to them, for example, or if a troubled family member is moving on to yet another placement. The traditional separations of responsibilities suggest that it will be the social worker or care manager's task to engage with the family and help them if necessary to recognise and cope with the range of feelings aroused by the person's impending transition. However, group care workers may also be able to offer collaborative support here, whether in terms of planned work or of informal contact with family members. Moreover, it is not only the family who may be affected by a departure, but the rest of the person's social network – friends, neighbours, and so on. The responsibilities of the team will include helping the individual to plan for all aspects of departure, including relationships between the individual and her family and other parts of her network.

Impact on the staff group

Just as group care workers may feel ambivalent over admissions, so they may have similar ambivalence when people leave. For example, they may ask themselves: 'Have we really helped this person? What else might we have done?', or 'Will she really be safe/happy/wanted where she is going?'. (They may also, of course, feel some of the same envy, loss or sense of being left behind that the other clients may feel.) Whether the person was a favourite member of the group who will be strongly missed, or a troublesome and awkward member whose departure might be felt initially as a relief, there may be a range of strong feelings within the team and within some individuals in particular. Since these feelings are often difficult to face directly, there is a natural tendency to deny or disown them, or to leave them to others to express, all of which can create extra tensions in the place. It will be most important that a real effort is made to recognise and deal with these feelings, perhaps through group support, because otherwise they may distort the processes of helping the individual or their family, or the rest of the group. As we have seen, the evidence from the client's perspective is that departure from care is often badly handled, and it seems likely that it is the unrecognised or unresolved feelings of the workers, as much as any external objective factors, which create some of the difficulties that arise over planning and handling departures.

The need for planning

Returning to the focus of work with the individual client, we have seen much evidence as to why departure may be difficult for the individual. All of these factors may feel worse if the person has not been helped to prepare for departure appropriately. By contrast, a 'good ending' will be one that has been anticipated and planned well in advance, and which represents the fruition of all the plans and programmes that have been carried out during the person's stay. As with admission, not all departures can be precisely anticipated, as people sometimes leave suddenly for unexpected reasons or simply stop attending without explanation – in which case the team still has to find ways of helping the rest of the group and the team itself to handle this fact. Moreover, not every leaving can be planned in the same way, although teams can evolve ready-made contingency plans to put into operation for certain specific situations. For example, in settings such as residential centres for older people or for people with degenerative diseases, departure may mean the death of the client, and the reality of this fact will need to be understood by the workers and faced with the clients (see Burton, 1993; Shemmings, 1998).

Tasks and stages

Having recognised that planning is all-important, it is necessary to be clear about what is involved. One way of approaching this planning, just as in planning an admission, will be in terms of a number of identifiable stages in the process of departure. For example, Brearley (1982) highlights five main stages in the handling of a departure: planning, review, preparation, departure and aftercare. In the light of the earlier material on admissions, this framework is fairly self-explanatory, and the reader is referred to Brearley's useful book for further discussion. As an alternative approach, it may be more helpful here to think in terms of tasks rather than stages.

The tasks facing an individual client when leaving a group care unit may be described as first to *evaluate* what has happened during her stay, so that she can be clear about what she is leaving behind, and about what has been good or otherwise about her stay; second to *disengage* from the place and from the wide range of people within it and involved in it, in order to be able to engage fully with the new arrangements; and third to *stabilise* herself in the new situation – to readjust to a new way of life, a different home-base or daytime routine, and so on.

Associated with each of these tasks, the team will need to consider what sort of help may be required if the whole process is to be handled satisfactorily – and in the light of the earlier discussion of the impact on others of any departure, attention will have to be given to work in each part of the system – with the individual client, with the group of clients as a whole and with individuals within it, as well as with the individual's family and social network and with the group care team itself.

It is in order to help with handling this complexity that Figure 3.2, 'Leaving group care', is offered. This is proposed as a guide for practitioners, similar to that offered earlier when discussing admissions, to help in planning the appropriate handling of departures. It might be used, for example, as the framework for a team discussion on planning a particular individual's departure, and it might also be used with the client herself, to help her anticipate what sort of support she may need with each task, and to help to clarify which areas will be other people's responsibilities rather than her own. Arising from such discussions, the team should aim to enter an appropriate comment or plan for their work within *each box* – some examples have been entered to indicate how the approach can be used. Equally, Figure 3.2 might be used as part of a training exercise to help a team identify and agree upon various approaches to good practice, or to help groups of students to appreciate the range of tasks facing somebody leaving a group care unit, and the associated skills required by the workers.

Figure 3.2: Leaving group care: schedule of the team's work with various groups (with examples)

	Evaluation	Disengagement	Stabilisation
Work with the individual			1. Regular follow-up visits from keyworker if appropriate 2. etc
Work with relatives and others			
Work with the existing client group	1. Raise subject at house meeting 2. Seek opportunities for informal discusson, especially in 'home-base' group	1. Party and small collection for leaving present 2. Making sure key people are there to say goodbye on the day	
Work within the staff group			1. Meeting for 'assessment' after departure 2. etc

Aftercare

The task of 'stabilisation' refers to what is sometimes known as 'aftercare'. Many group care units seem unable to provide an adequate service in this respect – sometimes because the teams just do not conceive of this task as part of their responsibilities, sometimes because they are not encouraged or resourced to do so by their agency. There is undoubtedly a problem here, in that the task of a group care unit is principally to provide a good service to those currently using the unit, and there will have to be some point at which the responsibilities of the team cease if they are not to have an ever-increasing workload. On the other hand, if the team is not in any way actively engaged in supporting clients after departure, they may never achieve the true potential of their work, and may become locked into an inward-looking pattern in which everybody avoids facing the future and planning properly for it. There are various ways in which team members can become productively engaged in supporting people after they leave the unit, whether through regular monitoring visits to individuals who have recently left (equivalent to the 'bridging' role' described under 'Admission'), or through group meetings with former clients either on the basis of a programme of planned meetings or on a 'drop-in' basis. For some people such arrangements may be needed only for a short time to help them stabilise in the next stage in their lives, whereas for others such as young people who have grown up in long-term residential care, there may be a much longer-term need, so that they can return even many years later to a place where they will be remembered and valued.

Principles for good practice

Just as there are certain principles for good practice in relation to the admission stage, so there are similar principles that apply to the departure stage:

(1) Each setting must have a clear procedure for reviewing and evaluating each client's 'progress', so that decisions about departure can be properly anticipated and planned.
(2) Each setting must have a clear policy as to what criteria will be used to decide when a client is ready to leave.
(3) Each client's admission agreement and programmes must include some explicit consideration of the plans for her departure.

(4) The workers should never underestimate the possible impact of departure on those leaving group care, and its ripples throughout the unit, including the team itself. They should always plan for appropriate support to be offered to the individual and their family during and after a departure. This support should take into account the issues of power, prejudice and dependency as experienced by those involved.

(5) Each person leaving needs a 'bridge person', just as at admission, to help them bridge the gap out of the place and into their next accommodation.

Conclusion

This chapter has followed the individual client's progress through the group care unit, drawing connections between the evidence on the client's experience and the responsibilities of the team. For the most part, we have focused here on the general responsibilities of the team as a whole, whereas in the next chapter, the focus switches to the individual responsibilities of each worker in the unit.

FOUR

The Worker's Shift

Introduction

Having examined group care work from the perspective of The Client's Stay, we now consider a third perspective, in which the focus is on the responsibilities of the group care worker in terms of her typical working day, beginning with the necessary preparation before arrival at work, through the various responsibilities of her work, to the handling of departure from the unit at the end of the day. Although it is a new way of describing the tasks of the group care worker, this perspective is also a synthesis of several strands drawn from related fields, and we shall begin by examining some of these strands, in order to explain the origin of this way of analysing the work.

I draw in particular on material from mainstream social work theory. One of the most useful frameworks for analysing practice is the concept of the social work 'process' (Payne, 2005a), in which there are identifiable phases of work progressing through time: 'assessment, planning, intervention and review' (Parker and Bradley, 2003, p ix), these corresponding to the beginning, middle and end stages of a 'case', that is, work with an individual or family. This simple basic formula has remained an underpinning framework in many classic social work texts from Butrym (1976) through to Adams et al (2005), and it underpins the UK requirements for social work training (DH, 2002). In its various forms this framework provides the student or worker with a straightforward means of planning and analysing their practice. Indeed, experience in social work training suggests that, unless students can operationalise some version of the process model, they are unlikely to be able to make constructive use of other more sophisticated models. It should therefore be helpful for those learning about working in group care to have an equivalent of this process model, which can help them to organise their thoughts and plan their practice.

However, there is a difficulty in using the process model in analysing group care work, since it is not immediately clear as to how the model applies in this setting. In one sense, group care may appear to have no clear beginning–middle–end sequence at all, because in most settings care is provided as a seamless ongoing programme. There may happen to be an admission or departure of a client on any given day, and these are certainly significant events not only for the individuals involved but also for the group as a whole. The approach taken in some of the literature has tended to suggest that the process in question should be taken to be this process of admission–care–discharge of the client – in other words, the process described in The Client's Stay perspective of this book. The problem is that while these stages in the client's career provide useful benchmarks for the discussion of the individual client's experience, they do not tell the whole story. Group care consists not simply of the parallel careers of a number of individual clients at the hands of a number of individual workers. In group care, the whole is much more than the sum of its parts, because there is also the group life of the whole place to consider – what has been described as 'the alchemy of all the members, staff and users, of the Centre' (Carter, 1988, p 108). This group life includes the innumerable combinations of interactions between all the individuals involved, and between various sub-groups, as well as the interactions between those on the inside and the outside of the unit. It is therefore group life – and team membership – that must also be taken into account when focusing on the 'process' of group care work.

On the other hand, if we look at 'group life' in terms of all the everyday interactions between all the participants, then group care may seem to have an unmanageably large and varied range of beginnings, middles and endings. We might apply the process framework to each of these interactions, analysing each in terms of its phases of assessment–action–evaluation, and indeed this is the approach taken elsewhere in this book to understanding 'Opportunity-led Work'. However, while this application is helpful for conceptualising work with 'slices of life' in group care, it does not help individual workers in the more 'macro'-focus on planning and sustaining their day-by-day work. Another approach is taken by Whitaker et al (1998), who use a framework based upon an 'action research cycle' to show how a staff team can *collectively* assess, plan, intervene and evaluate in relation to specific pieces of work such as helping an individual to integrate better with the group, or helping the unit as a whole to improve relationships with its neighbours (Whitaker et al, 1998, pp 133-52). This is a helpful formulation in terms of planning teamwork, although again it does not necessarily clarify the process from the individual worker's point of view. Thus the process model, which appears very clear in the context of fieldwork, is not easy to match exactly with the realities of group care work. How then should the worker structure and plan her own work?

One solution to this difficulty is to turn the focus temporarily away from the client and back on to the worker. The social work process can be seen as describing not only the client's encounter through time with a social worker, but also the worker's engagement through time in one 'unit of work'. The unit of work that is most usefully studied for a field social worker is an individual case, whereas perhaps the unit of a group care worker's work that can be most usefully described is a *day's work*, or shift. The worker arrives for her shift, engages in the work of the unit and her own tasks within it, then eventually disengages from it and leaves at the end of the shift, having completed one main unit of work. It is this unit, then, that will be analysed in terms of the process model in this chapter.

These theoretical difficulties, which might at first seem remote from practice, turn out to have considerable practical relevance, because they reveal a central contradiction inherent in much of this work, and especially in residential work. The problem is that the process for the client (admission–care–departure) and the process for the worker (arrival–shift–departure) do not correspond. Indeed, they often conflict, as constantly changing personnel, working unpredictable (to some clients) shifts, move in and out of the clients' lives in a way that risks disrupting and disordering their lives, rather than contributing positively to them. The film *John*, made by the Robertson Centre (1969), gives a graphic depiction of the consequences for the client (in this case a three-year-old boy) of such a mismatch. Another example was encountered by a social work student:

Example
A student on placement in a residential home for older people found that there was a changeover of shifts halfway through the residents' lunch – so that one set of workers served the first course, then disappeared through the kitchen door to be mysteriously replaced by another set of workers who proceeded to serve the second course!

This 'mismatching of the processes' has increased as the reorganisation of group care, and especially of residential care, has led to the widespread introduction of shiftwork and the 'industrial model' described in Chapter Two. The effect of these changes on the experience of residential care should not be underestimated. They have created the risk for the resident that life will become disjointed and confusing as different workers come and go each day, and the risk for the worker that although in one sense working conditions have greatly improved, in another sense job satisfaction may be diminished by the lesser degree and quality of involvement possible with individuals and groups. This problem places a responsibility on group care teams and managers to ensure that the arrangement of their shifts causes as little disruption as possible to the clients' lives, and a responsibility on each worker to recognise that she is entering and leaving a larger and longer process at the beginning and end of each shift, and to show appropriate sensitivity to the possible impact of this 'mismatching of the processes'.

While these problems inherent in shiftwork do not usually arise in day care settings, there are many related issues which do arise. For example, many day services have to develop complicated timetables for the week's activities, which will allow workers to move between a wide range of tasks both within and outside the centre itself, and which may thus give rise to some of the same conflicts that arise in a shiftwork system. The demands of teamwork are similar in both settings, such as the need for clear ongoing communication throughout the day's work and the need for workers to be able to transfer tasks and responsibilities between each other at short notice and without detriment to the clients.

Other implications that follow from taking 'The Worker's Shift' as the focus of this third perspective on group care practice are considered in the rest of this chapter as we work through the sequence from arrival to departure.

Arrival

Arriving for the start of a day's work in any occupation gives rise to mixed feelings: on the one hand there may be enthusiasm and a keenness to anticipate the day's events with constructive planning, while on the other hand there may be a sense of wariness and reluctance to face the day with all that it may bring. In group care, there are likely to be additional factors arising from the nature of the work, such as anxiety connected with the personal stress that this work can engender, or various powerful feelings that arise from the close personal involvement with one's clients that often occurs in this work. What will be important is the way in which the worker handles the process of arrival at the unit: qualities of preparedness, willingness and ability to communicate, good timekeeping and self-awareness will be as vital here as skills of assessment. Indeed, this stage has been termed 'arrival' rather than 'assessment' because, although assessment is an important function at this point, it is clearly not the only function, and it does not disappear from the group care worker's repertoire after this arrival stage: indeed it is one of the core skills required throughout the day's work.

In fact, the conscientious worker has often begun working before actually arriving at the unit. The task of mentally preparing oneself for the events and tasks of the day, and anticipating the likely emotional and other demands in prospect, is certainly real work. Many people will allow themselves time on their way to work to think through this anticipatory phase, using otherwise 'empty' travelling time on the bus or in the traffic jam to ponder on the likely events and demands of the day's work. This planning may not always be done in a conscious and deliberate way, but it will nevertheless be effective in that the worker will arrive on site ready to engage immediately with the tasks of the day. Even where this pre-arrival planning is not possible, the worker can make opportunities to begin planning on arrival by, for instance, quickly consulting with others and noting down key tasks for the day.

It is worth adding that the worker has a particular responsibility to arrive on time for work. We shall see the importance of the dimension of time throughout this chapter: staff teams can only operate and cooperate effectively if they can rely upon each other to be where they said they would be and when. The worker who habitually turns up for work half an hour late is undermining the work of the team, by opting out of the shared responsibility for communication and planning, and risks creating considerable tension and resentment in the team.

Upon arrival, the worker has to make an initial assessment of the climate of the place – the moods of individuals and groups, clients and staff – and to form a judgement from this assessment as to what might be an appropriate way in which to engage with each group. This is equivalent to what Whitaker et al (1998, p 140) call 'Taking a Reading of the Current Situation'. In order to make these judgements, the worker needs to gather a large amount of information about what has happened since the end of her previous shift, and to share thoughts and ideas about this information and about plans for the day's work with her colleagues. Some of this information-gathering can be carried out through discussion and reading logbooks, as we shall see below, but some of it happens on a much more intuitive level. The worker learns to use all five senses, plus a sixth sense of informed intuition, to gauge the climate of the place at the start of the day. Many experienced residential workers report that they can sense the mood of the unit at the start of a shift before they have talked in detail with any of the staff or residents – *although it might not be sensible to rely entirely on such intuition!*

It is hard to define what 'intuition' consists of in this context: perhaps it involves the subconscious recognition of certain combinations of minor details, such as sounds from far-flung parts of the building, odd silences, the ways in which people are seen to move around the building or hang back, and the behaviour of certain individuals who seem to act as barometers for the mood of the group as a whole. To the outsider, or to someone unfamiliar with this kind of work, the significance of these details may well go unrecognised (as would their equivalent in visiting someone else's family home), whereas to the well-established worker they may have a very powerful meaning:

Example

In a residential child care setting, workers gradually came to realise that one of the children, Andy, had an occasional habit of draping himself across a certain part of the staircase, and muttering to himself. They later discovered that he tended to do this when he had been on the fringe of some semi-delinquent behaviour initiated by other children, and uncertain as to whether or not to join in the delinquency. By the time the full significance of the behaviour had emerged, however, several workers had already independently come to recognise that when Andy was seen hanging around in that place, something was amiss in the overall life of the group as well as for Andy individually.

In addition to these elements, the worker also has a responsibility to be aware of her own personal state of mind at the start of the day's work, and to be prepared to put aside any distractions or difficulties arising from this state of mind. Sometimes she can make constructive use of such feelings, by sharing them with colleagues or with clients if appropriate. This may be especially appropriate in those settings where one aim of the work with the clients may be to enable them to recognise and handle their own and others' emotions. In these settings, there will be occasions when a worker who is feeling low or distracted would do better to at least inform colleagues and clients of this state of mind than to leave them guessing and perhaps confused.

Group care makes great personal demands upon the workers, and the worker's self is the main professional tool available to her. When we move on to discuss the responsibilities of the worker, a theme will be seen to emerge of each worker monitoring and managing her own physical and emotional energy, in order to remain effective throughout the day's work. Such self-management starts at or before the beginning of the day's work with this recognition of one's personal starting point.

Whatever a worker picks up intuitively upon arrival, she has a responsibility to establish contact with colleagues, and to begin to communicate with them in order to plan the day's work. There are many ways in which such preparation and planning may be done – in most residential settings the staff rota is organised so that there is some overlapping from one shift to the next, in which case the person 'bridging' the two shifts can be consulted in person. There is also likely to be a handover meeting at which all of the relevant information and feelings can be discussed.

In some settings, workers prefer to rely on a written Communications Book for passing on such information, although experience shows this to be a less than adequate means for real communication about the significance of events. Moreover, it has been shown that the mere existence of a handover meeting may not in itself lead to better standards of care, unless the meetings are properly led, and unless they are attended by the head of the unit – Raynes et al (1987) produced interesting evidence on this point in their research into the residential care of people with learning difficulties. This is a most useful research finding, which should give pause to those whose solution to any problem that arises is 'Let's have another meeting!'. What counts will be not so much the fact that a meeting happens, but rather the quality of communication achieved in the meeting, and the commitment and ability of the team members to 'own' and put into practice the issues discussed in the meetings.

The 'material' to be passed from one group or individual to the next consists of feelings and impressions as well as facts, and it is important that such planning meetings are handled in such a way as to facilitate the expression of the feelings-content as well as the business matters. This may be done, for instance, by dividing the meeting into two separate sections, or by building a shared agenda at the start of each meeting, to include both aspects; it will also require sensitive chairing that attends to more than just the facts being communicated. In some settings (for example therapeutic communities) it is common practice for handovers to be attended by the clients as well as by the workers, in order to encourage the full sharing of information and to maximise the opportunities for clients to reflect upon and evaluate their own experiences. Whichever method or combination of methods is used, it must be recognised that there are two parallel sets of responsibilities in the handover meeting: those at the end of their shift have a responsibility to hand material forward to the incoming group, while the incoming individuals each have an equal responsibility to seek out that information, check it out between them and make initial assessments as to what plans are appropriate.

Those working in day care settings face similar issues but in slightly different circumstances. One student whose previous experience had been in residential work found that when working on a day care placement in a family centre she was much better able to feel part of a team of workers, because ample time was allowed at the start of each day's work for the workers to meet together before the clients arrived. At this meeting, the workers could discuss plans and ideas for the day's work, and share any concerns or uncertainties, in a relatively relaxed but nevertheless purposeful atmosphere. The focus of this planning work may be different in day care settings from in residential work, in that the clients, as well as the staff, are coming to and from the centre each day, bringing new experiences from their home life. Accordingly, whereas residential workers can expect to pick up from their colleagues on the previous shift all of the relevant facts and feelings about their clients' world, day care workers will not usually begin to pick up new information until the clients arrive for their day or session at the centre. In these settings, therefore, the first meeting of the day may have an 'as-if' quality to it: the workers are planning their work as if they know what has happened overnight and what is likely to happen during the day, but in the full knowledge that they may well have to adapt their plans suddenly if different circumstances arise. In the family centre mentioned above, this issue was tackled by holding a further informal planning meeting over coffee each morning with the parents after they had arrived and had left their children supervised in the playroom for half an hour.

The shift itself: the responsibilities of the worker

During the course of the day's work, each group care worker has many types of task to perform, and she is responsible to herself, to the clients, to the team and to the agency for these tasks and for the way in which they are carried out. These tasks have been listed elsewhere in many different formulations (for example, Whitaker et al, 1998). Our concern in this chapter is not so much with the tasks themselves as with the responsibilities that they entail, in terms of the professional skills and personal commitment required of the worker. Some of the main responsibilities are set out below, and these responsibilities form the central part of our consideration of The Worker's Shift. It would be misleading to suggest, however, that these responsibilities necessarily follow each other in a day's work in the order in which they are given here. Although there is some sense of a sequence in the order in which they are presented, many of the responsibilities relate to tasks that may arise and recur many times during any given day's work – and, indeed, the conscientious completion of one task may entail several different responsibilities.

Assessing

Each individual is responsible for assessing people and situations both individually and on a shared basis. We have already considered (Chapter Three) the wide range of assessment activities in group care, from making an initial assessment of the mood of the group at the start of the day, to a situational assessment as to how to intervene appropriately when a critical incident is brewing, and to contributing to the group assessment of the needs of an individual client. Assessment is the starting point of all good practice, and it is the responsibility of each worker to contribute actively to this assessment, just as it is the responsibility of managers to facilitate such participation. Much assessment, however, is carried out informally by individuals in the course of their daily work. For example, a care worker teaching art classes in a day centre for adults with learning difficulties is reported as saying:

Example
'You've got to get to know people well. You take this group of eight people. This morning, I'll change my attitude for near enough every person in that group. I do it subconsciously almost. Initially, my own method of assessing people is to let them do almost anything they want while I just observe. Then I see what they like doing and take it from there.' (Carter, 1988, p 66)

On the other hand, as we saw earlier, assessment is not only an informal and intuitive activity, it is central to many of the formal tasks of the worker, such as the assessment of the needs of individual clients, review of the development of a group, and so on. It has been suggested that 'making sense' is the 'central task of the social worker' (England, 1986, p 57), and it can be argued that assessment is the main means by which workers 'make sense', both in the sense of understanding the complexities of their task, and in the sense of helping their clients to understand and resolve the complex issues facing them. In the group care context, making sense of one's tasks as a worker and helping the client to make sense of her own life and its challenges often amount to the same thing, and it may be especially important for the worker to recognise that both activities are taking place at one and the same time. In fact, so many different things may be happening at the same time that the worker will sometimes have to allow time to pass in order for things to gradually become clearer – which may mean resisting the urge or expectation to always make swift assessments of every situation.

Planning and anticipating

Each worker in the group care setting is of course responsible for thinking her own thoughts – but also for sharing and checking them out with colleagues. It is no excuse in this work to protest 'I didn't think ...' or 'I hadn't heard ...' when something goes wrong. The first stage of this thinking-work is the assessment described above; the second stage is the planning and anticipating of what needs to be done. As with assessment, some of this work can be done individually, but much of it involves being ready to share one's thoughts and feelings with other workers and with the clients. For example, assessment in its various forms might lead the team to the hypothesis that a particular older person in a residential home may be feeling anxious about a forthcoming visit from a relative, but whoever is the keyworker then has the responsibility to engage with that resident and probably with other people in helping to plan and prepare for the visit in such a way that the outcome will be more satisfactory both for her and for the visitor. This planning will not happen unless the worker responsible for this piece of work takes the initiative to make time and consult the appropriate people. The responsibility to plan and replan one's work as it progresses is also linked to the need to anticipate. We know that not all events can be predicted, but the experienced worker does develop the ability to anticipate likely developments in certain situations, and to prepare herself to handle the predicted outcome.

A different sense in which workers have a responsibility to plan and anticipate in their work is in setting aside time on a regular basis to consider the likely events of the forthcoming day, week or month, and to draw up whatever plans are necessary. Again, some of this work can be done individually, but much of it will be done collaboratively in the team. The difficulty of maintaining a planned approach to one's work when under pressure is considerable, and in order to maintain the professional quality of their work, both the individual worker and the team as a whole must find ways of building in planning time.

Whitaker et al's action research cycle provides a helpful model here (Whitaker et al, 1998, pp 133-52).

Engaging

Beyond assessment and planning, workers have to become involved in their work – to engage both with the people they are there to help and with the tasks that are required. This process of engagement will sometimes be relatively straightforward, but may often be quite difficult and may entail 'reaching out' in a very practical sense:

> **Example**
> A student on placement in a family centre, Maria, found that Norma, one of the mothers attending the centre, would not talk to her or even acknowledge her presence. Although other team members reported similar experiences, Maria was left feeling uncomfortable and puzzled. She shared this feeling with the staff team and with her practice teacher, and together they considered a range of ways in which Maria might reach out to achieve some contact with Norma. She tried various ways, unsuccessfully, until one day when Norma was going out to the shops for a few minutes. Maria asked if she could join Norma for the walk, but with no response. Eventually, she decided to run after Norma and walk alongside her: this did the trick – Norma responded with humour and openness, and from then on she was able to gain a great deal from the relationship that gradually developed with Maria.

Maria's strategy for engaging Norma in this example was perhaps unusual, and was only undertaken after careful assessment, but in this case it was very productive.

The group care worker has to handle many complex interactions with other people, and it is the responsibility of each worker to engage appropriately with a wide range of colleagues and clients – in the sense of achieving and sustaining communication with them. Communication may be seen as the 'key to group care work', but communication will never happen unless each worker takes it as her own responsibility to engage constructively with others, to monitor the effectiveness of that engagement, and to revise her strategy when problems are encountered. Sustaining this constant flow of communication will require the use of a range of skills, including, for example, group-membership skills for taking part in planning meetings, counselling skills such as 'active listening' to achieve communication with individual clients, and group-leadership skills for promoting communication within the larger group (Collins and Bruce, 1984).

Engaging with clients may also mean moving well beyond the superficial level of many everyday interactions and being willing to make contact at a much deeper level with what matters most to the person. When we reflect upon the disruption and rejection that may have brought many service users into the group care setting, and the pain and distress that this may have caused them, it is evident that many people will have very powerful feelings to cope with. These feelings may influence their individual behaviour and moods as well as the collective atmosphere of the unit, and it often falls to the group care worker to try to engage with people at this level in order to help them cope with their feelings about their lives, past, present and future. In the child care setting this has been called 'responding to pain and pain-based behaviour' (Anglin, 2002, p 107) and there will be equivalents in other settings. 'Engaging' therefore means being receptive and perceptive at many levels and developing the skills to make connections with people at each of these levels, including the skills of 'Opportunity-led Work'.

Taking action

It follows from the above that it is not enough for the worker merely to think about what to do and why: she also has the responsibility to take appropriate action, whether to enable somebody to say what they want to say, to prevent something from happening, to try to relieve some deeper distress or simply to meet a resident's need for some physical comfort. We have already seen that planning and anticipating may in themselves become significant forms of taking action, and that engaging with people or with the necessary tasks may be a considerable achievement in itself. In fact, 'taking action' may seem to encompass an impossibly wide range of types of event. Various attempts have been made to categorise the different types of activity of group care workers – including the distinction between 'direct' and 'indirect' work (Ainsworth, 1981), and (in the child care context) Whitaker et al's (1998) distinctions between what they call the five 'task arenas':

> Working with individual young people; working with the group of young people; working with and being managed by [the larger organisation]; working with people and

> organisations in wide networks; and surviving (maintaining
> viability) as a staff team. (Whitaker et al, 1998, p 25)

It is not always productive to draw such distinctions too precisely, however, since some activities that might be 'indirect' in one setting may be classed as 'direct' in a more participative regime, and the same piece of work may involve working in many 'task arenas' at once. Indeed, it is important to recognise that, even for 'junior' workers, group care work does include taking action beyond the immediate daily care of the clients. Thus to take action may mean to pick up the telephone and speak to a councillor about a political issue that has arisen, to initiate a staff discussion on an issue such as HIV/AIDS, which has broad implications for everyone in the group care setting, or to spend a morning working alongside the domestic staff to promote good communication between the various groups of staff in the unit.

These decisions about where to 'target' one's actions individually and as a team can be greatly helped by the use of the systems approach described in Chapter Five. Nevertheless, it is inescapable that a great deal of group care work includes tasks that may be seen by some as mundane, trivial or even demeaning, including physical and personal care. Those new to this work are often concerned about how they will handle tasks such as intimate care for people (Lawler, 1998), although many experienced staff find great job satisfaction from being able to offer people the basic personal care that they need. It is also not uncommon for social work students on group care placements to question whether such direct care activities are '*real* social work'. While this question raises greater issues about the nature of social work, it is important to note at this stage that offering direct care is definitely part of 'real social work': it has intrinsic value in its own right for clients who need everyday support and advice, and it is also often the vehicle through which other less tangible services such as emotional support may be offered. What will be important is that such tasks are thought about and reflected on in team meetings and valued as an essential part of the job.

On the other hand, taking action may at times mean deciding to do nothing – to allow a situation to develop further, for example, or to allow an angry individual to 'say their piece' before taking any other sort of action. The skill lies in judgement and timing: knowing when to act, when not to act, and when to allow others the space to act is an important skill in this work, and the Critical Incident Analysis format provides a useful framework for analysing the worker's decisions about taking action (Chapter Two this volume; Thomas, 2004).

Acting ethically, including countering prejudice

Within an overall aim of treating others fairly and with dignity and respect, it is clear that group care workers have a responsibility to confront racism, sexism, ageism, and other powerful prejudicial action wherever it is encountered in their work. This will involve challenging both overt expressions of such prejudice, and those more subtle and hidden forms embedded in, for example, admission or diagnostic criteria, or staff selection procedures. Workers will meet these challenges in a number of different ways – for instance, a worker may overhear a conversation between two clients which includes a racist remark, or a client may address such a remark to a worker, or perhaps a comment may be made within a staff team by one worker to another. There is evidence that many such issues pass unchallenged in group care work, just as they do in other professions (Barn et al, 1998), and this situation will continue unless each worker regards it as her own responsibility to take appropriate action to counter prejudice and to support and enable others to do so. Nevertheless, Barter et al (2004, pp 93-5) describe how in some residential child care settings, despite some worrying findings about the levels of violence between some young people, racism has become a much less prevalent occurrence and is simply not tolerated by staff.

There are many other aspects of 'acting ethically' in the group care setting, and each worker must take an active part in the shared responsibility for monitoring the ethical standards of the unit – and especially for guarding against the physical or moral degradation of clients by the workers, which may happen through several causes as part of a 'corruption of care' (Wardhaugh and Wilding, 1998). The problem of the prevalence of bad practice was noted in Chapter One, and particularly the problem of staff inertia in implementing models of good practice. Such inertia can also lead teams to tolerate practices that they know to be unethical or harmful: in a sense, bad practice can only be sustained through the collusion of the group care workers and/or the management. Each worker, then, has an individual responsibility to be aware of what is happening in the place, to make moral judgements about what is happening, and to take appropriate action.

A further example of the ethical judgements that individuals and teams have to make is in what might broadly be called discretion, or 'the management of secrets' (Bok, 1986). Each client has a right to privacy and to the confidentiality of personal secrets, and each worker has a responsibility to respect and uphold these rights, which may not be easy in the informal hurly-burly of group life. Being appropriately discrete, in interactions with both clients and informal staff groupings, can demand considerable strength of will on the part of the individual, and a disciplined approach within the team as a whole.

Finally, many of the judgements about acting ethically are not so straightforward as those described above. There is no single 'correct' value system by which such judgements can be made (see Stanley and Reed, 1999), and the team, together with their employers, will have to work out and agree upon a code of practice by which actions can be judged. Such a code will often be informed by government regulations and guidelines such as the General Social Care Council's Codes of Practice (GSCC, 2002; SSSC, 2002), and backed up by a system of inspection and a complaints procedure (Morgan, 2000). However, at the level of day-to-day practice, the responsibility lies with the individual worker to be conscientious, and to have the courage of her convictions when she encounters unethical practice (see Clough, 2000, for a useful chapter on ethical practice in residential work).

Being diligent and reliable

Being diligent and conscientious is a central responsibility of any professional worker. The group care worker is responsible to the clients and their relatives as well as to the agency and to society as a whole, and, in each case, she has the responsibility to be thorough and careful in carrying out all of the responsibilities listed here, so that others may depend on her. Being reliable is not always easy: some of the tasks required of group care workers are tiresome and petty, and we are all tempted at times to take short cuts and to try superficial solutions to deep problems. However, what we are paid to do is to take care, which means bothering to follow up on small issues even when we do not feel like doing so, and remembering to attend to an individual's minor personal request even though other needs of our own may feel more important or pressing:

Example

Jane was an experienced worker in a hostel for people recovering from mental health difficulties. At the start of a weekend's duty she agreed to a request from Matthew, a young man who (in addition to other difficulties) was agoraphobic, to accompany him at some point during the weekend to the DIY shop to buy some tools. In the midst of the busy weekend's work, this plan slipped her mind completely, until the Sunday lunchtime when Jane was about to go off duty, and Matthew reminded her quietly but reproachfully about it. Realising the importance for Matthew of this trip, Jane then stayed on after the end of her shift to drive out of town with Matthew for his trip.

Being reliable and diligent does not always mean being prepared to work beyond one's allotted hours, but, on the other hand, it may well involve the kind of flexibility and commitment indicated in Jane's work here.

Moreover, being reliable assumes extra importance in those branches of group care that involve caring for very vulnerable and dependent people who may have had unhappy experiences of being dependent upon others. Here, 'being reliable' will mean paying scrupulous attention to the detail of arrangements, even in terms of the minutiae of everyday life, and putting the highest premium on achieving consistency across the team and through time. It is important, therefore, that the team reflects together on what reliability really means and feels like, perhaps drawing upon the help of a team consultant, and reflecting on experiences in their own lives both of being able to rely on others and of being let down or undervalued. Unless they can do this, it may be hard to develop a genuinely dependable climate in the place, in which clients will really feel able to depend upon the team as a whole.

Monitoring

As action unfolds during the course of any particular day's work, and the worker carries out the various responsibilities described here, she will also monitor what is happening, both in terms of each individual strand of work, and of the day's work as a whole. This will involve monitoring individual clients and staff as well as monitoring the impact of one's own interventions: this monitoring is a form of the 'ongoing assessment' mentioned elsewhere in this book.

There are various methods of observation and recording, and many purposes to which these methods can be put (see Chapter Five), and in some units the regular recording of the day's 'work in progress' encourages the workers to develop their skills in observing and monitoring. Much of the monitoring in many units, however, is done at an informal (perhaps even unconscious) level, relying to some extent upon the kind of intuition described earlier in this chapter. An example of a worker monitoring her own work and the work of the unit is found in the following account of the start of a day's work:

Example

A senior residential worker, Sue, 'sits writing the diary at 9.15 a.m.' and 'reflects on the work so far accomplished'. She works through the list of plans which she had drawn up with the other staff at the start of the shift, and reviews the success or otherwise of each aspect of the plan. It is clearly necessary that any progress in these plans should be monitored and evaluated at this stage, even though it is not the end of that day's work, still less the end of the story for any of the individual residents. Much of this work remains 'work in progress' over long periods of time, and without conscientious monitoring the purposefulness of the work can ebb away. Sue does not simply sit in the office with her list, however; she consults again with each of her colleagues, going round to different parts of the building to find people who are still engaged on various tasks. (Adapted from Burton, 1982)

Monitoring is the raw material out of which more formal assessments and evaluations are made and further action/intervention is planned, and it must therefore be carried out by each worker, and shared within the team. Among the skills required for this monitoring will be what has been described as 'helicoptering ability', or 'the ability to switch perspectives' (Hawkins and Shohet, 2000, p 37), that is, to move rapidly between different areas of concern and different levels of awareness. This is what Whitaker et al (1998, p 25) describe as 'working within different task arenas at the same time'. The multidimensional nature of group care work is a theme throughout this book, and it is in the monitoring of what is happening throughout any given day's work that the worker's ability to manage the complexity of the work will be really tested. Although 'helicoptering' might appear to be primarily a managerial or supervisory skill, in group care everybody needs it, since monitoring what is happening is not a task that can be safely assumed to be the responsibility of others.

Pacing oneself

If we recognise the 'shift' as the unit of work of the group care worker, it follows that the worker is responsible for remaining as effective at the end of the shift as she was at the beginning. In such demanding work this is not straightforward: workers need to be able to 'manage' their own energy and emotions as well as those of others, and to measure out their responses and actions so that they will not be so fatigued towards the end of the shift that they cannot respond conscientiously and appropriately in each situation. They will need to monitor their own effectiveness, gauge the levels of energy required for each piece of work, and anticipate likely future demands.

Meinrath and Roberts (2004) discuss the difficulty of being a 'good-enough staff member' in a therapeutic community for adults, and their remarks apply equally in most group care settings:

> The demands of being a good or ideal staff member can take a tremendous toll.... Deprived clients often seem to ask for everything that they never had as a child and the community seems to demand an incredible dedication from the staff member. (Meinrath and Roberts, 2004, p 321)

The writers quote a list of suggestions from research into 'burnout' as to how those working in these settings can take care of themselves, such as: 'Each individual should plan a tolerable day for himself, as the whole staff group should plan a tolerable day for themselves' (Freudenberger, 1975, p 74).

In order that the worker can successfully achieve this 'planned tolerable day', it will be important, for instance, to find ways of building into the day some quiet moments of withdrawal and reflection, to allow for some self-monitoring and replanning (see Clough, 2000). The worker will still need to communicate with colleagues before taking such a break, of course, and in most teams a way of working will evolve in which people have a mutual respect for each other's thresholds and capabilities, so that they can allow and even encourage each other to pace themselves in this way. Newcomers to this work and students on placement sometimes find this aspect of the work stressful and puzzling, and may need sympathetic help and guidance from colleagues and supervisors to learn the relevant skills and habits. It will not always be easy to achieve this level of teamwork, however: financial and other constraints increasingly mean that many group care workers are working in conditions which risk leading to stress and burnout, partly through the lack of adequate time for reflection and self-monitoring. Here it will be the responsibility of the workers to take appropriate action to make management aware of the nature and extent of the pressures under which they are working, and to propose appropriate strategies for change. Equally, the emotional pressure that many group care teams face may, if not handled well, lead to extra stress as team members struggle to cope: it is therefore not just each individual but the team as a whole which needs to monitor its work and its stress levels and to pace itself.

Using supervision and consultation

The previous item has led us naturally to consider the need for supervision. Supervision is not just an activity that managers and practice teachers should offer, it is also something that each worker has the responsibility to seek out and use constructively. This means that the worker is responsible for bringing appropriate material for discussion, for making and taking opportunities for informal supervision and 'live' supervision, and for viewing supervision in the widest of terms. For example, much supervision of group care work is more appropriately handled in the staff team as a whole rather than in the one-to-one situation (see Frost and Harris, 1996), but making full use of this approach requires commitment, trust and risk-taking on all sides, not just on the part of the manager/supervisor. Supervision, then, cannot be regarded as an 'optional extra' in group care work – a luxury or indulgence that is only fitted in after everything else has been done. Without a comprehensive programme of supervision, it will be virtually impossible for the workers to carry out the responsibilities that have been described in this chapter (Frost et al, 1999).

In addition to whatever regular arrangements are made for supervision (see Chapter Five for further discussion), workers must be able to recognise when they are out of their depth and need either consultation, special advice or just the opportunity to think through a new or different aspect of their work. For example, a worker in a day centre for people with learning difficulties reported that, in running a drama group for the clients, she recognised the risks involved in working without proper supervision:

> 'I worked with our psychologist at the beginning. Then she was off sick for a few months, when things seemed to get very heavy. I knew there was something happening and wasn't sure whether I should carry on, whether it was dangerous emotionally. I had bad worries and asked if I could have supervision. Norman, the head of another centre and a group analyst agreed. Certain qualities are very important in leading groups and it made me look at what I was doing, in detail.' (Carter, 1988, p 81)

Evaluating

All professional workers should be able to evaluate their own work. In this context, group care workers have a responsibility, having monitored their work through the day, to form judgements about the quality and effectiveness of that work. Beedell (1970) makes the point that it may be difficult to distinguish between the effects of an individual's work and the work of the team as a whole, and this difficulty indicates the need for workers to talk to each other about these evaluations, and to engage in evaluation on both the formal and the informal level (see Collett and Hook, 1992).

Some people are too hard on themselves in the judgements that they make about their own work, and it can be a most useful exercise to ask for feedback from others about one's own performance: group care offers more opportunities for this feedback than many other work settings, since so much work is done alongside others:

> **Example**
> Shamira, a young worker in a day centre for adults with complex special needs, had made considerable efforts to establish a significant relationship with Corrie, a particularly isolated woman with profound speech difficulties and little apparent awareness of other people. When Shamira talked in a staff meeting about her sadness and frustration at not feeling able to 'reach' Corrie, several other workers commented on the great improvement that they had noticed in Corrie's morale since Shamira had taken a special interest in her, and one reported that Corrie's sister, who visited her weekly, had also mentioned noticing an improvement. Shamira was surprised and pleased at this positive feedback, and felt encouraged to sustain her efforts; her relationship with Corrie continued to develop, although it was painstaking work.

Not all workers are too hard on themselves, however: in some settings one would only wish that the workers could face making a more honest appraisal of their own limitations or faults. It is for this reason that self-evaluation is not enough: it must be done in the context of the team working together. Such evaluation may not come about without struggle and conflict, which is why there is such a strong need for a staff consultant in group care settings (see Silveira, 1991; Mawson, 1994). Just as in the example given above, it may be through the sensitive use of staff meetings that such evaluation may be best done, and when a staff team has access to a consultant there is much more chance that the evaluation by team members of their own and of the team's work will be accurate and productive.

The process of evaluation should not, then, remain a matter of purely internal reflection on the part of each individual: indeed it will be more valuable if it is shared and debated with others. Working in group care involves a lot of 'giving out', which means that workers need a lot of replenishment, both from each other and from within themselves. As Hollinghurst and many others have said, 'we owe it to the person we care for to look after our own well-being' (Hollinghurst, 1998, p 37).

Conclusion

The above items all refer to the responsibilities of the individual worker: it is clear that there are many other duties for each worker than have been described here, and that there is more that might be said about some of these responsibilities. However, the aim here has been to propose a way of describing group care work, rather than to create an exhaustive listing – readers might like to develop further thoughts on types of responsibilities.

Departure

Having considered the range of responsibilities of the group care worker during her shift or day's work, we now consider the issues facing her at the end of the shift. There is an even greater lack of literature on this area than on the 'departure' stage of The Client's Stay, although it is interesting to note that the one area in which this topic has been given some attention is in the literature on coping with stress and burnout (for example, Mattingly, 1981; Maslach and Leiter, 1997). The stress inherent in group care work is noted at several points throughout this book, and in the present context the literature suggests that the handling of the end of the shift is critical in any individual's or team's management of stress.

At the end of the shift, the worker has to decide what to do with the stressful feelings that may have been engendered by the day's work: what proportion of these feelings can be left in the workplace (and how can this be done), and what proportion must the individual worker take home? If the proportions are misjudged, one party or the other may be left 'carrying' problems that do not belong to them. An additional resentment may then build up on either side, which could result in extra difficulties the next time that person comes back on duty or the team reassembles.

Towards the end of the shift, even if the element of 'pacing oneself' has been handled well by both individual and team, the worker's energy level may be low, and it may be difficult to give sufficient attention to the issues involved in finishing the day's work. Nevertheless, the worker does have responsibilities in this area, some of which are set out below, arranged in sequence from preparation for leaving through to after departure.

The whole process of leaving the unit at the end of the day/shift might be summarised as a process of disengagement. We saw earlier that at the start of the shift the worker has to tune in to the mood of the place and to the specific needs and demands of the individuals and groups within it – similarly, the worker has to gradually 'tune out' again at the end of the shift. This will involve finding appropriate ways of bringing each piece of work to an end and leaving things satisfactorily both for incoming workers and for this worker's own subsequent return for her next shift; saying goodbye to those with whom she has been involved during the day; and finally managing the transition back home so as to leave work behind and keep it in perspective.

Preparation for leaving

Leaving things straight and clear with clients and others

The individual worker is responsible for concluding each piece of work with which she has been involved, and for seeing to it that no 'loose ends' have been left. Given the multifaceted nature of the work, it is very easy to lose sight of the later stages of some of the many interactions in which one has been involved, and to go off duty leaving behind a client or colleague who is unsure as to how and when that interaction will be concluded:

> **Example**
> The example was quoted earlier (pp 131-2) of Jane, who nearly forgot an undertaking that she had promised to Matthew, one of the residents, that she would go shopping with him; in this instance, Jane stayed on after the end of her shift to carry out her promise. Had she not done so, or had she gone off duty without being reminded of her promise by Matthew, she would have left Matthew potentially angry and disappointed at being let down, and the rest of the staff team possibly unaware of the

problem and unable to resolve it even if they had realised what had happened.

Such issues will arise in respect of groups as well as individuals, and colleagues as well as clients. The complex web of interactions in which each worker has been participating throughout the day therefore needs to be drawn together at the end of the day. As in other aspects of group care, some of this drawing together can be achieved individually, some in small groupings and some in the large group.

In some cases, an interaction at the individual level may need to be 'rounded off' in a group discussion, or vice versa: the worker carries the responsibility for deciding how to complete each piece of work, although this decision may be made in consultation with others. Where the worker is not able to 'round off' an incident satisfactorily by the end of the shift, all salient information about the facts and feelings of the incident clearly has to be passed forward to the incoming team and brought forward for the next day's work. Some workers find it helpful to spend a few minutes before the end of the shift reviewing the events of the day and checking that each piece of work has been properly concluded.

Checking on commitments for the next shift

Experienced workers learn to think several stages ahead, as well as to keep in mind the ongoing evaluation of earlier work. At the end of the day, the worker needs to be aware of what is planned for the following day's work both in terms of her own responsibilities and in terms of the work of the unit as a whole. In a shiftwork system, the worker also needs to know what is planned for the incoming shift, so that the end of the current shift can be managed so as to allow for a good transition. In most units the Unit Diary provides a central reference point for all workers to check on these future commitments, and the handover meeting is the forum for discussion and exchange of information about them, although much of the information is often relayed informally.

Handover meetings

The handover meeting should play an important part in helping individual workers to 'process' the day's work, and the proper use of a system of handover meetings will enable the team as a whole to bring the work of the shift to a satisfactory conclusion (Frost et al, 1999, pp 88–9), just as we have already seen that it provides the means of bringing people together at the start of the shift to share their planning and preparation. The main purpose of the handover meeting in many group care settings is to encourage the full exchange of information and feelings between all the workers, and thus to enable the day's work to be reviewed and evaluated in a shared forum. Where there is a complete changeover of shifts, the handover also has the function of conveying this material to the incoming workers, to enable them to tune in to the climate of the place. Indeed, Mason (1989) argues convincingly for the handover meeting to be conducted by the incoming shift, with a focus on what they need to know or understand in order to provide the most appropriate care during the coming hours.

In some day care settings, the equivalent to the handover meeting will be the 'feedback' or 'wash-up' session at the end of the day, when all the workers get together after the clients have left. Here there is no incoming team of workers to 'hand over' the material to, but there is still an important need to review and evaluate together, and often this meeting will be recorded in note form in a logbook, which can be consulted at the start of the following day's work: in a sense the team is 'handing over' material to itself:

Example

In one probation day centre run on therapeutic community principles (Cook, 1988), the workers' last meeting of the day was held after the clients had left, but was recorded openly for the clients to read on the following morning before the first community meeting of the day.

We saw earlier that in some therapeutic community settings the handover is conducted with all members present, including clients, and the same will be true in the end-of-day meetings in a therapeutic community day service. A particularly striking example of the sharing of responsibility for each other that some settings promote can be found in the account of the closing meeting between staff and users in a day therapeutic community for people with mental health difficulties (Higgins, 1997). Shortly before the end of the meeting the chairperson would always ask: 'Does anybody feel they need support tonight?', and if someone indicated that they were feeling particularly anxious or stressed, fellow members of the community would arrange to be available for telephone and sometimes other support to each other.

Departure

Saying goodbye

In this account of the worker's perspective, it is important that we do not overlook the experience and feelings of the clients. For example, how do the highly dependent clients in some residential settings cope with the feeling of being abandoned by a favourite worker who turns out after all to have preoccupations elsewhere? How do the clients in a day care setting cope with leaving the unit at the end of the day to return to a possibly risk-fraught situation at home, while the workers remain behind to discuss the clients and ultimately to return to their own supposedly well-ordered lives? It is clear that the clients, both individually and as a group, may be powerfully affected by the comings and goings of the workers in ways which some teams do not fully appreciate.

Nor should we assume that it is only the clients who may have these feelings: group care often demands such a powerful personal involvement on the part of the worker that it may be very difficult to face detaching oneself at the end of the day. The worker may, for instance, experience feelings of guilt at leaving behind a highly dependent individual in a residential unit, or feelings of anxiety as to what may befall the frail clients of a day centre for older people over a long and lonely weekend: while these clients are receiving care in the unit, such feelings may be submerged, only to surface again at the end of the shift. On the other hand, the end of the shift may, of course, bring the worker enormous feelings of relief. Most people are glad to come to the end of a day's work, but in group care the physical and emotional demands of the day may build up to such an extent that the worker is almost desperate to leave the building. The risk here is that the worker is thereby tempted to leave in haste, without saying proper goodbyes or rounding things off properly with colleagues or clients.

Such feelings may not always be expressed directly, but may emerge in more indirect forms. It is a well-recognised feature of group care work that the workers, either individually or as a team, often try to deal with the various powerful feelings associated with the work by denying these feelings, or by unwittingly 'acting out' the feelings in indirect or inappropriate ways (Menzies-Lyth, 1988). Such denial may be manifested in various forms – and sometimes so subtly that it is hard to detect any traces of the original feelings. The strong feelings that have been identified above as pertaining to the end of the shift may lead to a variety of difficulties:

> **Example**
>
> In a residential unit for adolescents in crisis, the staff team worked under such great emotional pressure that the workers found it very difficult to disengage from each other and from their work at the end of each shift. Members of the team began spending long drinking sessions in the local pub, and some of them became involved in a complex web of sexual relationships with each other, which led to powerful jealousies and rivalries. These conflicts fed back into the work of the unit, so that working at the unit became even more stressful. It emerged in a staff consultation group that one characteristic of the work of the unit was that the workers very rarely managed to say goodbye, either to each other or to the residents, at the end of their shift. In discussion, a link was established between this difficulty in saying goodbye, which mirrored the difficulties experienced by many of the adolescents in their families, and the 'acting-out' behaviour of many of the staff. Nobody could maintain clear boundaries, and the work of the unit could only begin to be sorted out once this situation had been confronted.

In order to prevent the development of such difficulties, workers will need to pay attention to how they handle taking leave of the clients and of each other at the end of the day. Do they go round the unit to each client, saying a personal goodbye, or is there an opportunity to say goodbye to the group of clients together, perhaps in an informal way? Are there any helpful rituals or customs in the place associated with departure, such as the outgoing team congregating briefly in the kitchen for a coffee at the end of an evening shift? As in other aspects of the work, it is the responsibility of team members both individually and collectively to work out appropriate ways of handling departure so that it can be used constructively rather than being denied or overlooked.

After departure

The literature on stress and burnout suggests that it is important for workers in any occupation to establish clear boundaries between work and home, in order that the stresses inherent in the demands of work do not overwhelm the worker's whole existence. These boundaries will be particularly necessary for group care workers because of the special demands of this work. Furthermore, since the majority of workers in many settings are women, who may also be carrying major caring responsibilities at home in addition to being more likely to be responsible for the 'caring' rather than the managerial tasks in the group care setting, it is especially important for these workers to draw clear lines between home and work.

To illustrate the need for the careful handling of this transition, Maslach (1982) draws an interesting analogy with the decompression time that a diver needs to spend in order to make the transition between working at high pressure and returning to normal conditions:

> In a similar way, people working in an environment of high emotional pressure need to decompress – to get completely out of the high-pressure environment before moving into the 'normal pressure' of their private life.... Decompression refers to some activity that: (a) occurs between one's working and non-working times, and (b) allows one to unwind, relax, and leave the job behind before getting fully involved with family and friends. (Maslach, 1982, p 102)

There will be many different ways of managing this transition. Maslach (1982) suggests spending some time engaged in a solitary hobby or non-intellectual activity as typical methods of achieving 'decompression', while Mattingly lists the following possibilities:

> settling the concerns of the day by talking about them, a rigorous closure on work which avoids any discussion of it, changing clothes, physical exercise, shopping, being alone, listening to music, playing a musical instrument, blocking work-related thinking by engaging in cognitive activities not related to work, having a drink in a social circumstance. (Mattingly, 1981, p 162)

It will be important for each worker to learn from experience which methods of handling the end of the day are effective for herself. These will vary according to the personal style and circumstances of the worker, and it is not appropriate for anyone else to insist on what will be the right method for that individual. For further discussion of burnout and ways of addressing it, see Maslach and Leiter (1997).

Re-evaluating

Despite the importance of unwinding and finding ways of leaving work behind at the end of the day, it is inevitable and in some ways necessary that the worker does not completely forget the events of the day. If the workers have evolved an effective system for evaluating together at the end of the day, most of the 'processing' of the day's events will have been completed before leaving, but this will not always be the case. Some of the day's events may have been particularly complex or stressful, and it may take time for the worker to satisfactorily process them.

In some instances it may only be after considerable time spent puzzling over the details, or perhaps attending to other matters altogether, that a worker starts to make sense of a difficult incident that occurred much earlier in the day. Gradually the pieces fall into place, and the worker realises the significance of some apparently minor detail that unlocks a previously little-understood event. In other cases, the worker may experience a delayed emotional reaction to some traumatic moment during the day's work, which may necessarily have been dealt with somewhat superficially at the time, but which may have had a much greater impact on the worker than she initially realised:

Example

Cathy was a confident and capable student who was working on placement in a secure unit for young adults with psychiatric problems. During the course of a livelier-than-usual game of basketball, she was pushed to the ground and kicked by one of the clients, unseen by the other workers, and had to withdraw from the game. Although she felt that she had to 'take this incident in her stride' at the time, it was only later that evening, long after the end of her shift, that she realised how upset and angry she was over this event, and that she decided how she would take the matter up in the following day's meeting with the residents. Discussion of this incident subsequently led to further debate in a team meeting on issues of personal support and on gender roles.

As in the above example, it may not always be through choice, but through necessity, that the worker continues to process the events of the day long after the end of the shift. In an ideal world, the worker would be able to make conscious decisions as to which matters to think through in this way, and which to leave until the next day or next shift, but in reality it is not always possible to behave so rationally. Moreover, much of the impact of the work will be experienced less physically than through the sly kick in the shins in the incident described above, and often happens through verbal or other means which may be experienced less than consciously but which may nevertheless pack a considerable emotional 'punch'. This will sometimes be the process known as 'projective identification', by which people in distress or emotional pain may unconsciously engineer situations or communications so that someone else (in this case the worker) ends up feeling their pain for them, but without knowing how or why (Shohet, 1999; Stokoe, 2003). It may be distorted or disconnected feelings such as these that we find ourselves left with after the end of a shift or day's work, and the key to unravelling them, as with so much else in this work, will be good supervision and consultation.

Finally, there is a special difficulty that may arise for residential workers when they come to the end of an evening shift. How can you unwind, 'decompress' and do any necessary re-evaluation of the day's work late in the evening, when your most urgent need may be for sleep, especially if you are sleeping on the premises and may be called up again during the night, and if you know that you will have to be ready again for the morning shift in only a few hours' time? Moreover, how can you unwind if you are a resident residential worker? Far fewer residential workers 'live in' on the premises these days, but there are still some places where this happens. This is a point at which shiftwork becomes particularly stressful, and it indicates the need for residential workers to develop special skills in self-management – for instance, through learning specific relaxation techniques. Both Mattingly (1981) and Maslach and Zimbardo (1982) have suggestions in this area, including items such as meditation techniques, physical exercises, and so on. Those working in group care teams may find it helpful to compare notes with each other and share ideas as to how to cope with times such as this.

Conclusion

We have considered how workers and teams may handle the end of the day's work, in terms of a sequence of preparation for leaving, departure and after departure. It is perhaps surprising that there is so much to say about what might at first sight seem like a minor aspect of any day's work, but the evidence that we have considered here suggests that, if departure is not carefully handled, it may bring complications and has the potential to develop into a major problem.

Here we also conclude the chapter on the individual worker's perspective on a day's work throughout the shift. The aim of this chapter has been to present a way of describing the responsibilities of the individual group care worker in terms of the 'process' of work from start to finish. The recurring theme, however, has been that an 'individual' model, while a necessary starting point, cannot adequately describe group care work, with all its complexities of interlocking groups and groupings. In the next chapter, therefore, we shall develop this material further in the teamwork context: how does individual work connect with the work of the team as a whole, and what is the role of those with more senior roles in terms of supporting, managing and supervising this work?

FIVE

The Team and its Task

Introduction

Having examined the responsibilities of the individual worker through a shift or day's work, we now change the perspective again. The material in Chapter Four was largely focused on the worker's responsibilities towards her clients and towards herself, although many of the examples also inevitably touched on her interactions with colleagues. By contrast, we shall now focus much more on the team as a whole and on its task, looking in particular at the worker's interactions with other team members. The perspective taken in this chapter is therefore different from the previous one in that we are now considering the worker's part in the whole organisation. Although this is a book about *working* in group care rather than specifically about leadership in group care, it will be argued that much group care work does require familiarity with the skills and concepts of leadership and management. In the first part of the chapter we shall be looking at the skills of team membership and the various ways in which individuals' work connects with the work of the team and of the unit as a whole; in the second part we shall consider how a 'systems' approach provides a useful conceptual framework for sorting out these connections; and in the third part we move on to look at the application of these skills and concepts to leadership and management roles at whatever level in the formal hierarchy.

Working as a team member

The skills of team membership

To understand the skills required for working as a team member in group care, we must return briefly to the distinctions made in Chapter One between group care and office-based social work. It will be recalled that among the distinguishing features of working in group care are the following which relate to teamwork:

- *Interdependence*, in that all members of the team rely directly on each other and on the team as a whole for the effectiveness of each person's work;
- *Public practice*, in that much of one's work is visible and open to comment by clients, colleagues and others; and
- *Multiple relationships*, in that each client may have distinct and sometimes contrasting relationships with more than one worker, as well as with other clients and with the place as a whole.

It follows that, for a group care worker to work successfully as a team member, she must be able to take full account of these factors in her work.

With regard to 'interdependence', she must be able to contribute positively and constructively to the work of colleagues, to accept help from others in her own work, and to cope with the frustrations that arise when there is conflict in the team or when the interdependence seems to be breaking down or under threat. She must therefore be able to 'decentre' from her own individual tasks sufficiently to be aware of the complementary and interlocking tasks of her colleagues, but without 'taking her eye off the ball' in terms of her own work. This may become especially difficult if conflict within the team leads people to undervalue or misinterpret each other's work, and even more so if such conflict remains unspoken or unresolved for long periods of time. All team members must strive towards open communication and the unravelling of personal agendas and interpersonal conflict within the team – if this is not done, both clients and workers will suffer. It is also clear that individual workers cannot abdicate responsibility for resolving these conflicts by waiting for someone else to put them on the agenda.

The demands of 'public practice' are that the worker must bear in mind the likely wider effects of any interaction between herself and another individual or group. In particular she must be able to be honest and accurate in her feedback to colleagues about how she views their practice, and be able to receive and even encourage others' feedback on her own performance without feeling too threatened. In addition, she must be able to communicate clearly with the group of clients about how they perceive her work and the work of the whole team. If these requirements start to sound impossible for most mere mortals to achieve, that is because they *are* difficult for individuals in isolation to achieve. What is needed is an open climate of acceptance and communication within the unit as a whole, encouraged and supported by management. Nevertheless, the absence of such a climate should not be used by the worker as an excuse for not trying, since 'our communication problem is mine as well as yours'. Teamwork is rarely uncomplicated: for many teams it remains a constant struggle, and it is probably never experienced as the 'ideal state' implied in some of the texts on the subject. It is also worth adding that many opportunities arise while working alongside colleagues to check out facts and feelings and to make the necessary reassessments and readjustments 'on the hoof'. So much is happening at once in most group care units that people have to be able to depend on each other for a quick, straight response on matters of concern.

Furthermore, the public nature of much group care work means that workers need to be able to communicate in this way in the presence of their clients: for many people this is surprisingly difficult, in that they feel it would be wrong to admit in public to any disagreement or uncertainty as to what to do next and why. Perhaps this difficulty stems from the felt need to present a 'unified front', perhaps sometimes from a patronising attempt to protect clients from seeing the workers' conflicts or vulnerabilities. For example, some time ago in one highly regarded children's establishment, an unwritten rule developed that staff should never disagree with each other in front of the children, for fear of unsettling them – a policy that effectively prevented the children from learning how to resolve differences constructively!

In terms of 'multiple relationships' the worker must be able to tolerate sharing her work with others without becoming possessive about her relationships with 'her' clients or envious or resentful about her colleagues' relationships with 'their' clients. Handling this complex pattern of relationships is not easy. For example, having to offer personal care to people with high dependency needs tends to evoke a range of strong feelings in any worker – sometimes a deep desire to help and even 'rescue' that person, sometimes an instinctive or perhaps unconscious desire to push away and even harm the person, for fear that their needs will become quite overwhelming. In group care, many of these powerful feelings will be swirling around just below the surface, and it is very easy to become caught up in unhelpful reactions to them – criticising another worker's apparent overindulgence of a needy individual whom others see as manipulative, for example, or unconsciously 'setting up' a situation so that a vulnerable individual's request for help will be ignored or misinterpreted by the team. By contrast, a team that is working well together will capitalise on the many interlocking relationships between workers and clients. Moreover, the pattern of relationships extends well beyond the boundaries of the unit itself, to include relatives and friends of the clients, other professionals, neighbours, and many more.

The skills of being an effective team member in this context can therefore be very demanding in terms of personal maturity and equanimity under pressure. The worker has to manage the balance between her own individual work, the work of the team and the functioning of the whole establishment, and in order to do this she has to monitor not only her own work but also that of her colleagues, and she has to be able to communicate openly and constructively about any difficulties that arise. This juggling act of self-management is at the heart of the mode of working referred to earlier as 'working alongside', and becomes one of the worker's core skills: it is also the foundation of all more advanced or complex management skills.

The place of individual work in group care

The team provides the context for all individual work, and unless the interrelationships of the team are understood, valued and worked at by everyone, individual work will suffer. Such work will then either become 'semi-detached' from the group life of the place, or it may be taken over by the more dominant team members. Where this happens, the risk is that the team will undervalue and eventually lose the contributions of those members with less power, status or self-confidence. Newcomers and students at the start of a placement sometimes score low on all three counts, and may thus run into particular difficulties – a factor that may well contribute to the rapid turnover of junior staff in some settings. It is therefore a matter of great importance that the team as a whole 'owns' individual work, and that individuals are enabled to feel closely tied in to the task of the whole team. We shall look at two aspects of these connections – first, examining the 'keyworker' role, and, second, distinguishing between 'role' and 'function'.

Keyworkers

The place of individual work in the team is often arranged through a keyworker system, in which each client is assigned an individual worker. The term 'keyworker' has been used in many different contexts to cover many different things, which is not surprising, as it refers to a function that will differ enormously according to its context. In some places a keyworker provides the individual client with the coordination of personal care, in others she may offer counselling, or act as an advocate, or help to maintain links with family and others outside the unit; in some settings, meanwhile, these various functions are combined in what can become an excessively vague and shapeless role. Some places operate a 'co-keyworking' system, so that there are always two individuals sharing the focus on each client, with a greater chance that there will usually be one of them on duty. There is no 'right way' of operating a keyworker system, since it must always be tailored to match the needs of the clients with the task of the unit *and* with the skills and availability of the workers, all of which factors vary greatly from one unit to another. At the same time it should be emphasised that although the keyworking role involves an individual personal relationship, it is not primarily a friendship but a professional relationship, tied in to the supervision system and to the work of the team. In each unit the general expectations of the keyworker role should be carefully thought out by the team, and each particular allocation of a keyworker to a client should be based on a thorough assessment and agreement, as described in Chapter Three. Laverty and Reet (2001) have a useful and practical example of the operation of a keyworker system in respite care for children with disabilities.

The 'matching' of keyworkers to clients is especially important: who chooses whom and how? The implications for a client of being 'allocated' to a particular individual for keyworking support may be quite different from the message given by being free to identify a member of the staff team with whom he or she feels comfortable. These decisions (and the way they are made) should be discussed within the context of team meetings and supervision, and where appropriate with the group of clients as well (Worthington, 2003). If the interdependent team is to truly function as such, each worker will need to know and understand something about each other worker's pattern of 'key' relationships with individuals and with the group as a whole: readers of this book will have gathered by now that all roads lead to the staff meeting and it is here that the place of individual work in the team should be debated.

Role and function

The place of individual work in the team may be further clarified by an understanding of the concepts of role and function. The organisation of group care, like any other work, requires that people hold certain responsibilities according to their given job or function: night staff have one set of jobs to carry out, team leaders another, and so on. It is essential that these formal roles are as clear as possible, so that everybody understands the extent and limits of their own and each other's responsibilities. Without such arrangements, things would never reliably get done. However, such parcelling-out of functions, while necessary, can never tell the whole story in work such as this, which often requires such close involvement with one's clients, and which frequently has to be 'opportunity-led' rather than always conforming to tight schedules. How, then, can Opportunity-led Work be managed within the acknowledged need for structure?

Dockar-Drysdale (1968), writing a long time ago about residential work in a therapeutic school, makes a useful distinction between what she calls 'assigned function and created role'. She argues that whereas the unit as a whole assigns people their formal *functions* such as residential worker or teacher, the clients may 'create' more personal and meaningful *roles* for individual workers according to the relationships which develop, and according to the needs of the clients and the potential of the workers. Thus one child may need the security of a relationship with a strongly 'containing' individual who can offer very firm boundaries on behaviour while nevertheless remaining amenable to much direct personal communication, whereas another child may need to find a relationship with someone who can tolerate extremes of difficult behaviour without constantly seeking to restore order. The two workers may have the same job title or 'assigned function', but this child may relate to them and their 'roles' very differently.

Roles such as these may assume considerable importance, and indeed form the basis of much individual work in group care, but they may also clash at times with the formal functions — including that of keyworker. Dockar-Drysdale (1968) gives the example of a boy in a strong dependent relationship with his class teacher who suddenly needs the teacher's help in an emotional crisis: the teacher has to decide at a critical moment whether to retain his function as class-group teacher or to fulfil the role that the boy requires of him — in this case a pastoral or what she terms a 'maternal' role. Whichever way he decides, he might need to call on a colleague to take over whichever function he decides he must temporarily abandon — that is, 'holding' the boy and his emotional needs, or 'holding' the class and sustaining its learning environment.

The term 'role' is being used here to indicate the more personal and sometimes symbolic quality of the relationships that develop in much group care work, and it is important that we understand the interplay between these symbolic roles, based on more or less dependent relationships, and the 'given' functions of the formal organisation. Such roles arise not only in work with children, of course: in many other group care settings the individual worker may come to assume a special and personal significance for the client, and may be treated almost as if she were a parent, sibling or trusted friend, for instance. The worker needs to be able to recognise her importance both to the individual and to the group, in order that she can know how to deal with the feelings aroused in herself and in the client, as well as in her colleagues – and how to hold on to both the real intensity of the feelings but also to the reality that she is *not* the client's relative or personal friend. This may happen not only to members of the 'professional team', since other staff including domestic and ancillary workers who have informal contact with clients may find themselves invested with particular 'roles' that may need to be at least acknowledged even if not always acted upon.

In these situations the worker therefore needs to be able to recognise (partly through consulting with colleagues) her importance both to the individual and to the group, in order that she can know how to manage the range of feelings aroused. This is not an argument for the kind of patronising relationships that develop in some settings to meet the needs of the staff, but a call for the recognition of the emotional undertones that may arise in any situation where intensive and sustained personal care is offered by one person or group to another. It also follows that the team as a whole needs to be tuned in to this aspect of their work, so that they can help each other respond constructively to people's expectations of them – whether this will involve engaging with an individual's deeper needs or gently but firmly redirecting such demands.

Group care workers are very often faced with decisions such as this, weighing up the competing 'role' expectations of individuals within the group, and of the group as a whole, against the 'function' expectations of other workers and perhaps of still other people beyond – other professionals, parents and relatives. Faced with such a situation (which may sometimes arise quite suddenly), the worker has to assess the competing demands and decide where her energies are best directed. At times considerable flexibility is called for – the worker may need to ask a colleague to temporarily take over her 'function' in relation to the group in order that she can respond to an urgent individual need, or vice versa (Whitaker et al, 1998).

These decisions are complicated by the fact that in the context of the 'multiple relationships' in group care, there may be a large number of combinations of individual relationships within the group, not all of them immediately evident. It will not be sufficient for such decisions always to be left to guesswork or intuition: the team needs to set aside time regularly to assess the balance of needs in the group, the pattern of interrelationships between individuals and groups, and the scope for flexibility – since although there will always need to be flexibility in terms of workers' roles, there will also need to be clear cut-off points, beyond which individuals are not empowered to act.

Communication within the team

As we saw earlier, there is little chance of successful individual work unless it is closely connected with the work of the team as a whole, which means that there must be consistently good communication. The chief means of achieving this communication will be for people to meet together regularly and work at it, in staff meetings and supervision. There is also an important place for both informal and formal written communication, but although each of these will have its place in sustaining and confirming what has been achieved in meetings and supervision, without regular and effective meetings nothing else can happen.

Staff meetings

Staff meetings have many different functions in group care, and the first requirement of a successful meeting is that everyone knows and agrees the function of the meeting. It seems useful here, therefore, to itemise the main types of staff meeting (see Box 5.1); the titles used will vary from one unit to another, of course – my aim here is simply to clarify some basic distinctions.

Box 5.1: The functions of staff meetings

(1) *Business Meeting:* to ensure that all are aware of facts and decisions concerning the day-to-day running of the unit and the lives of its members. These meetings can also be used to maximise the opportunity for each worker to take responsibility for some aspect of the everyday work of the place (see Burton, 1993, 1997).

(2) *Assessment and Care-Planning Meeting:* to debate and agree upon the needs of and programme for individuals and groups of clients, using the pooled resources and experiences of the team as a whole. This meeting may also be used for the retrospective assessment of the way people and incidents were handled by the team.

(3) *Policy and Resources Meeting:* to review, evaluate and revise longer-term strategies and policies, such as the referral system, patterns of supervision, ethical issues, and so on. The status of such a meeting needs clear acknowledgement, to avoid confusions and frustrations as to what power the meeting has to make decisions (see Baldwin, 1990, p 94).

(4) *Support/Supervision Group:* to enable workers to share positive and negative feelings about their work, about themselves and about each other, and to give and take feedback, validation and emotional support. It is especially effective when facilitated by an external consultant.

(5) *Training Group:* differs from the Support Group in style as well as content, in that an agenda is agreed in advance, covering a set topic and usually involving a trainer – sometimes involving other outsiders (see Douglas and Payne, 1988), although the most effective are often closely tied in to the everyday concerns of the staff (see, for example, Clifford, 1998).

(6) *Problem-Solving Meeting:* used either as part of the long-term debate of policy and resources types of issues, or as one-off short-notice analyses of critical incidents. Sometimes this is a joint meeting between staff and clients.

(7) *Handover Meeting:* to ensure clarity and fullness of communication between workers on different shifts or with largely separate areas of responsibility (see Chapter Four; Mason, 1989).

(8) *Community Meeting:* includes both staff and clients together, and may include functions such as problem solving, support, business, handover, and so on.

The successful running of a group care unit will require a pattern of various types and frequencies of meeting for various groups and sub-groups, sometimes involving 'outsiders' as well as 'insiders'. The work of designing and implementing a pattern of staff meetings is touched upon later in this chapter; here we are concerned with the ways in which the individual worker needs to participate in these meetings.

We have seen several examples in this book of workers bringing important issues for discussion at staff meetings – such as feelings arising from conflict in the team, and thoughts about proposals for change. Bringing such items to a meeting and subsequently debating them requires considerable skill, such as the ability to listen to other people's expression of strong feelings without needing to interrupt or retaliate, the ability to assert one's own judgement without undermining others' confidence, and the ability to give attention to the 'process' of group interaction as well as to the content of the discussion. Very often when people complain about 'communication problems' in staff teams, such difficulties can be traced to the lack of skills such as these, the lack of confidence to use such skills even when people do have them, or the lack of leadership in such communication. Training and supervision in the use of such skills – either in separate training sessions or 'live' through the use of a consultant to facilitate communication in the team – can therefore make an enormous contribution to the work of any team. This whole discussion serves to underline the essential contribution of groupwork skills to group care practice.

Using supervision

Bringing issues to staff meetings may sometimes be even harder than suggested above, because it can feel impossible to know exactly what one needs to bring, apart from a general feeling that 'something isn't right'; on the other hand, in meetings people sometimes bring (or indirectly draw attention to) issues quite unintentionally – by getting unnecessarily heated over an apparently minor matter, for example, and thus hinting at deeper anxieties or tensions. Staff meetings may not always be the best place to unravel such uncertainties – they may be better raised first in supervision, which will sometimes be the best place to begin exploring uncertainty.

Supervision in group care covers a wide range of practice, in terms of both content and method, including team supervision and 'live' or 'opportunistic supervision' (Collie, 2002). There may therefore be some overlap between the functions of staff meetings, supervision and general support, and these distinctions will vary from unit to unit. I am using 'supervision' here, however, to refer specifically to a *planned programme of meetings between an individual or group of workers and a manager or supervisor*, with the focus being on the workers' learning about their own work and about themselves as workers as well as on understanding the details of the situation or case being discussed. In the case of the worker or team needing to explore uncertain ground, or trying to move beyond what may feel like a 'stuck' or circular situation, a deeper understanding of what happens between people in supervision can help.

In particular, I want to focus briefly on the part played by what has been termed the 'reflection process' (Mattinson, 1975; Hawkins and Shohet, 2000). This is the phenomenon by which workers may unconsciously bring into supervision material relating to their own feelings about their relationship with their clients. Thus, in the simplest example, when feeling under particular stress, the worker may tend to treat her supervisor in much the same way as her client treats her, for example making her feel powerless, or despairing, or perhaps very special. These may be unconscious feelings, affecting people's thoughts and behaviours without them being fully aware of what is happening or why. The task of the supervisor will be to become aware of such phenomena as they arise, and to help the worker become aware of them, so as to unlock some of the complicated and confusing interactions that can lead to people feeling 'stuck' in their work.

While this reflection process has been identified in the supervision of casework and individual psychotherapy, it is a phenomenon which also arises in group care, although in different and more complex ways. Simple examples would include the staff team which begins to re-enact the difficulties of a group of clients, or the team which treats its managers with the same mistrust and hostility that it experiences from the client group; however, given the complexity of group care, some of these reflections may become very complicated indeed and hard to trace back to their source. An understanding of such processes can contribute not only to maximising the learning from supervision, but also to enabling the team to help the clients resolve the anxiety or difficulty that was originally being expressed. In the light of this phenomenon, 'using supervision' may take on a different meaning, in the sense of each person, and the team collectively, being ready to examine what happens in supervision – the 'process' as well as the content – for clues as to what is happening in the unit as a whole (see Hinshelwood, 1987, 2001; Hawkins and Shohet, 2000).

Informal communication

Beyond the formal arrangements of meetings and supervision, an enormous amount of the communication that happens within group care teams happens at the informal level. Such communication flow is essential if the team is to function collaboratively, and much of what is talked about might appear trivial to an outsider – the detail of how a mealtime ended, or of a minor argument between two people over a bar of soap, for instance. Yet these details will have meaning for the workers, and the conversation will often serve the function of helping people to work out what was trivial and what held greater significance, and thus eventually to knit together all the strands of individual interactions into a meaningful whole.

Where there is so much informal communication, often conducted during or shortly after times of stress, the tendency towards gossip and backbiting is powerful. In order to cope with their strong feelings, people may start to say things that they would not say to an individual's face, or make fun of others' fears or failings. However, such behaviour is contagious as well as unprofessional, and it can spread swiftly through a group to the point where a 'subculture' develops which runs quite against the avowed aims of the unit. It is therefore the responsibility of team members to monitor the tone as well as the content of their communication so that they always show respect for the dignity of those being discussed, whether clients, their families or colleagues: this means refusing to abuse the position of power that group care workers hold. It is a rare team indeed where this is always achieved, but unless there is a commitment in the team to keep communication fair and open, things deteriorate rapidly, and 'on-task' work can quickly become 'anti-task' (Menzies, 1988). The whole point of using group care as a helping environment is that it involves making purposeful use of all the possibilities in the informal times as well as in the formal arrangements, and this applies to staff interaction as much as to any other aspect of the place.

Recording

The recording of work in group care takes many forms and fulfils many functions. Here we are concerned with its role in connecting the work of individuals with the work of the team, and in holding the work of the whole unit together. Most group care teams are required to keep some form of daily 'logbook' covering the salient events of each day – visitors, outings, celebrations, significant changes; in some places this logbook is also used to describe the atmosphere of the day's work, the mood of the group of clients and staff and of key individuals. It usually forms the main record of the cumulative experience of the whole group, and will often be used by the incoming team members to help them tune in at the start of a shift. A word of caution, however: referring to the logbook is no substitute for proper handover meetings – even the most detailed written record of a day's work cannot give the full flavour of the life of the unit, and in particular is not 'interactive' enough to allow the incoming workers to ask questions, give and take support, or try out hypotheses as to why certain things have happened or not happened. Indeed, in some teams, the logbook is only written up after the handover meeting, as an agreed record of what has been 'handed over'. Nevertheless, the logbook does serve a useful purpose in providing a daily 'freeze-frame' of the flowing stream of the life of the unit, and thus in enabling team members to keep track of events over longer periods of time, by building up a cumulative picture of the evolving life of the group.

Individual work itself will often be recorded on case files or 'continuity sheets', and these records are likely to include not only any planned one-to-one sessions that may be held as part of an individual programme, but also those unscheduled but significant developments that arise during daily living, as well as the periodic summary of the person's progress through their stay. With the advent of legal requirements for clients to have access to their own records on request (1998 Data Protection Act), many units have implemented systems of 'open recording', in which what is written down is an agreed record of a discussion between the client and the worker, rather than the purely subjective view of the individual worker. The implications for group care practice of this change to open recording are enormous, especially in terms of addressing the issue of power identified earlier in this book, although they have been largely unexplored in the literature. Finally, within appropriate limits of confidentiality, individual recording also provides a record for the benefit of other workers in the unit who may need to understand more about the individual client's situation and needs and about the work being undertaken with them, and thus it adds further to the linking of each team member's work into the task of the whole team.

Team, system and task

Introduction

Much of this book is focused on the 'interconnectedness' of group care work and a principal theme is the responsibility of the worker to hold together all of these connections. The range and diversity of factors needing to be connected is so great that some kind of theoretical framework is needed that can help the worker to hold them all together, and to explain and predict the effects of one part of the network on another. One such framework, especially useful since it focuses precisely on the connections within and between complex networks, is the 'systems' approach, and in the following pages we shall be considering some elements of this approach, together with a range of its applications to various aspects of group care practice. This section is accordingly the most 'theoretical' part of the book describing a number of different versions and applications of the principles of systems thinking.

The 'systems' approach

What is a system?

The basic premise of the systems approach is that any human organisation, such as a family, work group, or in this case a group care unit, may be viewed as a 'system' consisting of many parts. All of these parts are interconnected and affect each other, and the whole system is in some senses greater than the sum of its parts, and can be said to have characteristics of its own. Straightforward examples of systems in group care would be: the unit as a whole, the staff team or the family system of any given client. The systems approach can help to explain the ways in which 'systems' such as these operate both within themselves and in interaction with each other.

What sort of characteristics do systems have?

We shall look briefly at four main characteristics that systems are said to have. First, a system may be said to be *open* or *closed*, according to how openly and actively it relates with its surroundings – for example, the extent to which people or things regularly join and leave the system. Most group care units are clearly open systems in that both clients and staff regularly join and leave the system. A closed system, by contrast, would be one in which nothing comes in or goes out – and no group care unit could continue to function on that basis (see Bruggen and O'Brian, 1987, p 56).

Second, a system may be said to have *boundaries*, which 'define' the system, and which will be crossed by the people or things joining and leaving. For instance, in order to define a day centre as a system, and thus to understand its component parts and characteristics, we have to temporarily exclude from our thinking the other households on the same street, or the other day centres in the area, and place these outside the 'boundary' of this day centre. Such boundaries are in the mind of the beholder, of course, because we could equally decide to define the whole group of day centres in the area as a system in its own right if we wanted to concentrate on, for instance, the interactions between them. To identify any particular grouping as a system, then, is simply a way of 'framing' one's thinking in order to learn more about how that grouping works.

A third characteristic of systems relates to the issue of *change*. The systems approach is based on the view that since all the parts of a system are connected, change in any one part is likely to affect all other parts of the system. The implications of this simple idea are enormous, especially in social work, where change is usually a central preoccupation.

A fourth characteristic of systems, which also relates to change, is the idea of *homeostasis*: all systems are said to be inherently geared towards preserving themselves intact by keeping their various parts in a state of balance or homeostasis – this characteristic has been called the 'self-maintaining and adaptive capacity' of systems (Preston-Shoot and Agass, 1990, p 45). Taking these last two characteristics together may help us to explain, for example, why an attempt to change a whole residential unit by 'pushing' all the parts at the same time may meet inbuilt resistance and thus fail, while by contrast a simple 'nudge' of one small part of the system may set in motion much greater changes in the system as a whole.

What is 'systems thinking'?

The connections between the parts of a system, and the ways in which these parts influence each other, can all be studied within the systems approach, although the approach itself does not presuppose any single theoretical basis for the connections. Thus, rather than asking, for instance, 'why did this worker lose her temper with that resident?', systems thinking might lead us to ask: 'what was the pattern and history of relationships throughout the unit, where do this worker and this resident fit into that pattern, and what was currently happening between this resident and her family or network, or, for instance, between this worker and the team as a whole, which might have contributed to this outbreak of tension?'. This is a much more complicated question, but a group care unit is a complicated place, and using this approach may lead to a more productive answer than a simple 'single cause and effect' approach. Avoiding the pitfalls of seeking simplistic explanations is one of the chief benefits of using the systems approach or 'systems thinking' (see Payne, 2005, pp 157-8).

Applying the systems approach to practice

Of the many ways in which systems thinking can be applied to group care work, we shall look at three, focusing first on the internal workings of the group care unit as a 'system', second at the connections between the unit and other relevant systems, and third at the implications of systems thinking for defining the task of the unit.

The unit as a system

First, we focus on the unit itself as a system with its own sub-systems. In the example of the worker losing her temper with the resident, we analysed a simple 'situational assessment' in terms of some of the interlocking factors that may have contributed to that incident. One way in which a systems approach can help the team to make sense of their work, therefore, is in broadening the base for assessing any situation so that a much wider range of factors than usual can be taken into account. Such a broadening might also affect assessment in other ways: in the case of assessing the needs of an individual client, for example, systems thinking might lead the team to meet jointly with the person, her family and friends, in order to look at the range of resources in the neighbourhood and their potential for being adapted to help her, rather than relying solely on the familiar but limited 'checklist' approach of listing personal symptoms and problems. The systems approach is thus also an approach that fits well with the holistic view proposed in this book and with a 'strengths' perspective (Saleebey, 2005).

Similarly, viewing the whole unit as a system of interlocking parts will contribute usefully to the planning of admissions and departures. This is why the emphasis in Chapter Three was on taking full account of the impact of an admission or departure on all the various sub-systems of the unit (see Box 3.1 and Figure 3.1). The reality is that we may as well plan to take such effects into account, since, even if we do not, the effects will nevertheless still happen, and it is better to anticipate and understand events than to be constantly surprised and puzzled by them.

Wider systems and group care: family systems and the 'unitary approach'

A second way of applying systems thinking involves looking beyond the boundaries of the unit, and defining the range and limits of the unit's work – how far can group care work usefully include planned contact with the clients' families and other networks, or with the local neighbourhood? In other words, what are the connections between the unit as a system and the other systems around it?

The most obvious 'other system' in relation to group care is the family system of the individual client. Looking at the family as a system enables us to understand more about the ways in which family members influence and affect each other. Thus, change in one individual may have a profound effect on other family members, and the family system as a whole may try to protect itself from the impact of this change by trying to retain its balance or established order at all costs. Sometimes, for example, a family tries to maintain this balance by pushing out an individual who is seen as challenging it: this is a pattern that sometimes turns out to lie behind the referral through family pressure of an individual to a group care setting. A systems-based response to such a referral might include a full exploration with the family as to why this individual is identified as having the greatest problem, and why this problem is seen as being better addressed by removing the individual from the family home than perhaps by exploring or adjusting other aspects of the family system. Such an approach might result in solutions other than a group care placement, or it might still lead to such a placement, but with a clearer focus on the real reasons for admission and thus on the task of the unit in relation to this individual and her family. There is a substantial body of theoretical assumptions and working methods based on the family systems approach, some of which have been applied directly to group care (see Bruggen and O'Brian, 1987). For further examples, see Colette Richardson's (2003) account of the application of the theory and practice of systemic family therapy to the general work of a residential therapeutic community for adolescents; see also Yvonne Bailey-Smith's (2001) description of a systemic approach to working with black families.

A second, and in some ways more far-reaching, way of applying systems thinking to the broader task of group care derives from the so-called 'unitary approach' to social work. This approach involves a further piece of reframing, since the 'systems' identified here are not necessarily the predetermined ones of the unit, the family or the staff team, but are formulated in terms of the main systems that can be identified in any piece of social work intervention. These main systems can be summarised as follows: the change-agent system (the helpers), the client system (those asking for help), the target system (those at whom the help is directed), and the action system (the new 'system' formed around the change agent and target systems in order to effect change). The team's first task, as part of the assessment phase of the work, will be to determine precisely who or what lies within each of these systems. Using the 'unitary approach' encourages teams to be as clear as possible in identifying, and if necessary assembling, the appropriate resources and approaches for any given piece of work. Although the terminology may be complex to a newcomer, once one becomes familiar with it, it can certainly help teams to structure an appropriate response to a call for help. For example, distinguishing between the client system and the target system should lead to help being targeted on those areas that are most amenable to change, and should thus lead to more effective change.

Both of these applications of systems thinking offer ways of viewing the group care task more broadly, and can lead to more imaginative and productive help for individuals – by mobilising the resources of family and friends, by promoting change beyond the immediate boundaries of the group care unit, and particularly by encouraging maximum clarity and openness in the assessment of referred problems. Fur further discussion of these aspects of systems thinking see Malcolm Payne's useful chapter on 'systems and ecological perspectives' (Payne, 2005b).

The Primary Task and the 'open systems' model

A third way of using systems thinking in group care work is in defining the task of a unit. However, before looking at what the systems approach can contribute to this matter, we shall first consider why it is not only important, but also difficult, to be clear about the task of a unit.

It is not hard to see that, if the work of a group care team is to be effective, team members must be clear about what they should be doing and why – and not just in general terms, but specifically, in relation to what the outcome of their efforts is expected to be. It follows that, for these individual functions to be clear, the collective task of the unit as a whole must first be established. The argument of this book has so far proceeded as if it was straightforward to state the unit's task, and from there another easy step to list the functions of each team member. In reality, defining the precise task of the unit may be far from simple: for example, is the real task of a probation day centre the one which is proclaimed in the official brochure by the local chief probation officer, or is it based on the blueprint of the head of the unit, the collective aims of the staff team, or the hopes of the users and their families? How does it take into account government policy on the one hand and the views of the local neighbourhood on the other hand? How can we reconcile the fact that each of these groups may have conflicting views about the task of the unit? Furthermore, how can the task be expressed more precisely and productively than in such generalised aims as 'rehabilitation', 'normalisation', and 'prevention of reoffending' – none of which is precise enough to lead to clear guidance on the tasks of the workers?

It is in order to address some of these questions that we turn to the *open systems* model. Within this approach, each group care unit is viewed as an 'open system' with one central or Primary Task, 'the task which the enterprise must perform in order to survive' (Rice, 1963, p 42; Kahn, 2005). An 'open system', as we have seen, is one which is open to its surroundings in the sense that it has a throughput of materials – in the case of group care, this usually refers to the arrival and departure of clients. The unit takes in or 'imports' people at one end, provides care or treatment for them or 'transforms' them, then sends them out or 'exports' them again at the other end (Miller and Gwynne, 1972). This throughput therefore refers to the approach taken in the perspective of 'The Client's Stay' in Chapter Three of this book. The Primary Task of the unit is defined in relation to this throughput: it is the function which the unit must perform in achieving this throughput, for society and for the funding body, as well as for the clients using the service. Readers may begin to feel that the language of this approach is rather cold and concrete for a book that has been seeking to emphasise the human relations approach to group care, although in fact thinking 'systemically' can contribute greatly to one's understanding of and engagement with the complex patterns of human interaction in group care. What the concept of the Primary Task offers is a way of staying focused on the 'bottom line' of group care: a group care unit must admit the right people for the right reasons, must offer them the right sorts of care and support, and enable them to eventually move on to whatever the next step in their lives will be.

This approach to defining the task focuses attention on the tensions between the functions expected of the unit by various parties, and thereby encourages teams to be explicit and unambiguous about what exactly they are there to provide. It is thus much more hard-edged than some of the 'vision statements' and 'mission statements' that some organisations promote. The Primary Task must be expressed as a clear and precise statement of intent, which will enable the team to make firm connections between the intended outcome of The Client's Stay and the stated functions and actual roles of individual workers and of the team as a whole. Thus, for example, when the team of the probation day centre define their Primary Task, they may have to take account of the views of the general public and the court system, whose aims for the centre may include 'to keep offenders off the streets', 'to prevent offenders from reoffending', and 'to provide a constructive alternative to custodial sentences', but the eventual formulation will be of most use if it includes a statement about the planned outcome for the users such as 'to enable people who have offended (and are likely to reoffend) to become more constructive members of society (and *less* likely to reoffend), but without totally removing them from society'. It should be noted that even this formula only applies to a hypothetical case, whereas in reality such organisations may have an even more complex task with more precise hoped-for outcomes. Defining and redefining the task is an essential and ongoing process.

Defining the Primary Task of a unit therefore requires the balancing of many different factors, both internal and external. These will include sorting out which of the many tasks of a unit is fundamental to its continued existence, and how the other tasks relate to it, as well as facing up to the inherent conflict when the Primary Task is doomed to be constantly undermined because of barriers to good practice such as those outlined elsewhere in this book (see Menzies, 1988). Further discussion and detailed applications of this approach are to be found in Obholzer and Roberts (1994a) and Kahn (2005).

Conclusion

This section has provided an introduction to a wide range of applications of systems thinking to group care. For the most part, this approach has been set out in general terms here, and it will be for readers to apply this approach to the particulars of their own situation, perhaps after following up some of the recommended reading. As stated earlier, the systems approach does not provide the answers, it provides different ways of framing the questions. Finally, systems thinking has particular applications for those with management or leadership responsibilities. Many people, when they start working in group care, feel baffled by the complexity of the task, and at first feel that they 'can't see the wood for the trees', but as they learn their way around the complexity of the system, they discover much more about how things fit together. One particular contribution of systems thinking can therefore be to enable people to operate more effectively at a management level – since management always involves some element of holding and understanding complicated situations, plus the essential element of bringing about or coping with change.

Managing the system

Introduction

Having looked at what is involved in working in a group care team, and having opened up some of the possibilities offered by a systems approach, we shall finally look at how an understanding of teams, tasks and systems can help to inform the specific responsibilities of leading such a team. It will not be possible here to do justice to the whole range of management tasks, since this is a book on *working in group care* rather than specifically on managing it. This section involves a further change of focus from the earlier material, in that most of the book thus far has been focused on the work of the 'basic-grade' group care worker, whereas now we are looking at the tasks of more senior workers who hold some leadership and/or management responsibilities. This change of focus in itself highlights the issue of hierarchy in group care teams, a subject which gives rise to much strong feeling in some teams. There will be some discussion of the role of the manager or leader of the whole unit, although I also have in mind the other team members who hold leadership roles. This intermediate or 'practitioner-manager' level of working in group care carries its own particular strains and demands, which often go unrecognised both in practice and in the literature, and just as in many other branches of social work, people are often promoted into these roles with little or no preparation for their new responsibilities. As a prelude to this section, therefore, it is worth considering briefly the individual's transition into a management role in group care.

The transition into management

The transition into a leadership role may be a challenging time all round (Reynolds, 2003): it is likely to involve the individual in re-evaluating her relationships with other team members, both those more senior and those more junior to herself, and thus to involve a certain amount of change on everyone's part. Among the themes that may arise are the three 'key issues' of power, prejudice and dependency highlighted throughout this book. Taking on a management role requires the individual to address these issues anew in relation to both colleagues and clients. Thus it has been pointed out that for a woman the transition into management may be made especially difficult because of the way others may continue to underestimate or belittle her abilities (Coulshed, 2006). Black workers moving into management may encounter a similar renewed 'onslaught of the stereotypes', despite evidence that, for black clients in particular, such an appointment may have a powerful positive impact – see, for example, the discussion of the importance of black role models by Jones and Waul (2005).

In particular, the new team leader may encounter an entirely new and different set of responses from former peers – those who distance themselves from anyone in authority over them, for example, or those who quickly become dependent on any leader for guidance and personal support. On the other hand, she may feel hampered in taking on her new role by those colleagues who seek to deny the change by treating her exactly the same as before, or by a general reluctance in the whole system to adapt sufficiently to an individual's change – this may be the downside of the 'homeostasis' or tendency to resist change in some organisations. In coping with this range of responses, she may also discover new aspects of her own work style, some of which may feel less easy to deal with than others.

Becoming a 'practitioner-manager' will often involve changing one's main reference group from being 'one of the workers' to being part of a management team, and this new reference group may bring new sources of validation and support. Even in those settings where formal hierarchies are considerably flattened, something of this effect is still likely to be felt. On the other hand, being a practitioner-manager is an ambiguous position, since you have a foot in both camps. The new manager is unlikely to drop all of her previous functions in terms of direct work with clients, but she *is* likely to have to take on extra functions especially in relation to other staff, such as supervision, leading a shift and holding more administrative responsibilities. This dual role may be quite difficult at times, and managing the balance of loyalties right across the system is one of the great challenges of any management role in this work. Even the most experienced manager can feel torn between responding to the needs and demands of individual workers and pursuing the agreed goals of the unit as a whole, and in the temporary state of personal 'crisis' while becoming a new manager these conflicts may feel particularly acute. Indeed, the reason for my emphasis here on this transition is that the principles of crisis intervention work (for example, Roberts, 2000) suggest that the kinds of solutions to these dilemmas that people evolve in their early days of becoming a manager may set the pattern for much of their future work – we are creatures of habit and once we have carved ourselves a path we are likely to follow it again the next time we feel unsure or under threat. This is why it is so important that the transition into management is monitored carefully both by the individual and within the context of supervision and professional development. As with other transitions, keeping a personal/professional journal can be most helpful for the individual in keeping track of what is happening, observing one's own reactions and responses to challenge, and learning new ways of making sense and taking action (Bolton, 2001).

Management

In one sense, it can be argued that all group care work involves some element of management – managing oneself and managing situations as well as managing people and buildings. At a superficial level this is an attractive argument, since, while not all of these activities are usually thought of as management, in group care 'managing' will never be a completely separate activity from the other responsibilities of the worker. On the other hand, such a broad concept does not necessarily make for clear thinking, and if group care is to be truly purposeful and effective in achieving its task, it is better to retain some clear distinctions between management and other responsibilities; such distinctions will be explored further in the coming pages.

The simplest definition of management is that it is about sorting out 'who does what – why, when and how?'. All of the theories of management really boil down to elaborations on these simple questions. For example, whose job is it to supervise mealtimes in a day centre, and how should that supervision be carried out – indeed, does the mealtime really need supervising? Whose task is it to ensure that issues such as this are decided upon at all, rather than left to chance and the goodwill of whoever happens to be around? What responsibilities are held by the person who makes or coordinates such decisions to ensure that they are made fairly and consistently and in accordance with a due awareness of the issues of power, prejudice and dependency outlined elsewhere in this book? While the answers to these questions may be straightforwardly identified and agreed upon in some settings, in many units things are less clear. It often appears that all the functions of formal management are held by the manager, whose personal style thus dictates how everything shall be done in the place – whether that means a 'hands-on' and prescriptive approach or a more 'laid-back' and perhaps vague approach. However, while the influence of the designated leader should not be underestimated, the functions of management are never completely confined to that person.

Levels of management

There are many levels of management in group care (see Box 5.2), and while these levels do not correspond exactly with the rungs of the formal hierarchy, there is a clear progression implied in their formulation. The levels of 'managing oneself' and 'managing the practicalities' have been included here for the sake of completeness, although it will be argued that 'real' management only begins at level 3. It will also be apparent that these levels cover only the internal life of the unit – the external management of the group care system extends to several further levels, which cannot be covered here.

> **Box 5.2:** Levels of internal management in group care
> 1. ('Managing' oneself as an individual worker.)
> 2. ('Managing' the practicalities of everyday life, including managing situations and critical incidents.)
> ....
> 3. Managing the shift: coordination and deployment of resources.
> 4. Managing the team: holding things together through time and across the team.
> 5. Managing the unit, including managing the Primary Task, managing the work context, managing resources, and so on.

At the individual level, each worker carries responsibility for *'managing' herself* – as we saw in Chapter Four, individuals are primarily responsible for their own working day, for starting and finishing the day's work appropriately, and for working within a range of responsibilities as set out in that chapter. There are clear connections here with other parts of the system: individuals must coordinate their work with others, they must work towards a commonly held Primary Task, and they must plan and evaluate their work. However, while such 'self-management' has been seen as an aspect of management (Harris and Kelly, 1991), it is probably more productive to view it simply as part of the professional responsibilities of any qualified social worker (Expert Group, 1992). The distinction is between taking responsibility for one's own work and having accountability for others' work, in the sense of managing the team or the unit as a whole – which is where true management responsibilities arise.

Similarly, in terms of the daily work of the unit, while all workers are involved in *'managing' the practicalities* of everyday life, we again need to be clear about the way in which the term 'management' is being used. The example of the supervision of mealtimes was given above. Here it is the event that requires 'managing': the people eating the meal need the food to be provided appropriately, in a suitable atmosphere and with practical and personal support where this is required. Various elements of this task may be provided by kitchen staff, other domestic staff and care staff, and some by the clients themselves, who will help themselves and each other, and all of this needs planning and coordination. If a problem arises – in the form of a critical incident, for example – a worker or team will have to *manage the situation* by responding appropriately and in accordance with any pre-planned policies for handling such incidents, coordinating their efforts as the situation develops, and evaluating their work afterwards. As above, however, while it can be argued that 'managing the practicalities and managing incidents' are part of the formal management task of a unit, it is probably more productive to view such tasks as part of the standard repertoire of group care skills, and to retain the term 'management' for other types of responsibility.

The point at which it becomes more appropriate to describe group care work as involving management is where a worker is responsible for *coordinating* all the tasks and events in the unit at any one time: this point is indicated by the dotted line in Box 5.2. Such coordination is provided by the senior worker on the shift or whoever it has been agreed will carry this responsibility on this occasion. This coordinator will try to ensure that all of the parts of the operation are carried out as they should be, that people are aware of each other's roles and contributions and aware of the extent and limits of these contributions, and that whatever difficulties arise are sorted out satisfactorily. Moreover, it will be important that the way today's coordinator carries out these responsibilities is the same as the way tomorrow's and yesterday's coordinators work, *and* that this way of working fits with the Primary Task and working methods of the unit. It is therefore at the third stage in Box 5.2 that we begin to consider 'real' management in the sense of leadership, administration and the coordination and deployment of resources.

The need for the bringing together of the day-by-day coordination into a consistent and coherent overall pattern indicates one main role of the team leader: *holding things together through time and across the team.* This role relates directly to the contexts of working in group care, as set out in Chapter Two: time, place, teamwork. Everyone in group care has to allow for these contextual aspects of their work, but those with management responsibilities have to pay particular attention to the overall effect of these aspects on the clients, the workers and the task itself. The image of *holding* expresses this function most clearly: it is based on the metaphor used by Winnicott (1990) to describe the parental (usually maternal) function of providing both physical and emotional holding for an infant as a way of not just reassuring but also enabling growth and development. Winnicott himself applied this metaphor to the residential context, in terms of both the 'holding' of the troubled feelings and sometimes difficult behaviour of young people and others in distress, and in turn the holding that a staff team under pressure may need if they are to retain the ability to think creatively and respond appropriately to the needs of the residents. For more detailed applications of this metaphor in the group care context, see Ward and McMahon (1997), Musgrave (2001) and Ward et al (2003). The manager carries the greatest 'holding' responsibilities over time, although other individuals – and the team collectively – carry parts and versions of these same responsibilities.

Among the many responsibilities involved in *managing the whole unit*, of central importance is the management of the Primary Task. This will mean establishing, implementing and monitoring policies and procedures for the stages of The Client's Stay (see Chapter Three), and ensuring that these are all coordinated towards the achievement of the unit's task, through the appropriate systems for dependence, independence, and so on. There is also the management of the work context including, for example, managing personnel, and coordinating the various programmes, rotas and routines of the place into an integrated whole. These broader responsibilities of management are likely, in most units, to be held by the manager and deputy rather than being shared around equally among the team, and represent what is more commonly thought of as management.

There is much more to be said than will be possible here about managing the whole unit – in particular, the whole area of budgetary control, which has assumed increasing importance in the workload of many managers, sometimes to the detriment of other important areas (see Gallop, 2003, for a useful chapter on budgets and 'Best Value'). An area that deserves some mention is that of 'quality assurance', that is, the responsibility of the manager to ensure that the service provided to clients and their families is of an appropriate quality. Here I would argue that, while the manager does have clear responsibilities to implement a quality assurance programme, every worker in the system has equal responsibilities towards achieving that quality of service – thus the argument in this book for workers to understand and carry out their individual and team responsibilities, to understand the workings of the system as a whole, to adhere to the principles of professional group care, and to address the key issues of power, prejudice and dependency. The particular contribution of the manager to a quality assurance programme is likely to be the implementing of a system for regularly reviewing and evaluating all aspects of the practice of the unit, including hearing the views of the clients. Without such monitoring, and without measuring the achievements of the unit against its objectives and proclaimed methods, claims about quality assurance will remain 'empty rhetorical statements' (Harris and Kelly, 1991, p 83).

Responsibilities of management

Despite what has been said about the point at which 'real' management responsibilities begin, in practice people often have to function at many different levels during the course of a day's work – for example, even relatively inexperienced staff can contribute to 'holding things together through time' by taking an active part in handover meetings, while the elements of 'managing oneself' and 'managing situations' apply to managers as much as to 'junior' staff. In addition, in a system in which management functions are properly delegated, people at each level may contribute by holding key responsibilities for certain areas or aspects of the work, such as running the system for ordering food, monitoring the maintenance of the building, and overseeing 'outreach' work with families or with the local community. The range of tasks and functions is too great to cover here in detail: instead we shall focus on three central concerns of management at any level, managing conflict, managing decision making and power, and managing change.

Managing conflict

While many of the examples given in this book have shown individuals working at establishing or improving the links between their own work and other parts of the system, the starting point for most of these examples has been conflict. Conflict is not, of course, peculiar to group care, but because of the complexity of the situation there is enormous scope for conflict: for example, conflict within the client group or the staff team, or between clients and workers, or between the unit and the outside world. There is scope for conflict on grounds of competing needs, or incompatible philosophies, or conflicting loyalties; there may be power struggles between members of the team or conflict over 'difficult' team members (Obholzer and Roberts, 1994b; Ward, 2003a, pp 52-3). The responsibility of all the workers, but especially those at the higher levels of management, will be to identify potential conflicts as they arise, to consult with the various parties involved, and to bring them together to work at resolving the conflict. The manager herself cannot always undertake to resolve the conflict – that will be the responsibility of the people involved, although she may have to use some authority in imposing a settlement where people cannot agree.

Many situations also arise in which compromise cannot be easily achieved: where conflicting needs are inherent in the task of the unit, for example, or where the parties involved feel that more is at stake than the superficial issue being discussed, or where the conflict goes 'underground' in the sense that people join factions which resent and compete with each other, thus enacting rather than resolving the conflict. This last scenario is the most damaging of all, because the covert conflict can have unpredictable effects on other parts of the system, as the 'reflection process' leads one group to re-enact the problems that another group is not resolving. This was the case in the situation described in Chapter Four, where the staff group dynamics of an adolescent unit mirrored the unresolved conflicts in the resident group.

Diagnosing the exact source and real location of conflict may therefore be the hardest task. Once this has been achieved, however, resolving the conflict still requires considerable knowledge as well as skill, and especially an understanding of the ways in which groups, sub-groups and individuals interact (see Coulshed, 2006). At both the diagnostic and the 'resolving' stages, the use of an external consultant to the staff team or to the manager can help by providing a forum and opportunities to examine all the possibilities.

In the process of conflict management it is especially important that managers do not lose sight of the principles of professional group care, or of the issues of power, prejudice and dependency that have been highlighted in this book. For example, some of the conflicts that develop within staff teams can lead to the team becoming so preoccupied with itself that the needs of the client become quite submerged in the process – here the responsibility of the manager will be to remind people of their Primary Task (which, it will be remembered, is always expressed in terms of the 'hoped-for outcomes' for clients), and to insist on restoring an appropriate balance of priorities. On the other hand, managers who lack the confidence or skill to facilitate compromise out of conflict sometimes end up imposing inappropriate solutions that may 'work' in the short term, but which cause deeper conflict simply because they have been imposed. In other words, if working in group care should be informed by the principle of empowerment, then the task of the manager will be the quite distinctive task of managing an empowering system.

Managing decision making and power

Part of managing any conflict will involve making decisions – about whose view or needs should prevail, for example, or about what strategy should be employed to prevent future conflict. At each of the levels of management identified above, decisions have to be made, and if people are to be able to make productive decisions, they will need to understand not only the details of the matter being decided, but also the ways in which decisions influence both groups and individuals throughout the various 'systems' of group care. What is most important may be not so much the outcome of the decision as the way in which it is made – who is consulted, who has the power to influence, argue and even veto? My own working assumption is that an appropriate approach to managing the team in group care will be a fully participatory approach, in which everybody can contribute to the debate on decisions at all levels (Rogers and Reynolds, 2003a). Although this system might sound laborious, it need not be so: each decision rests most sensibly with the group which it affects most, and there is a wide range of constructive and creative ways of using a participatory approach to management (see Douglas et al, 1988).

Decision making therefore brings us back again to the way in which issues of power are handled. Leaders have a responsibility to ensure that their style of leadership matches the working methods expected of the staff team, as well as the Primary Task of the unit. For example, if the Primary Task of a unit for adolescents is to encourage growth towards independence, it may be counterproductive for the leader of the unit to play an excessively 'charismatic' role that might encourage strong dependency among either staff or users. Similarly, if staff are expected to be absolutely reliable in their dealings with users, then leaders must be similarly reliable, otherwise a negative 'modelling' effect is likely to undermine the practice of the team. Managers also have a responsibility to examine the effects which their exercise of power has on others within the system, whether clients or their relatives, other workers or their families and communities, and so on. The theme of power is therefore a pervasive one, and for a team of workers to be able to trust and respect each other at the level required for the intensive nature of group care work, issues of personal power will have to be addressed directly in team meetings, supervision and consultation.

Managing change

Many of the decisions that need to be managed in group care relate to the theme of change. We saw earlier that there must be change in order for the unit to function at all – people must arrive, stay and depart, and workers must come and go for their shifts. In addition, any group care unit that has an aim of providing 'treatment' as well as care is concerned with promoting and facilitating change in the individual. All of this change has to be 'managed' throughout the system in two senses – it has to be planned for, and it has to be coped with. A curious paradox also arises here, because of the simultaneous need for both continuity and change: for many clients, group care units aim to provide constancy in a turbulent world, but at the same time they aim to facilitate change in individuals, families and systems. How can these two aims coexist, especially for those clients for whom the only constancy in their earlier lives may have been chaotic change and unpredictability? Experience shows that it *is* possible for these aims to coexist, but this coexistence will be helped by people being aware of the paradox.

Another type of change that has to be managed is innovation. This may be on a small scale in the sense of introducing a new way of using part of the building or a new or changed element in the routine of the day – although even these changes can have considerable impact throughout the system. Innovation also happens on a larger scale: for example, there may need to be a change in the focus of the Primary Task because of pressures from within the unit or from shifts in social policy; or changes in the composition of the team because of people's developing careers and training needs. Any of these changes may lead to a need for the practice in the unit to change, which will mean individuals and groups managing the transition from one way of living and working to another. A helpful example of planning an innovation – in this case the introduction of a new system of supervision – is offered by Atherton (1986, pp 115-26), and a very useful account of the processes of change and innovation can be found in Smale (1996).

Change requires adjustment: people have to get used to what is new or developing, and they have to face losing what they have left behind. In every major change there will be some loss, and we often fear change because the idea of loss is too threatening; thus we may try to sustain even the most untenable of situations (Marris, 1986). There is therefore a significant 'human factor' to be taken into account when trying to manage change or help others manage it: some people resist or deny the reality of change, others easily become enthusiastic about it and omit to make a proper ending in their eagerness to move forward – only to find later that there are regrets or confusions about what has happened. Whatever the scale or nature of the change being planned, therefore, the plans must take into account the details of managing the people who are being asked to change – their fears, doubts and resistances, their hopes and enthusiasms. Furthermore, since systems thinking tells us that change in one part of the system may have unforeseen consequences in other parts, we also have to allow for these other possible changes, for example the knock-on effects on outsiders whose work or lives may be altered by a change in the Primary Task of a group care unit.

The theme of managing change acquires a central importance in the light of the findings reported earlier (Chapter One) about the failure in many units to translate good ideas into practice:

> One of the barriers to convincing staff that good practices are workable and could be implemented in their home is organizational inertia. People often balk at the effort involved in bringing about change. (Booth et al, 1990, p 128)

Clearly, the quality of the service provided to clients may depend directly on the ability of managers at all levels to sell ideas and to demonstrate the workability of new approaches. People therefore need the opportunity to learn about a variety of approaches to managing change as well as about the details of good care practice. For further discussion of managing change in care settings, see Rogers and Reynolds (2003b).

Systems for management

Having looked at the different levels of management and three central concerns of management, we shall now turn briefly to some of the 'systems' that managers will need to establish in order to accomplish these functions. In particular, we will look at systems for supervision, consultation and staff meetings, treating each of these separately, even though in practice there may be considerable overlap between them.

Supervision

The main function of management with regard to supervision is to develop and sustain a culture of supervision and training that will permeate the system. Permeation is important because the complexity and intensity of the work means that every aspect of the team's work must be reached by supervision – for the sake of the thorough achievement of the Primary Task, but also for the sake of all the individuals involved. People in group care are vulnerable, workers because their actions may be misinterpreted and because in some settings they may even be assaulted, and clients because they themselves may be abused or neglected. Only if the workers have consistent and regular access to support, and only if they are regularly and personally accountable for their work, will both groups be properly protected from these risks (Brown and Seden, 2003).

In order for supervision to permeate practice, the model of supervision used must be appropriate both to the mode of practice and to the needs of the workers – and in most group care units this is likely to mean something more flexible and sophisticated than the traditional 'one-to-one' session borrowed from field social work. For example, since most group care teams are interdependent and involved in a complex network of relationships with clients, most work with clients will need to be discussed in group or team supervision rather than individual sessions, so that all of those involved can explore and challenge and contribute to each other's perceptions and views (Challender, 1999). On the other hand, there will still be a place for individual supervision within the overall pattern – for example, newcomers or those undertaking new responsibilities may need an extra opportunity for individual sessions, and all workers may need some individual discussion, perhaps of one-to-one sessions with clients (see, for example, Rafferty, 1998), or of more personal feelings about certain aspects of their work. The pattern of needs for different types of supervision among individuals and teams thus varies according to many different factors, and it is clearly not possible to offer a set of rules here for how the pattern should operate in any given unit, but there are several helpful texts in this field that are recommended to those drawing up such a pattern (for example, Atherton, 1986).

Beyond the formal arrangements of supervision there are other elements in the pattern. Since group care involves so much 'Opportunity-led Work', some of the support that the workers need will be required at short notice, and the supervision system must therefore allow for and even encourage team members to seek help and guidance from each other as and when it is needed. This may involve anything from being in the background and available for consultation while an incident is developing, to actively intervening in a situation that is getting out of hand (Collie, 2002).

The pattern of supervision needs to be comprehensive, covering all groups of staff in the unit, and allowing for a wide range of needs to be addressed. In particular, where issues of power and prejudice have a direct effect upon groups of staff within the team, there may be a need for 'targeted' supervision or other meetings for these groups. For example, in some settings Black Workers' Groups have been formed to provide mutual support, while in others the women in the team meet regularly as a group to discuss common issues in their work – although some have suggested that there are risks involved here in establishing what could become a 'split-off' sub-system within the team (Furnivall, 1991). Waking night staff in residential units are sometimes excluded from supervision arrangements, thus reinforcing their potential isolation from the rest of the team and risking their possible drifting away from an awareness of and commitment to the Primary Task of the unit. Moreover, apart from the 'professional team', other members of the 'full team' should be included in the pattern of supervision. This will include, for example, providing appropriate support for domestic and secretarial staff, both in terms of their given tasks and in terms of the roles that they may find themselves involved in.

In all but the smallest units, the range of supervision needs among the various groups is likely to mean that the planned individual and group supervision sessions will need to be delegated within the senior staff team, while the role of the manager is likely to be one of coordinating the network of supervision and consultation rather than of always being the supervisor. As with administrative tasks, there is much to be gained all round from delegating the work of supervision throughout the senior staff team, with the manager mainly supervising the other supervisors. Designing, introducing and sustaining a comprehensive system for supervision is thus one of the key responsibilities of the manager and the management team, within an overall context of managing professional development (Peel, 2003).

Consultation

Supervision is, by definition, 'in-house', and can be designed to address most of the issues that arise within the unit and across its boundaries. However, there are some issues that can only be adequately addressed through the use of an external consultant – either a consultant to an individual or, more likely, a consultant to the staff team. The function of the consultant will often be to join with the staff team for a series of regular support meetings (see item 4 in Box 5.1), aiming to influence the work of the whole team by improving communication and understanding between team members. The consultant may be a psychotherapist or psychiatrist, but may equally be a groupworker or experienced group care worker – in the light of all that has been said here about the distinctive nature of group care work, it will be important that the person has a good understanding of the particular pressures and complexities of the group care context (see, for example, Cardona, 1994).

Consultation may help in any aspect of the work of the team that is becoming 'stuck' – very often teams become too inward-looking and lose the capacity to stand back and analyse their situation, and the managers themselves are just as prone to this phenomenon as anyone else. A skilled and knowledgeable consultant can help to 'free up the system' so that the team can refocus on its work and come up with fresh solutions to old problems. It is not necessarily the role of the consultant to propose solutions – that can be quite counterproductive, since it tends to suggest that the team itself is incapable of solving its own problems. The role of the consultant is to facilitate the team in resolving its own issues – in other words, the consultant should never fully join the system, but be engaged as a change agent to help the system work out its own changes (see Furnivall, 1991). Nor is it being argued here that all consultation is by definition a 'good thing': unless is it carefully negotiated in advance, and unless the task of the consultants is clear and agreed between all parties, little may change (see Coulshed, 2006).

It is regrettable that, despite convincing evidence of its value from the work of Obholzer and Roberts (1994a) and others, staff consultation is still a great rarity in group care, being common only among certain specialist units. For the average group care unit, the notion of bringing in a consultant to the staff team is frequently seen as an indulgent and unnecessary luxury – and a consultant may only be called in when something has already gone wrong. By contrast the proper use of consultancy is often to help the unit and the team to stay on task and actively to anticipate and prevent things going wrong.

Staff meetings

The third of our 'systems for management' is the design and implementation of a pattern of staff meetings. We saw earlier in this chapter that there is a wide range of types of meeting, some of them involving the whole professional team, some also involving the clients, some involving outsiders. The task of the management team will be to consider in consultation with all parties what sort of pattern of meetings will be appropriate to the task of the unit, taking into account factors such as the following:

- How much time can be made available for meetings of the full staff team, and of sub-groups?
- Which types of meeting are likely to be most useful, bearing in mind the task and objectives of the unit?
- At what frequency should each type of meeting be held?
- Which meetings will require the presence of an 'outsider', such as a consultant, line manager or trainer?
- Will the overall pattern of meetings have coherence and predictability as well as the flexibility to allow for change and emergency?

These questions relate to designing the pattern of meetings: subsequent stages of the manager's work will include 'selling', negotiating and implementing the pattern, decisions about the appropriate leader and leadership style for each meeting, the structuring, recording and reviewing of each type of meeting, and so on. A useful guide to the role of meetings and the planned implementation of a system of meetings can be found in Harris and Kelly (1991).

Those who have worked extensively in group care will know that some places develop a 'culture' of meetings, so that all decisions, conflicts, proposals, and so on are automatically and openly brought for discussion at staff meetings, whereas other units never quite manage to operate in this way. In these latter units, people sometimes protest that 'we are too busy to have meetings', 'we're too large a team to have meetings', or 'we're only a small team, so we don't need to have meetings', and so on. None of these reasons is an adequate excuse for not having meetings, however, and I would state bluntly that, unless it has a reliable programme of regular planned team meetings, a professional group care team cannot function properly, and cannot achieve its Primary Task.

In addition, given the acknowledged powerlessness of the client in the group care system, we must not forget the role of the client in the system of meetings. As we saw earlier, there is enormous potential for empowering the client through the use of joint meetings of staff and clients, whether in community meetings, residents' forums or handover meetings, and perhaps the question that the team needs to ask itself is: 'Which meetings *must* the clients be excluded from and why?'. I am not arguing here, as some might fear, for an inappropriate blurring of boundaries, but for the implementing of a system for managing the work of the unit that fully acknowledges that the clients themselves have an important contribution to make to that work.

Conclusion

This chapter has moved from an account of the skills of team membership to an analysis of some aspects of the system for management in group care, with a final note on the role of the client in this system. There are many aspects of the system of group care and of managing the system that we have not been able to cover here, especially leadership, and the ways in which leadership at various levels can influence the work of the team, the interactions between staff and client groups, and thereby the overall success of the Primary Task of the establishment. There is also the very important area of the external line management of residential services (Whipp et al, 2005), which is beyond our scope here.

SIX

Full circle: making group care work

Introduction

This book has ranged over extensive territory, and in these final pages we shall briefly look back across that territory to review and evaluate the material covered, then look at some further applications of this material and some implications for training, before concluding with a re-examination of the principles of professional group care and the associated requirements on workers and managers.

Review of the four perspectives

The aim of the book has been to construct a theoretical and practical framework within which group care workers can analyse their work. The method used has been first to present an outline of the context of the work, and then to show how this context influences the tasks and responsibilities of the workers, using several different approaches or perspectives. The four perspectives that have been covered are Opportunity-led Work, The Client's Stay, The Worker's Shift, and The Team and its Task, and I have argued that these are not alternatives but complementary views: in order to have a full understanding of their task, a worker or team must hold all four perspectives in view together.

The value of the *Opportunity-led Work* framework is that it encourages workers to identify and use the wide range of possibilities for responsive and supportive work that can be offered in the context of everyday living in group care. It has only been possible here to give a brief introduction to the approach, whereas in daily practice many workers do some of their most valuable work in this mode; it is the responsiveness and attention to detail on the part of the staff that can make all the difference to the quality of the client's experience in group care.

The value of *The Client's Stay* perspective is that it encourages the worker to focus on the experience of the individual client – her needs, rights and wishes – which is entirely in keeping with the principle of 'placing the client at the heart of the system'. When taken together with the 'systems approach' outlined in Chapter Five, this perspective also encourages the worker to be aware of the client's family and community network – and much of the evidence on the client's experience of group care suggests that such an awareness is essential for successful care. As we saw in Chapter Three, this perspective emphasises the importance of planning at all levels, of partnership with clients and their networks, and of the client's right to participation in decision making. While some aspects of this perspective have been addressed widely in the literature, there remains much work to be done on appropriate models for planned programmes of care for individuals and groups, especially programmes that properly address the issues of power, prejudice and dependency.

The value of *The Worker's Shift* perspective, on the other hand, is that it draws on the daily experience and tasks of the worker to outline a different model of the 'process' of group care. This perspective focuses on the professional responsibilities of the worker from preparing for the start of a shift to unwinding at the end of the day, with a particular emphasis on the qualities required for professional practice such as being reliable and discrete, and acting ethically, and on the need for each individual to monitor her performance and pace herself through the day's work. This perspective also highlights the risk of 'mismatching' between the worker's experience and the client's experience – especially in those shift systems where the two sets of experiences and needs frequently collide and compete.

The fourth perspective, *The Team and its Task*, takes a broader view than the other three, looking at the skills and structures required for successful teamwork, and using the systems approach in a number of different ways to explore and explain the connections between the various elements operating in any group care setting. The value of this approach is that it encourages individuals and teams to think broadly, and to be prepared to reframe their thinking in order to understand the complexity of their work. It is therefore an especially valuable perspective for those with management responsibilities, in offering a range of frameworks for 'holding together' the work of the whole unit, although I have also argued that all group care workers need to be able to 'manage' in some senses. In particular, the concept of the Primary Task is central to the planning of purposeful group care, in that it highlights the need to aim for a good 'fit' or correspondence between the Task of the unit and the working methods and management systems used (see Obholzer and Roberts, 1994a).

These four perspectives, then, each contribute to an overall understanding of the work. None of the perspectives would be sufficient on its own as a model for practice, but taken together they cover most of the important issues. There will be some group care settings where the work involved does not easily fit into every aspect of this framework: for example, drop-in or self-help day centres or other day services, or those few residential settings, mostly in the voluntary sector, that have resisted the move to shiftwork and which continue to operate in the fullest sense as a community in their own right, although even in these places there will still be many aspects of the overall framework that do apply.

It is also worth noting that this has not been an exhaustive listing – there are other variations on these perspectives that might be equally fruitful in adding to one's understanding of the work. For example, while we have considered The Client's Stay, we have not given much attention to the worker's own 'career' in a group care unit, from appointment and starting work to eventually leaving the place. Do workers experience their 'stay' in a unit in any similar ways to the ways in which clients do? Ruth Emond's account (2005) of her time working and researching as a participant observer in two children's homes suggests that this might be the case. Similarly, while we have looked at The Worker's Shift, we have not paid much attention here to the parallel process of 'The Client's Day' – from waking to bedtime (or from arrival to departure on any given day in day care). This is a theme that has been covered well in some of the client-specific literature (for example, Carter, 1988), and it has been touched upon in some of the material here about routines and the use of time, but there is much more that might usefully be said.

On being a group care worker

There has been a theme running through this book of the need for clarity about the roles and professional responsibilities of the group care worker, but what perhaps still requires further emphasis is the overlap of the personal and the professional in this work. This is not the sort of work where you can leave your feelings behind when you start work – indeed, being a group care worker requires you to be fluent in the language of emotions, since, as we have seen, there are powerful feelings raised by many aspects of the work. In the sections on the experience of the client we have considered some of the strong feelings associated with entering and leaving group care, and especially feelings raised by the issues of power, prejudice and dependency. Such events and issues also have their effect upon the workers – for example, we will all have feelings about dependent and independent people, about people over whom we have some power or against whom we may feel prejudice, in addition to those deeper feelings associated with our inner motivations to do this sort of work. Moreover, these are not only individual but also shared feelings, since within and between the various groups in the unit there may be a complex interplay of feelings – love, hate, sadness, joy, rivalry, isolation, and so on. Finally, there will be spoken as well as unspoken feelings, and unconscious as well as conscious feelings, as we saw when considering the role of supervision (see Hardwick and Woodhead, 1999; also Simmonds, 1988).

The worker and the team will need to be able to understand and reflect upon this wide range of feelings, and sometimes to help the unspoken to be said and the unrecognised to be seen, so that the work of the unit will not be inhibited by powerful unresolved feelings among clients, workers or others. The group care worker therefore needs to be a 'reflective practitioner', reflective in the sense of both re-examining and learning from what has happened but also in the sense of thinking carefully as the work proceeds – in the midst of a 'critical incident', for instance. However, in the light of all that has been said about the nature of teamwork in this setting, it is not just the individual but the whole team and in some senses the whole unit which needs to be 'reflective' – to be able to think things through, re-evaluate them and make new connections where appropriate (Worthington, 2003). Reflecting together as a team or as a whole unit makes demands upon each person in terms of their ability and willingness to share thoughts and feelings, to listen to others' hopes, doubts and fears, and to come up with creative responses and reframings (Gould and Baldwin, 2004). It will be the responsibility of management to try to create the sort of atmosphere in which such shared reflection can develop: again, this is not an optional extra but a central element in the discipline of professional group care work.

Furthermore, however much is shared in the team, when incidents and challenges arise in the course of everyday group care work, it is often left to the individual worker to rely on her own self and sometimes on her own intuition to respond appropriately. The purposeful 'use of self' is a feature of most of the helping professions (England, 1986), but as we have seen throughout this book, group care practice makes particularly great and intense demands on the self of the worker, and everyone practising in this setting needs to develop their knowledge and skills in the use of self. It is probably the literature on therapeutic practice and mental health work that has addressed the use of self most fully (for example, Barnes et al, 1998). The somewhat undervalued art of intuition can sometimes feel like the group care worker's only real guide to practice when things get difficult (McMahon and Ward, 1998), although intuition can also be an unreliable guide at times. The more that the team can do to pool, compare and explore their intuitive responses the closer they will come to producing a genuinely reflective and holistic approach to practice.

Training for group care workers

Mention of intuition connects us to the question of training for group care workers. The undervaluing of group care work, which was acknowledged in the Introduction, is nowhere more sharply seen than in the patterns and provision of training (see Expert Group, 1992). Indeed, a real vicious circle operates, whereby group care is still seen as low-status, low-skilled work, for which professional training is often thought to be either unnecessary or irrelevant; workers in these settings are often expected to be 'naturally gifted' or intuitive carers, rather than qualified professionals. The full potential of group care is thus rarely achieved, since there is never likely to be a fully qualified team of workers available to do the work.

There is, in fact, no reason – other than financial – why every group care unit should not have a fully qualified professional team, although there will always be some debate as to what are the appropriate levels of qualification. The scheme of National Vocational Qualifications (NVQs) is intended to support and inform appropriate training at each level of the work, although some have expressed reservations about the application of this rather mechanistic scheme to group care work (for example, Payne and Kelly, 1990; Crimmens, 2000). The entire argument of this book has been that the skills of group care work need to be recognised in all their complexity and subtlety, rather than being reduced to mere technical 'competences'. In contrast to those who argue that group care work principally involves simple 'tending', it can be argued that it is the multifaceted context of group care which means that the professional responsibilities involved in 'tending' will never be simple. Whatever level you work at in professional group care, you are still working in a highly complex system, and in order to be able to offer a good-quality service to the clients, you need to be able to understand that system, work within it and influence it where appropriate.

I have argued elsewhere (Ward, 1991; Ward and Preston-Shoot, 1998) for training in group care to be treated as an equal and integral part of every social worker's training, and in particular I have supported the proposition that every social worker on a qualifying course should have to undertake a full assessed placement in a group care setting, whether or not they ultimately intend to work in group care. I would continue to support this view even though it can be argued that group care is not really part of social work at all (Milligan, 1998). Experience of operating such a system (Ward, 2005) suggests that the gains are considerable: *all* students have the opportunity to gain a fuller understanding of the experience both of the workers and of the clients in these settings, trainers and academics are required to address the positive aspects of group care, and the clients ultimately gain because they are cared for by a better-trained staff team with higher morale and self-respect. The supposed problems in implementing such an approach, especially locating suitable placements and practice teachers, may present a challenge in some areas, but this challenge may be reframed to represent an opportunity for training to contribute directly to the improvement of practice – by targeting experienced group care workers to train as practice teachers. The context for this debate may develop further, however, as the boundaries between social work, social care and other/newer professional identities change and evolve.

The curriculum for training group care workers will have to be elaborated and discussed elsewhere. In one sense this book has offered a framework upon which such a curriculum might be based, although the detail of curriculum design involves far more than a mere intellectual framework. The curriculum for residential work training has been addressed by the Residential Forum (1998) and others, while the curriculum for day care training has been very little discussed, and the curriculum for group care training only rarely (see CCETSW 1983; Expert Group, 1992) since the concept of group care itself is still under-recognised. Moreover, of equal importance as the curriculum will be the way the whole programme is conceived and delivered, and the degree to which the student experience can be felt as relevant and connected to the practice being learned (Ward and McMahon, 1997).

Making group care work

Finally, we return briefly to the questions addressed at the start of the book about the preconditions for successful group care, and about the principles upon which such care should be based. While some might wish here for a set of specific guidelines as to what precise arrangements and practices will make for good-quality group care, such as advice on staffing levels or a training curriculum, my response is that these are available elsewhere, and that what I will offer instead is a summary of the principles upon which such guidance should be based, with an overall recommendation that all of those responsible for organising group care services should engage in their own task of designing and implementing high-quality care bearing principles such as these in mind.

Placing the individual at the heart of the system

The successful implementation of this simple principle has been shown to be infinitely complex and fraught with distractions, such as the barriers identified in Chapter One and the 'cooling effect' described by Booth et al (1990). What is required is an unswerving commitment at every level in the organisation to identifying the needs, rights and wishes of those for whom the service is provided, to negotiating and renegotiating an appropriate response, and to delivering a high-quality service to each individual. At every level in the organisation there will be other factors pulling against this commitment, and for group care to be successful, these factors will consistently have to be re-examined and then repositioned below the priority of the well-being of the individuals in the system. Central to this work will be the implementation of a comprehensive system for listening to the voice of the client and incorporating this voice in the design and operation of the system itself.

Demonstrating an active commitment to anti-oppressive practice

The factors operating against this principle are, first, the in-built power base of the welfare system and those working within it, second, the prejudices that permeate most human organisations and, more broadly, society itself, and the consequent oppression experienced at a personal and institutional level by many of those using group care services, and finally the anxieties that arise at every level about handling others' dependency needs. The operation of effective anti-oppressive practice again requires firm commitment on the part of individuals, teams and agencies, and a determination to constantly monitor and improve practice. The nature of the power relationships is such that, while there is much that individuals and teams can do at the micro-level of direct practice with clients, there is an overriding need for those responsible for external management, inspection and training in respect of group care services to address the issue more fully. The risk is that unless change can be brought about at this level, other changes, whether at the level of direct practice or at the level of glossy governmental policy documents, may remain largely cosmetic.

Underpinning professional caring with a team approach

The implications of the teamwork context of group care have been seen throughout this book. For teamwork to thrive in group care, not only do the systems of supervision, staff meetings and informal communication need to be expertly managed and operated, but people also need to be working in an overall system that facilitates interdependence: for example, working with clarity about their shared task and their individual roles, working in a shift system or rota of responsibilities that helps rather than hinders the achievement of the task. In addition, the 'team' means not only the professional team of the unit, but also the others working in the place and especially the others outside the unit with whom the work must be planned in partnership. In particular, it is essential that both the internal and the external managers of a group care unit understand and facilitate the task facing the team, and that the whole external system of management is designed to enable them to do so (Whipp et al, 2005).

Taking a holistic or 'systems'-based approach

The range of ways in which systems thinking can contribute to an understanding of group care was explored in Chapter Five, although it was acknowledged that this was just a beginning. The pressures *against* using such an approach are surprisingly great: the sheer impact of the demands of daily practice both as a worker and as a manager in group care, and the extensive range of issues faced at every level, mean that people tend to feel compelled to keep responding at the immediate micro-level, rather than being able to stand back sufficiently to notice and explore the connections between different types of demand and between different elements in the various systems. Yet again, what is required is a commitment and determination, in this case, to think broadly, to make connections, to use systems principles to design and implement the service and to bring about change where necessary. Linked to this element is the need for an emphasis on a holistic approach, which brings us back full circle to the central focus on the client herself, and to the imperative of seeing her as a real, whole person rather than as a problem requiring a 'care package'.

In conclusion

My aim in writing this book has been to bring together and examine a wide range of ideas about group care, in order to offer those involved in this work a framework for their thinking and thus for their practice. I have assembled material from many different sources, both theoretical and practical, and I have tried to ensure that whatever statements I have made about this work are rooted firmly in the realities of practice and consistent with the actual needs and rights of the people using the service. The constant refrain has been that this is complex and demanding work, requiring understanding, skills and professional teamwork of a high order. I have also been keen to emphasise the positive potential of this work to make a real difference to people's lives, and the need for group care workers to sustain this belief and to be supported in it, even through times of difficulty and crisis. I acknowledged at the start that I would be drawing more heavily on examples and literature from a residential child care perspective than from some others, since that has been my own working and teaching experience, but I hope that the material has been applied with sufficient depth and breadth to reach right across the spectrum of group care in all its many contexts. The framework is now in place, and the implied challenge has been issued: can such a framework help people to understand their work better and to provide better services to those using group care? I wish readers well in their efforts to achieve these aims.

Bibliography

Adams, L., Beadle-Brown, J. and Mansell, J. (2006) 'Individual planning: an exploration of the link between quality of plan and quality of life'. *British Journal of Learning Disabilities*, 34 (2), pp 68-76.

Adams, R., Dominelli, L. and Payne, M. (eds) (2005) *Social Work Futures: Crossing Boundaries, Transforming Practice*. Basingstoke: Palgrave Macmillan.

Ahmed, S., Small, J. and Cheetham, J. (eds) (1986) *Social Work with Black Children and their Families*. London: Batsford.

Ainsworth, F. (1981) 'The training of personnel for group care with children', in F. Ainsworth and L. Fulcher (eds) *Group Care for Children: Concepts and Issues*, London: Tavistock, pp 225-44.

Ainsworth, F. (1997) *Family Centred Group Care: Model Building*. Aldershot: Ashgate.

Ainsworth, F. and Fulcher, L. (eds) (1981) *Group Care for Children: Concepts and Issues*. London: Tavistock.

Allott, M. and Robb, M. (eds) (1998) *Understanding Health and Social Care: An Introductory Reader*. London: Sage/Open University.

Anglin, J. P. (2004) *Pain, Normality and the Struggle for Congruence: Reinterpreting Residential Care for Children and Youth*. New York & London: Haworth.

Astor, R. and Jeffereys, K. (ed) (2000) *Positive Initiatives for People with Learning Difficulties*. Basingstoke: Macmillan.

Atherton, J. S. (1986) *Professional Supervision in Group Care*. London: Tavistock.

Atherton, J. S. (1989) *Interpreting Residential Life: Values to Practice*. London: Tavistock.

Bailey-Smith, Y. (2001) 'A systemic approach to working with black families', in L. McMahon and A. Ward (eds) *Helping Families in Family Centres: Working at Therapeutic Practice*, London: Jessica Kingsley, pp 117-35.

Baldwin, N. (1990) *The Power to Care in Children's Homes: Experiences of Residential Workers*. Aldershot: Gower.

Ball, C. (1984) 'Developing an understanding of the educational and cultural needs of an Asian child', in I. Mallinson and G. Thomas (eds) *Examples of Developing Practice Skills in Residential and Day Care: Learning from Experience*, Surbiton: Social Care Association, pp 21-5.

Barn, R. (1993) *Black Children in the Public Care System*. London: BAAF/ Batsford.

Barn, R., Sinclair, R. and Ferdinand, D. (1997) *Acting on Principle: An Examination of Race and Ethnicity in Social Services Provision for Children and Families.* London: BAAF.

Barn, R., Sinclair, R. and Ferdinand, D. (1998) *Acting on Principle: An Examination of Race and Ethnicity in Social Services Provision for Children and Young People.* London: BAAF.

Barnes, C. (1990) *'Cabbage Syndrome': The Social Construction of Dependence.* Basingstoke: The Falmer Press.

Barnes, C. and Mercer, G. (2006) *Independent Futures: Creating User-led Disability Services in a Disabling Society.* Bristol: The Policy Press.

Barnes, E., Griffiths, P., Ord, J. and Wells, D. (1998) *Face to Face with Distress: The Professional Use of Self in Psychosocial Care.* Oxford: Butterworth-Heinemann.

Barter, C., Renold, E., Berridge, D. and Cawson, P. (2004) *Peer Violence in Children's Residential Care.* Basingstoke: Palgrave Macmillan.

Beedell, C. (1970) *Residential Life with Children.* London, Routledge & Kegan Paul.

Berridge, D. (2002) 'Residential care', in D. McNeish, T. Newman and H. Roberts (eds) *What Works for Children? Effective Services for Children and Families,* Buckingham: Open University Press, pp 83-103.

Berry, J. (1972) 'The experience of reception into care', *British Journal of Social Work,* 2 (4), pp 423-34.

Berry, J. (1975) *Daily Experience in Residential Life.* London: Routledge and Kegan Paul.

Bettelheim, B. (1950) *Love is not Enough,* New York: Free Press.

Bettelheim, B. (1974) *A Home for the Heart.* London: Thames and Hudson.

Bok, S. (1986) *Secrets: Concealment and Revelation.* Oxford: Oxford University Press.

Bolton, G. (2001) *Reflective Practice: Writing and Professional Development.* London: Paul Chapman.

Bond, M. (1989) 'Management in the homes'. *Community Care,* 9 March, pp 20-21.

Booth, T., Bilson, A. and Fowell, A. (1990) 'Staff attitudes and caring practices in homes for the elderly'. *British Journal of Social Work,* 20 (2), pp 117-32.

Brandon, D. (1981) *Voices of Experience.* London: Mind.

Brandon, D. (1991) *Innovation without Change.* London: Macmillan.

Brandon, D. and Brandon, T. (2001) *Advocacy in Social Work.* Birmingham: Venture Press.

Brearley, C.P. (1990) *Working in Residential Homes for Elderly People.* London: Tavistock/Routledge.

Brearley, P., Black, J., Gutridge, P., Roberts, G. and Tarran, E. (1982) *Leaving Residential Care.* London: Tavistock.

Brearley, P. (1982) 'The experience and process of leaving', in P. Brearley, J. Black, P. Gutridge, G. Roberts and E. Tarran (ed) (1982) *Leaving Residential Care,* London, Tavistock, pp 11-34.

Brearley, P., Hall, F., Gutridge, P., Jones, G. and Roberts, G. (1980) *Admission to Residential Care.* London: Tavistock.

Brechin, A. and Swain, J. (1989) 'Creating a 'working alliance' with people with learning difficulties', in A. Brechin and J. Walmsley (eds) *Making Connections: Reflecting on the Lives and Experiences of People with Learning Difficulties.* London: Hodder & Stoughton, pp 42-53.

Brechin, A. and Walmsley, J. (eds) (1989) *Making Connections: Reflecting on the Lives and Experiences of People with Learning Difficulties.* London: Hodder & Stoughton.

Brown, A. (1990) 'Groupwork with a difference: the group 'mosaic' in residential and day centre settings'. *Groupwork,* 3 (3), pp 269-85.

Brown, A. and Clough, R. (eds) (1989) *Groups and Groupings: Life and Work in Day and Residential Settings.* London: Tavistock.

Brown, E., Bullock, R., Hobson, C. and Little, M. (1998) *Making Residential Care Work: Structure and Culture in Children's Homes.* Aldershot: Ashgate.

Brown, H. and Seden, J. (2003) 'Managing to protect', in J. Seden and J. Reynolds (eds) *Managing Care in Practice.* London: Routledge/Open University, pp 219-47.

Bruggen, P. and O'Brian, C. (1987) *Helping Families: Systems, Residential and Agency Responsibility.* London: Faber and Faber.

Bruggen, P., Byng-Hall, J. and Pitt-Aitkens, T. (1973) 'The reason for admission as a focus of work for an adolescent unit'. *British Journal of Psychology,* 122, pp 319-29.

Bullock, R., Little, M. and Millham, S. (1993) *Residential Care for Children: A Review of the Research.* London: HMSO.

Burton, J. (1982) 'Don't panic, plan it'. *Social Work Today,* 3 August, p 10.

Burton, J. (1989) 'Institutional change and group action: the significance and influence of groups in developing new residential services for older people', in A. Brown and R. Clough (eds) *Groups and Groupings: Life and Work in Day and Residential Settings.* London: Tavistock, pp 59-79.

Burton, J. (1993) *The Handbook of Residential Care.* London: Routledge.

Burton, J. (1998) *Managing Residential Care.* London: Routledge.

Butler, B. and Elliott, D. (1985) *Teaching and Learning for Practice.* Aldershot: Gower.

Butrym, Z.T. (1976) *The Nature of Social Work.* London: Macmillan.

Campling, P., Davies, S. and Farquharson, G. (eds) (2004) *From Toxic Institutions to Therapeutic Environments: Residential Settings In Mental Health Services.* London: Gaskell.

Cardona, F. (1994) 'Facing an uncertain future', in A. Obholzer and V. Z. Roberts (eds) *The Unconscious at Work: Individual and Organizational Stress in the Human Services.* London: Routledge, pp 139-46.

Carter, J. (1981) *Day Services for Adults: Somewhere to go.* London: George Allen and Unwin.

Carter, J. (1988) *Creative Day Care.* Oxford: Blackwell.

Carter, J. (2003) 'The meaning of good experience', in A. Ward, K. Kasinski, J. Pooley and A. Worthington (eds) *Therapeutic Communities for Children and Young People.* London: Jessica Kingsley, pp 133-47.

CCETSW (Central Council for Education and Training in Social Work) (1983) *A Practice Curriculum for Group Care.* CCETSW Paper 14.2. London: CCETSW.

Challender, D. (1999) 'Support and supervision', in A. Hardwick and J. Woodhead (eds) *Loving, Hating and Survival: A Handbook for all who Work with Troubled Children and Young People.* Aldershot: Ashgate, pp 79-93.

Clark, C. (ed) (2001) *Adult Day Services and Social Inclusion: Better Days: Research Highlights in Social Work 39.* London: Jessica Kingsley.

Clifford, D. (1998) 'Psychosexual nursing seminars', in E. Barnes, P. Griffiths, J. Ord and D. Wells (eds) *Face to Face with Distress: The Professional Use of Self in Psychosocial Care.* Oxford: Butterworth-Heinemann, pp 152-62.

Clough, R. (1982) *Residential Work.* London: Macmillan.

Clough, R. (1987) *Living Away from Home: A Report on Research into Residential Child Care for the ESRC.* Bristol: University of Bristol.

Clough, R. (ed) (1994) *Insights into Inspection: The Regulation of Social Care.* London: Whiting and Birch.

Clough, R. (2000) *The Practice of Residential Work.* Basingstoke: Macmillan.

Clough, R., Bullock, R. and Ward, A. (2006) *What Works in Residential Child Care: A Review of Research Evidence and Practical Considerations.* London: National Children's Bureau.

Collett, S. and Hook, R. (1992) 'Evaluating group care: should we leave it to the experts?'. *Practice*, 5 (2), pp 111-20.

Collie, A. (2002) 'Opportunistic staff development strategies in therapeutic communities'. *Therapeutic Communities*, 23 (2), pp 125-32.

Collins, T. and Bruce, T. (1984) *Staff Support and Staff Training*. London: Tavistock.

Cook, R. (1988) 'A non-residential therapeutic community used as an alternative to custody'. *International Journal of Therapeutic Communities*, 9 (1), pp 55-64.

Corby, B., Doig, A. and Roberts, V. (2001) *Public Inquiries into Abuse of Children in Residential Child Care*. London: Jessica Kingsley.

Corden, J. and Preston-Shoot, M. (1987) *Contracts in Social Work*. Aldershot: Gower.

Coulshed, V. (2006) *Management in Social Work* (3rd edition). Basingstoke: Palgrave Macmillan.

Crimmens, D. (2000) '"Things can only get better!': an evaluation of developments in the training and qualification of residential child care staff', in D. Crimmens and J. Pitts (eds) *Positive Residential Practice: Learning the Lessons of the 90s*. Lyme Regis: Russell House Publishing, pp 78-94.

Crimmens, D. and Milligan, I. (eds) (2005) *Facing Forward: Residential Child Care in the 21st Century*. Lyme Regis: Russell House Publishing.

Crimmens, D. and Pitts, J. (eds) (2000) *Positive Residential Practice: Learning the Lessons of the 90s*. Lyme Regis: Russell House Publishing.

Dartington, T., Miller, E. J. and Gwynne, E. V. (1981) *A Life Together: The Distribution of Attitudes around the Disabled*. London: Tavistock.

Davenport, S. (2004) 'A gender-sensitive therapeutic environment for women', in P. Campling, S. Davies and G. Farquharson *From Toxic Institutions to Therapeutic Environments: Residential Settings in Mental Health Services*. London: Gaskell, pp 88-98.

Davis, A. (1989) 'Women and local authority residential care', in C. Hallett (ed) *Women and Social Services Departments*. Hemel Hempstead: Harvester Wheatsheaf, pp 103-31.

DH (Department of Health) (1982) *Residential Care for Children in London*. A Report by DHSS Social Work Service, London Region.

DH (1990) *Caring for Quality: Guidance on Standards for Residential Homes for Elderly People*. London: HMSO.

DH (2002) *Requirements for Social Work Training*. London: DH.

DH (2005) *Independence, Well-being and Choice: Our Vision for the Future of Social Care for Adults in England*. Norwich: The Stationery Office.

Dockar-Drysdale, B. F. (1968) 'The relation of assigned function to created role in a theraputic school', in B.F. Dockar-Drysdale, *Therapy in Child Care*. London: Longman, pp 52-66.

Dominelli, L. (2002) *Anti-oppressive Social Work Theory and Practice*. Basingstoke: Palgrave Macmillan.

Douglas, R. and Payne, C. (1982) *Developing Supervision of Teams in Field and Residential Social Work*. London: National Institute for Social Work.

Douglas, R. and Payne, C. (1983) 'Down the wrong street'. *Social Work Today*, 6 December, p 21.

Douglas, R. and Payne, C. (1985) *Developing Residential Practice: A Sourcebook of References and Resources for Staff Development*. London: National Institute for Social Work.

Douglas, R., Ettridge, D., Fearnhead, D. and Payne, C. (1988) *Helping People Work Together: A Guide to Participative Working Practices*. London: National Institute for Social Work.

Douglas, T. (1986) *Group Living: The Application of Group Dynamics to Residential Settings*. London: Tavistock/Routledge.

Duffy, B. and McCarthy, B. (1998) 'From group meeting to therapeutic group', in M. Allott and M. Robb (eds) *Understanding Health and Social Care: An Introductory Reader*. London: Sage/Open University, pp 145-54.

Emond, R. (2002) 'Understanding the resident group'. *Scottish Journal of Residential Child Care*, 1, pp 30-40.

Emond, R. (2005) 'An outsider's view of the inside', in D. Crimmens and I. Milligan (eds) *Facing Forward: Residential Child Care in the 21st Century*. Lyme Regis: Russell House Publishing.

England, H. (1986) *Social Work as Art: Making Sense for Good Practice*. London: Allen & Unwin.

Expert Group (1992) *Setting Quality Standards for Residential Child Care: A Practical Way Forward* (Final Report of the Expert Group). London: CCETSW.

Fariss, N. (2000) 'Partners in parenting: safe reunification', in M. Chakrabarti and M. Hill (eds) *Residential Child Care: International Perspectives on Links with Families and Peers*. London: Jessica Kingsley, pp 81-92.

Firth, W. (2004) 'Acute psychiatric wards: an overview', in P. Campling, S. Davies and G. Farquharson (eds) *From Toxic Institutions to Therapeutic Environments: Residential Settings in Mental Health Services*. London: Gaskell.

Fisher, M., Marsh, P., Phillips, D. and Sainsbury, E. (1986) *In and Out of Care: The Experience of Children, Parents and Social Workers*. London: Batsford.

Flower, J. (1983) 'Creating a forum'. *Community Care*, 21 April, pp 20-1.

Freudenberger, H. J. (1975) 'The staff burn-out syndrome in alternative institutions'. *Psychotherapy Theory, Research & Practice*, 12, pp 73-82.

Frost, N. and Harris, J. (1996) *Managing Residential Child Care*. Brighton: Pavilion.

Frost, N. and Wallis, L. (2000) 'Empowering children and young people? The possibilities and limitations of the complaints system', in D. Crimmens and J. Pitts (eds) *Positive Residential Practice: Learning the Lessons of the 90s*. Lyme Regis: Russell House Publishing, pp 110-27.

Frost, N., Mills, S. and Stein, M. (1999) *Understanding Residential Child Care*. Aldershot: Arena.

Fulcher, L. (1981) 'Team functioning in group care', in F. Ainsworth and L. Fulcher (eds) *Group Care for Children: Concepts and Issues*. London: Tavistock, pp 170-97.

Fulcher, L. (1998) 'Acknowledging culture in child and youth care practice'. *Social Work Education*, 17 (3), pp 321-38.

Fulcher, L.C and Ainsworth, F. (eds) (1985) *Group Care Practice with Children*. London: Tavistock.

Fulcher, L. and Ainsworth, F. (eds) (2006) *Group Care Practice with Children and Adolescents Revisited*. New York: Haworth.

Furnivall, J. (1991) 'Peper Harow – consultancy – a consumer's view', in W. R. Silveira (ed) *Consultation in Residential Care*. Aberdeen: Aberdeen University Press, pp 123-46.

Gallop, L. (2003) 'Managing budgets and giving Best Value', in J. Seden and J. Reynolds (eds) *Managing Care in Practice*. London and New York: Routledge and Open University, pp 165-91.

Gardner, J. and Glanville, L. (2005) 'New forms of institutionalization in the community', in K. Johnson and R. Traustadottir (eds) *Deinstitutionalization and People with Intellectual Disabilities: In and Out of Institutions*. London: Jessica Kingsley, pp 219-30.

Goffman, E. (1968) *Stigma: Notes on the Management of Spoiled Identity*. Harmondsworth: Penguin.

Goodwin, A. M. and Gore, V. (2000) 'Managing the stresses of nursing people with severe and enduring mental illness: a psychodynamic observation study of a long-stay psychiatric ward'. *British Journal of Medical Psychology*, 73, pp 311-25.

Gould, N. and Baldwin, M. (eds) (2004) *Social Work, Critical Reflection and the Learning Organization*. Aldershot: Ashgate.

GSCC (General Social Care Council) (2002) *Code of Practice for Social Care Workers*. London: GSCC.

Gunaratnam, Y. (2001) 'Working across cultures of difference: ethnicity and the challenge for palliative day care', in J. Hearn and K. Myers (eds) *Palliative Day Care in Practice*, pp 23-42. Oxford: Oxford University Press.

Hardwick, A. and Woodhead, J. (eds) (1999) *Loving, Hating and Survival: A Handbook for All who Work with Troubled Children and Young People.* Aldershot: Ashgate.

Harris, J. and Kelly, D. (1991) *Management Skills in Social Care: A Handbook for Social Care Managers.* Aldershot: Gower.

Hawkins, P. and Shohet, R. (2000) *Supervision in the Helping Professions* (2nd edition). Buckingham: Open University Press.

Hearn, J. and Myers, K. (eds) (2001) *Palliative Day Care in Practice.* Oxford: Oxford University Press.

Higgins, B. (1997) 'Does anybody feel they need support tonight?'. *Therapeutic Communities*, 18 (1), pp 55-61.

Hill, M. (2000) 'Inclusiveness in residential child care', in M. Chakrabarti and M. Hill (eds) *Residential Child Care: International Perspectives on Links with Families and Peers.* London: Jessica Kingsley.

Hinshelwood, R. (1987) *What Happens in Groups.* London: Free Association Press.

Hinshelwood, R. D. (2001) *Thinking about Institutions: Milieux and Madness.* London: Jessica Kingsley.

Hollinghurst, V. (1998) 'A 'tangled web' of emotions', in M. Allott and M. Robb (eds) *Understanding Health and Social Care: An Introductory Reader.* London: Sage/Open University, pp 36-9.

Holloway, J. (1999) 'The other world', in P. Barker, P. Campbell and B. Davidson (eds) *From the Ashes of Experience: Reflections on Madness, Survival and Growth*, pp 37-53. London: Whurr.

Holman, R. (1988) *Putting Families First: Prevention and Child Care.* London: Macmillan Education.

Horobin, G. (1987) *Why Day Care?* (Research Highlights in Social Work 14). London: Jessica Kingsley.

Hosking, S. and Haggard, L. (1999) *Healing the Hospital Environment: Design, Management and Maintenance of Healthcare Premises.* London: E & FN Spon.

Hunter, S. and Watt, G. (2001) 'Trends and aspirations in day services for older people', in C. Clark (ed) *Adult Day Services and Social Inclusion: Better Days. Research Highlights in Social Work 39.* London: Jessica Kingsley Publishers, pp 133-57.

Jack, R. (ed) (1998) *Residential versus Community Care: The Role of Institutions in Welfare Provision.* Basingstoke: Macmillan.

Jenkins, J., Felce, D., Toogood, S., Mansell, J. and De Kock, U. (1988) *Individual Programme Planning: A Mechanism for Developing Plans to Meet the Specific Needs of Individuals with Mental Handicaps.* London: BIMH Publications.

Johnson, K. and Traustadottir, R. (eds) (2005) *Deinstitutionalization and People with Intellectual Disabilities: In and Out of Institutions.* London: Jessica Kingsley.

Jones, A. and Waul, D. (2005) 'Residential care for black children', in D. Crimmens and I. Milligan (eds) *Facing Forward: Residential Child Care in the 21st Century.* Lyme Regis: Russell House Publishing.

Jones, H. (1979) *The Residential Community: A Setting for Social Work.* London: Routledge & Kegan Paul.

Jones, K. and Fowles, A. J. (1980) *Ideas on Institutions: Analysing the Literature on Long-term Care and Custody.* London: Routledge & Kegan Paul.

Kahan, B. (1979) *Growing up in Care.* Oxford: Blackwell.

Kahn, W.A. (2005) *Holding Fast: The Struggle to Create Resilient Caregiving Organisations.* Hove and New York: Brunner-Routledge.

Kennedy, R. (1987) 'The work of the day', in R. Kennedy, A. Heymans and L. Tischler (eds) *The Family as In-patient: Families and Adolescents at the Cassell Hospital.* London: Free Association Books, pp 27-48.

Kesey, K. (2003) *One Flew Over the Cuckoo's Nest.* London: Penguin Books.

Laverty, H. and Reet, M. (2001) *Planning Care for Children in Respite Settings.* London: Jessica Kingsley.

Lawler, J. (1998) 'Body care and learning to do for others', in M. Allott and M. Robb (eds) *Understanding Health and Social Care: An Introductory Reader*, pp 236-45. London: Sage/Open University.

London Borough of Islington (1986) *Networks* (video). Available from Concord Films.

Maier, H. (1979) 'The core of care'. *Child Care Quarterly*, 8 (3), pp 161-73.

Maier, H. W. (1981) 'Essential components in care and treatment environments for children', in F. Ainsworth and L. Fulcher (eds) *Group Care for Children: Concepts and Issues.* London: Tavistock, pp 19-70.

Mallinson, I. and Thomas, G. (eds) (1984) *Examples of Developing Practice Skills in Residential and Day Care: Learning from Experience.* Surbiton: Social Care Association.

Manthorpe, J. and Stanley, N. (1999) 'Conclusion: shifting the focus from 'bad apples' to users' rights', in N. Stanley, J. Manthorpe and B. Penhale (eds) *Institutional Abuse: Perspectives across the Life Course*, pp 223-40. London: Routledge.

Marris, P. (1986) *Loss and change.* London: Routledge & Kegan Paul.

Martin, P. (1978) 'I only came for the flower show'. *Social Work Today.* 9 (39), pp 8-10.

Maslach, C. and Leiter, M. P. (1997) *The Truth about Burnout: How organizations Cause Personal Stress and What to Do About It*. San Francisco, CA: Jossey Bass.

Maslach, C. with Zimbardo, P. G. (1982) *Burnout: The Cost of Caring*. Englewood Cliffs, NJ: Prentice-Hall Inc.

Mason, B. (1989) *Handing Over: Developing Consistency across Shifts in Residential and Health Settings*. London: DC Publishing.

Mattingly, M.A. (1981) 'Occupational stress for group care personnel', in F. Ainsworth and L. Fulcher (eds) *Group Care for Children: Concepts and Issues*. London: Tavistock, pp 151-69.

Mattinson, J. (1975) *The Reflection Process in Casework Supervision*. London: Institute of Marital Studies.

Mawson, C. (1994) 'Containing anxiety in work with damaged children', in A. Obholzer and V. Z. Roberts (eds) *The Unconscious at Work: Individual and Organizational Stress in the Human Services*. London: Routledge, pp 67-74.

Mazis, S. and Canter, D. (1979) 'Physical conditions and management practices for mentally retarded children', in D. Canter and S. Canter (eds) *Designing for Theraputic Environments*. Chichester: Wiley & Sons, pp 111-58.

McCaffrey, G. (1998) 'The use of leisure activities in psychosocial nursing', in E. Barnes, P. Griffiths, J. Ord and D. Wells (eds) *Face to Face with Distress: The Professional Use of Self in Psychosocial Care*. Oxford: Butterworth-Heinemann, pp 71-82.

McDerment, L. (1988) 'Stress is a feminist issue'. *Care Weekly*, 28 October.

McIntosh, B. and Whittaker, A. (1998) *Days of Change: A Practical Guide to Developing Better Day Opportunities for People With Learning Difficulties*. London: King's Fund.

McIntosh, B. and Whittaker, A. (2000) *Unlocking the Future: Developing New Lifestyles with People who have Complex Disabilities*. London: King's Fund.

McMahon, L. and Ward, A. (1998) 'Helping and the personal response', in A. McMahon and A. Ward (eds) *Intuition is not Enough*. London: Routledge, Ch 2, pp 28-39.

McMahon, L. and Ward, A. (eds) (2001) *Helping Families in Family Centres: Working at Therapeutic Practice*. London: Jessica Kingsley.

Meinrath, M. and Roberts, J. (2004) 'On being a good enough staff member'. *Therapeutic Communities*, 25 (4), pp 318-24.

Menzies-Lyth, I. (1988) 'Staff support systems: task and anti-task in adolescent institutions', in I. Menzies-Lyth (ed) *Containing Anxiety in Institutions. Selected Essays, Vol 1*. London: Free Association Books.

Menzies-Lyth, I. (1988) *Containing Anxiety in Institutions: Selected essays, Vol. 1*. London: Free Association Books.

Miller, E. V. and Gwynne, G. V. (1972) *Life Apart: A Pilot Study of Residential Institutions for the Physically Handicapped and the Young Chronic Sick*. London: Tavistock.

Millham, S., Bullock, R., Hosie, K. and Haak, M. (1986) *Lost in Care: The Problems of Maintaining Links between Children in Care and their Families*. Aldershot: Gower.

Milligan, I. and Stevens, I (2006) *Residential Child Care: Collaborative Practice*. London, Sage Publications.

Moos, R. H. (1974) *Evaluating Treatment Environments: A Social Ecological Approach*. New York: Wiley.

Morgan, R. (2000) 'Positive residential practice: the contribution of inspection', in D. Crimmens and J. Pitts (eds) *Positive Residential Practice: Learning the Lessons of the 90s*. Lyme Regis: Russell House Publishing, pp 55-77.

Moriarty, J. and Levin, E. (1998) 'Respite care in homes and hospitals', in R. Jack (ed) *Residential versus Community Care: The Role of Institutions in Welfare Provision*, pp 124-39. Basingstoke: Macmillan.

Musgrave, S. (2001) '"Holding" as a way of enabling change in a statutory family centre', in L. McMahon and A. Ward (eds) (2001) *Helping Families in Family Centres: Working at Therapeutic Practice*. London: Jessica Kingsley, pp 148-59.

NISW (National Institute for Social Work) (1982) *Social Workers: Their Role and Tasks* (The Barclay Report). London: NISW.

Norman, A. (1985) *Triple Jeapordy: Growing Old in a Second Homeland*. London: Centre for Policy on Ageing.

Nzira, V. (1989) 'Race: the ingredients for good practice', in T. Philpot (ed) *The Residential Opportunity: The Wagner Report and After*. London: Reed Business Publishing and Community Care.

O'Brian, C., Bruggen, P. and Dunne, C. (1985) 'Extra meetings: a tool for decisions and therapy'. *Journal of Adolescence*, 8 (3), pp 255-61.

Obholzer, A. and Roberts, V. Z. (eds) (1994a) *The Unconscious at Work: Individual and Organizational Stress in the Human Services*. London: Routledge.

Obholzer, A. and Roberts, V. Z. (1994b) 'The troublesome individual and the troubled institution', in A. Obholzer and V. Z. Roberts (eds) *The Unconscious at Work: Individual and Organizational Stress in the Human Services*, pp 129-38. London: Routledge.

O'Hagan, K. (1986) *Crisis Intervention in Social Services*. London: Macmillan.

Okitikpi, T. (2004) 'Anti-discriminatory and anti-oppressive practice: working with ethnic minority children in foster and residential care', in H. G. Eriksson and T. Tjelflaat (eds) *Residential Care: Horizons for the New Century*, pp 130-43. Aldershot: Ashgate.

Oldman, C., Quilgars, D. and Carlisle, J. (1997) *Living in a Home: The Experience of Living and Working in Residential Care in the 1990s*. London: Anchor Trust.

Oswin, M. (1973) *The Empty Hours: A Study of the Weekend Life of Handicapped Children in Institutions*. London: Penguin.

Oswin, M. (1984) *They Keep Going Away*. London: King's Fund.

Page, R. and Clark, G. A. (eds) (1977) *Who Cares? Young People in Care Speak Out*. London: National Children's Bureau.

Parker, J. and Bradley, G. (2003) *Social Work Practice: Assessment, Planning, Intervention and Review*. Exeter: Learning Matters.

Patel, N. (1990) *A 'Race' against Time? Social Services Provision to Black Elders*. London: The Runnymede Trust.

Paulus, A. T., van Raak, A. and Keijzer, F. (2005) 'Informal and formal caregivers' involvement in nursing home care activities: impact of integrated care'. *Journal of Advanced Nursing*, 49 (4), pp 354-66.

Payne, C. and Scott, T. (1985) *Developing Supervision of Teams in Field and Residential Social Work*. Paper No 17. London: National Institute of Social Work.

Payne, C. and Kelly, D. (1990) *Making NVQs Work for Social Care*. London: National Institute for Social Work.

Payne, M. (2005a) 'Social work process', in R. Adams, L. Dominelli and M. Payne (eds) *Social Work Futures: Crossing Boundaries, Transforming Practice*. Basingstoke: Palgrave Macmillan, pp 21-35.

Payne, M. (2005b) 'Systems and ecological perspectives', in *Modern Social Work Theory* (3rd edn). Basingstoke: Palgrave Macmillan, pp 42-60.

Peel, M. (2003) 'Managing professional development', in J. Seden and J. Reynolds (eds) *Managing Care in Practice*. London and New York: Routledge and Open University, pp 303-28.

Phillipson, J. (1989) 'Race and gender: a woman's right to choose', in T. Philpot (ed) *The Residential Opportunity: The Wagner Report and After*. London: Reed Business Publishing and Community Care.

Pincus, A. and Minahan, A. (1973) *Social Work Practice: Model and Method*. Itasca, IL: Peacock.

Postle, K. (2001) 'The social work side is disappearing. I guess it started with us being called care managers'. *Practice*, 13 (1), pp 13-26.

Postle, K. (2002) "Working between the idea and the reality': abiguities and tensions in care managers' work'. *British Journal of Social Work*, 32 (3), pp 335-52.

Preece, D. (2002) 'Consultation with children with autistic spectrum disorders about their experience of short-term residential care'. *British Journal of Learning Disabilities*. 30, pp 97-104.

Preston-Shoot, M. and Agass, D. (1990) *Making Sense of Social Work: Psychodynamics, Systems and Practice*. London: Macmillan.

Rack, P. (1982) *Race, Culture and Mental Disorder*. London: Tavistock.

Rafferty, M. (1998) 'Clinical supervision', in E. Barnes, P. Griffiths, J. Ord and D. Wells (eds) (1998) *Face to Face with Distress: The Professional Use of Self in Psychosocial Care*. Oxford: Butterworth-Heinemann.

Raynes, N.V., Sumpton, R.C. and Flynn, M.C. (1987) *Homes for Mentally Handicapped People*. London: Tavistock.

Redl, F. (1966) *When we Deal with Children*. New York: Free Press.

Redmond, B. (2004) *Reflection in Action: Developing Reflective Practice in Health and Social Services*. Aldershot: Ashgate.

Residential Forum (1998) *A Golden Opportunity?* London: National Institute for Social Work.

Reynolds, J. (2003) 'Becoming a manager: acting or reacting?', in J. Seden and J. Reynolds (eds) *Managing Care in Practice*. London and New York: Routledge and Open University, pp 3-32.

RIBA Client Forum (1999) *Therapeutic Environments for Mental Health*. London: Royal Institute of British Architects.

Rice, A. K. (1963) *The Enterprise and its Environment*. London: Tavistock.

Richardson, C. (2003) 'The contribution of systemic thinking and practice', in A. Ward, K. Kasinski, J. Pooley and A. Worthington (eds) (2003) *Therapeutic Communities for Children and Young People*. London: Jessica Kingsley.

Roberts, A. R. (ed) 2000) *Crisis Intervention Handbook* (2nd edition). New York: Oxford University Press.

Robertson Centre (1969) *Young Children in Brief Separation: 'John'* (film). Available from Concord Films.

Rogers, A. and Reynolds, J. (2003a) 'Leadership and vision', in J. Seden and J. Reynolds (eds) *Managing Care in Practice*. London and New York: Routledge and Open University, pp 57-82.

Rogers, A. and Reynolds, J. (2003b) 'Managing change', in J. Seden and J. Reynolds (eds) *Managing Care in Practice*. London and New York: Routledge and Open University, pp 83-110.

Rollinson, R. (1992) 'Myths we work by: the 1991 David Wills lecture'. *Therapeutic Care and Education*, 1 (1), pp 3-21.

Rose, M. (1990) *Healing Hurt Minds: The Peper Harow Experience*. London: Tavistock/Routledge.

Ruch, G. (2005) 'Relationship-based practice and reflective practice: holistic approaches to contemporary child care social work'. *Child and Family Social Work*, 10, pp 111-23.

Sadler, M. (1984) 'Setting up a residents' committee', in I. Mallinson and G. Thomas (eds) *Examples of Developing Practice Skills in Residential and Day Care: Learning from Experience*. Surbiton: Social Care Association, pp 6-12.

Saleebey, D. (2005) *The Strengths Perspective in Social Work Practice* (4th edition). London and Boston, MA: Allyn & Bacon.

Scottish Executive (2000) *The Same as You? A Review of Services for People with Learning Disabilities*. Edinburgh: Scottish Executive.

Seden, J. and Reynolds, J. (eds) (2003) *Managing Care in Practice*. London and New York: Routledge and Open University.

Seed, P. (1987) 'Salient practice issues', in G. Horobin (ed) *Why Day Care? (Research Highlights in Social Work 14)*. London: Jessica Kingsley.

Shemmings, Y. (1996) *Death, Dying and Residential Care*. Basingstoke: Macmillan.

Shemmings, Y. (1998) 'Death and dying in residential homes for older people', in R. Jack (ed) *Residential versus Community Care: The Role of Institutions in Welfare Provision*, pp 154-65. Basingstoke: Macmillan.

Shohet, R. (1999) 'Whose feelings am I feeling? Using the concept of projective identification', in A. Hardwick and J. Woodhead (eds) (1999) *Loving, Hating and Survival: A Handbook for All who Work with Troubled Children and Young People*. Aldershot: Ashgate, pp 39-53.

Silveira, W. R. (ed) (1991) *Consultation in Residential Care: Children in Residential Establishments*. Aberdeen: Aberdeen University Press.

Simmonds, J. (1988) 'Thinking about feelings in group care', in G. Pearson, J. Treseder and M. Yelloly (eds) *Social Work and the Legacy of Freud: Psychoanalysis and its Uses*. Basingstoke: Macmillan Education.

Sinason, V. and Hollins, S. (2004) 'The ideal home and community for people with learning disabilites', in P. Campling, S. Davies and G. Farquharson (eds) *From Toxic Institutions to Therapeutic Environments: Residential Settings in Mental Health Services*. London: Gaskell.

Sinclair, I. and Gibbs, I. (1998) *Children's Homes: A Study in Diversity*. Chichester: John Wiley & Sons Ltd.

Singh, S. (2005) 'Thinking beyond 'diversity': black minority ethnic children in Scotland', in D. Crimmens and I. Milligan (eds) *Facing Forward: Residential Child Care in the 21st Century*, pp 45-56. Lyme Regis: Russell House Publishing.

Slater, R. and Lipman, A. (1980) 'Towards caring through design', in R.G.Walton and D. Elliott (eds) *Residential Care, A Reader in Current Theory and Practice*, Oxford: Pergamon Press.

Smale, G. (1977) *Prophecy, Behaviour and Change: An Examination of the Self-fulfilling Prophecies in Helping Relationships*. London: Routledge and Kegan Paul.

Smale, G. G. (1996) *Mapping Change and Innovation*. London: National Institute for Social Work.

Smith, M. (2005) 'Rethinking residential child care: a child and youth care approach', in D. Crimmens and I. Milligan (eds) *Facing Forward: Residential Child Care in the 21st Century*. Lyme Regis: Russell House Publishing, pp 115-26.

Smith, W. (2005) *Reflections on Death, Dying and Bereavement: A Manual for Clergy, Counsellors and Speakers*. Amityville, NY: Baywood.

SSSC (Scottish Social Services Council) (2005) *Codes of Practice for Social Services Workers and Employers*. Dundee: SSSC.

Stalker, K. (ed) (1996) *Developments in Short-term Care: Breaks and Opportunities* (Research Highlights in Social Work 25). London: Jessica Kingsley.

Stanley, D. and Reed, J. (1999) *Opening up Care: Achieving Principled Practice in Health and Social Care Institutions*. London: Arnold.

Stanley, N., Manthorpe, J. and Penhale, B. (1999) *Institutional Abuse: Perspectives across the Life Course*. London: Routledge.

Stein, M. (2002) 'Leaving care', in D. McNeish, T. Newman and H. Roberts (eds) *What Works for Children? Effective Services for Children and Families*. Buckingham: Open University Press, pp 59-82.

Stevens, I. (2000) 'Family reconstitution and the implications for group care workers: an American perspective', in M. Chakrabarti and M. Hill (eds) *Residential Child Care: International Perspectives on Links with Families and Peers*. London: Jessica Kingsley, pp 117-24.

Stokoe, P. (2003) 'Group thinking', in A. Ward, K. Kasinski, J. Pooley and A. Worthington (eds) (2003) *Therapeutic Communities for Children and Young People*. London: Jessica Kingsley, pp 82-98.

Taylor, B. J. (2000) *Reflective Practice: A Guide for Nurses and Midwives*. Buckingham: Open University Press.

Tester, S. (1989) *Caring by Day: A Study of Day Care Services for Older People*. London: Centre for Policy on Ageing.

Thomas, J. (2004) 'Using 'critical incident analysis' to promote critical reflection and holistic assessment', in N. Gould and M. Baldwin (eds) *Social Work, Critical Reflection and the Learning Organization*. Aldershot: Ashgate, pp 101-16.

Thompson, N. (2002) *Anti-discriminatory Practice* (3rd edition). Basingstoke: Macmillan.

Tibbitt, J. (1987) 'Day care – a 'good thing'?', in G. Horobin (ed) (1987) *Why Day Care? (Research Highlights in Social Work 14)*. London: Jessica Kingsley, pp 16-24.

Timko, C. and Moos, R. H. (2004) 'Measuring the therapeutic environment', in P. Campling, S. Davies and G. Farquharson (eds) *From Toxic Institutions to Therapeutic Environments: Residential Settings in Mental Health Services*. London: Gaskell, pp 143-56.

Tobin, S. S. and Liebermann, M. A. (1976) *Last Home for the Aged*. San Francisco, CA: Jossey Bass.

Tomlinson, P. (2004) *Therapeutic Approaches in Work with Traumatized Children and Young People: Theory and Practice*. London: Jessica Kingsley.

Trevithick, P. (2003) 'Effective relationship-based practice: a theoretical exploration'. *Journal of Social Work Practice*, 17 (2), pp 163-76.

Van der Ven, K. (1985) 'Activity programming: its developmental and therapeutic role in group care', in L. Fulcher and F. Ainsworth (eds) *Group Care Practice with Children*. London: Tavistock, pp 155-83.

von Sommaruga Howard, T. (2004) 'The physical environment and use of space', in P. Campling, S. Davies and G. Farquharson (eds) *From Toxic Institutions to Therapeutic Environments: Residential Settings in Mental Health Services*. London: Gaskell, pp 69-78.

Wade, B., Sawyer, L. and Bell, J. (1983) *Dependency with Dignity: Different Care Provision for the Elderly*. London: Bedford Square Press/NCVO.

Wagner, G. (1988) *Residential Care: A Positive Choice*. London: HMSO.

Walton, R. G. and Elliott, D. (eds) (1980) *Residential Care: A Reader in Current Theory and Practice*. Oxford: Pergamon.

Ward, A. (1984a) 'All you can do is bring your own self'. *Community Care*, 17 May.

Ward, A. (1991) 'Training for group care', in *The Teaching of Child Care in the Diploma in Social Work*. London: CCETSW.

Ward, A. (1993a) *Working in Group Care: Social Work in Residential and Day Care Settings*. Birmingham: Venture Press.

Ward, A. (1993b) 'The large group: the heart of the system in group care'. *Groupwork*, 6 (1), pp 63-77.

Ward, A. (1995a) 'Establishing community meetings in a children's home'. *Groupwork*, 15 (1), pp 4-23.

Ward, A. (1995b) 'Opportunity led work: 1. introducing the concept'. *Social Work Education*, 14 (4), pp 89-105.

Ward, A. (1996) 'Opportunity led work: 2. the framework'. *Social Work Education*, 15 (3), pp 40-59.

Ward, A. (2003a) 'On managing the team', in J. Seden and J. Reynolds (eds) *Managing Care in Practice*. London and New York: Routledge and Open University, pp 33-55.

Ward, A. (2003b) 'Using everyday life: opportunity led work', in A. Ward, K. Kasinski, J. Pooley and A. Worthington (eds) *Therapeutic Communities for Children and Young People*. London: Jessica Kingsley, pp 119-32.

Ward, A. (2005) 'Total immersion: using group care placements to maximise practice learning'. *Social Work Education*, 24 (4), pp 423-38.

Ward, A. and McMahon, L. (eds) (1998) *Intuition is Not Enough: Matching Learning with Practice in Therapeutic Child Care*. London: Routledge.

Ward, A. and Preston-Shoot, M. (1998) 'Editorial: special issue: training and education for residential child care'. *Social Work Education*, 1 (3), pp 269-74.

Ward, A., Kasinski, K., Pooley, J. and Worthington, A. (eds) (2003) *Therapeutic Communities for Children and Young People*. London: Jessica Kingsley.

Ward, L. (1975) 'Communication plus: the key to residential work'. *Social Work Today*, 6 (2), pp 34-7.

Ward, L. (1980) 'The social work task in residential care', in R. G. Walton and D. Elliott (eds) *Residential Care: A Reader in Current Theory and Practice*. Oxford: Pergamon, pp 25-36.

Wardhaugh, J. and Wilding, P. (1998) 'Towards an explanation of the corruption of care', in M. Allott and M. Robb (eds) *Understanding Health and Social Care: An Introductory Reader*. London: Sage/Open University, pp 212-29.

Warren-Adamson, C. (ed) (2001) *Family Centres and their International Role in Social Action: Social Work as Informal Education*. Aldershot: Ashgate.

Wendelken, C. (1983) *Children In and Out of Care*. London: Heinemann.

Wertheimer, A. (ed) (1996) *Changing Days: Developing New Day Opportunities with People who have Learning Difficulties*. London: King's Fund: National Development Team.

Wheal, A. (2000) 'Speaking for themselves: two care leavers' experiences of residential care', in D. Crimmens and J. Pitts (eds) *Positive Residential Practice: Learning the Lessons of the 90s*. Lyme Regis: Russell House Publishing, pp 101-9.

Whipp, R., Kirkpatrick, I. and Kitchener, M. (2005) *Managing Residential Child Care: A Managed Service*. Basingstoke: Palgrave Macmillan.

Whitaker, D., Archer, L. and Hicks, L. (1998) *Working in Children's Homes: Challenges and Complexities.* Chichester: Wiley.

Whittaker, A. (1997) *Looking at our Services: Service Evaluation by People with Learning Disabilities.* London: King's Fund.

Who Cares? Scotland (1998) *Listen Up: Young People Talk about Mental Health Issues in Residential Care: Who Cares Scotland Mental Health Project Report.*

Willcocks, D.M. (1987) *Private Lives in Public Places: A Research-Based Critique of Residential Life in Local Authority Old People's Homes.* London: Tavistock.

Willow, C. (2000) 'Safety in numbers? Promoting children's rights in public care', in D. Crimmens and J. Pitts (eds) *Positive Residential Practice: Learning the Lessons of the 90s,* pp 128-40. Lyme Regis: Russell House Publishing.

Winnicott, D.W. (1990) *The Maturational Processes and the Facilitating Environment: Studies in the Theory of Emotional Development.* London: Karnac.

Women in Mind (1986) *Finding our own Solutions: Women's Experience of Mental Health Care.* London: MIND.

Worthington, A. (1990) 'The function of the community meeting in a therapeutic community for pre- and young adolescents'. *International Journal of Therapeutic Communities,* 11 (2), pp 95-102.

Worthington, A. (2003) 'Relationships and the therapeutic setting', in A. Ward, K. Kasinski, J. Pooley and A. Worthington (eds) (2003) *Therapeutic Communities for Children and Young People.* London: Jessica Kingsley, pp 148-60.

Wright, F. (2000) 'The role of family care-givers for an older person resident in a care home'. *British Journal of Social Work,* 30, pp 649-61.

Index

S

Social work and people with dementia
Partnerships, practice and persistence
Mary Marshall and *Margaret-Anne Tibbs*

Current community care policies and increasing numbers of older people needing assistance mean that all social workers must be up-to-date in their knowledge, skills and attitudes towards people with dementia and their carers. This book, written by experienced social workers, provides guidance on best practice in a readable and jargon-free style.

This book is essential reading for social work and social care students, social workers undertaking CPD, and social and care workers transferring to dementia care from other fields.

PB £17.99 US$29.95 **ISBN-10** 1 86134 702 2 **ISBN-13** 978 1 86134 702 2
HB £55.00 US$75.00 **ISBN-10** 1 86134 703 0 **ISBN-13** 978 1 86134 703 9
234 x 156mm 256 pages November 2006
A BASW/POLICY PRESS TITLE

Older people and the law
Ann McDonald and *Margaret Taylor*

The book is a much-needed revised and updated edition of *Elders and the law* (PEPAR Publications, 1993). It describes the legal framework for working with older people following the modernising agenda in health and social care

Drawing on their extensive experience, the authors cover the range of legal issues affecting the welfare and financial security of older people in the community and residential settings. Emphasising the empowering nature of legal knowledge the book describes and explains the application of law and policy relating to older people in the context of social work practice.

Older people and the law is aimed at all professionals working with older people, but particularly social workers. Its clarity of style means that older people themselves and carers will find it accessible.

PB £16.99 US$29.95 **ISBN-10** 1 86134 714 6 **ISBN-13** 978 1 86134 714 5
HB £55.00 US$75.00 **ISBN-10** 1 86134 715 4 **ISBN-13** 978 1 86134 715 2
234 x 156mm 184 pages November 2006
A BASW/POLICY PRESS TITLE